"An unflinching memoir of a spy during a tumultuous time and unsavory alliances. Dobson recounts her recruitment, training, and espionage with rare self-awareness."

HENRY R. SCHLESINGER, AUTHOR OF *HONEY TRAPPED*

ABOUT THE AUTHOR

Sue Dobson was born in South Africa and witnessed Apartheid first hand. Wanting to contribute to a democratic South Africa for all, she joined the African National Congress (ANC) and was trained as an intelligence officer/ spy in the Soviet Union. She was deployed in South Africa and infiltrated the government propaganda department, interviewed Apartheid ministers and had a honey trap affair with a police chief involved with the Namibian independence process. She was 'burned' when she failed an enhanced security check for the State President's office, prompting her escape across southern Africa with the security police at her heels.

SUE DOBSON

BURNED

THE SPY
SOUTH AFRICA
NEVER CAUGHT

This story is dedicated to D.B. Thank you for handing me the key to a door I had tried to close for-ever. I had no idea the story wasn't over. This story is also dedicated to those South Africans who fought and died in the struggle for a new South Africa and who continue to do so.

I acknowledge too, all those who believed in me as I told my story, especially my agent, Tom Cull, who did not give up on me, George, Guy, Finola, S.T., and my children, who are slightly horrified at what their Ma got up to.

Burned (espionage parlance), when a field agent's identity is compromised.

Burned (noun), to be to subject to misfortune, mistreatment, or deception.

Burn (slang), a cutting remark intended to embarrass or humiliate someone.

AUTHOR'S NOTE

The story told within these pages is my own. This book tells of the events that I experienced, and I do not claim to speak for anyone else in my telling of them.

Mine is a fundamentally South African story. It is a story about a perfectly ordinary woman who got herself caught up in the extraordinary history of her country at a time when everything was changing and nothing seemed certain. The story of apartheid has many authors, and the story of how it ended has even more. What follows is my own story, my personal story—just one entry in the anthology of South Africa's most painful collective memory.

It has taken me over thirty years to share this, the true account of my role as a soldier in the war against apartheid. It is still as clear today as it was back then that the world must never be allowed to forget the atrocities committed in that beautiful, troubled, fool's paradise perched on the tip of the African continent. That is why I have chosen to share my story.

Mine is a tale of extremes: of love and betrayal, beauty and cruelty, passion and loss. South Africa herself is a land of contrasts and contradictions, unbearable beauty concealing a brutality beyond the limits of comprehension. South Africa, in all her splendour and spite, is a central character in my story. I want you to understand that her presence thrums beneath every page and echoes every day in my own life. She demands to be seen and felt.

There are many other South Africans like me, of varying colours and creeds, whose stories align with my own. Many of my comrades gave their lives in the struggle for freedom and dignity. Many more would have gladly given theirs if it meant we could tear down the old South Africa and build a new, better nation in its place. I salute them and admire them—each and every one. Their lives are all meaningful and the deeds they carried out significant. It all mattered.

All I ask is that they are not forgotten.

PROLOGUE: A FINE PLACE FOR A BULLET, 1989

THERE WAS A SPOT BETWEEN HIS EYES THAT, as we lay together in bed, seemed like a fine place for a kiss. Or a bullet.

I looked up at the Colonel and stroked his cheek with my forefinger. A bead of sweat glistened on his top lip. Two White bodies tangled among the thin sheets, among each other.

The Namibian climate was unbearable at the best of times, but tonight the heat was something else. There was a dampness, too, suspended in the air so thick you could taste it. I was burning up, but I was ready to do what I had been trained to do.

I had lain in wait for long enough; I was a coiled snake—a Cape cobra—and I was finally ready to release the venom that had slowly, silently built up within me since my political awakening many years before.

The man drowsing beside me was a major player in the espionage game, a police chief whose jackbooted cronies had committed crimes ranging from murder and intimidation to election rigging and sabotage. He was a trained and experienced spy, and now he was here to tamper with the UN-mandated independence process in Namibia, then one of the most fraught countries in the world. What he didn't know was that I was a spy too, working on the other side for South Africa's freedom-fighting opposition and Nelson Mandela's African National Congress (ANC). I seduced the Chief and let him think I was just a silly blonde floozy, his harmless bit on the side. He stepped into my trap, and now it was within my power to decide if this would be the last mistake he would ever make.

The year was 1989, and Namibia was a tinderbox. The country was in the throes of revolution, and its birth as a nation was proving difficult. The UN, and the wider world, had its eyes trained on Africa's western coast. A UN resolution mandated the independence process, but free and democratic nations aren't so easily conceived.

Already, too much blood had been spilled. The Nationalist government of South Africa was stretched thin to begin with, barely upholding the system of apartheid that sustained it. And now the UN wanted it to give up Namibia as well, even if that meant prising it from the apartheid state's death grip. The rulers of my country were like cornered animals, besieged on all fronts—and all the more dangerous for it. They weren't going to just hand over Namibia, no matter what the foreign meddlers at the UN said. Agents of the apartheid government were everywhere, crawling through the desert and using every dirty trick they had to frustrate the independence process. I was in bed with one of those agents.

I traced his eyebrows with my finger and moved to the spot above his nose, right between his eyes. I drew a small circle with my fingertip. For the bullet, I thought. A nice, neat hole. No mess. The exit wound would be different, of course. Blood could get so sticky in this damn heat.

Half asleep, he shifted towards the bedside table where he had left his lighter and his cigarettes. And his gun, which he always kept loaded.

"Penny for your thoughts, Mrs. Kid?"

He lit up and sucked in a mouthful of smoke before exhaling luxuriously and sighing in that typically male, self-satisfied way. He always got like this after sex. It made him slow, languid. It made him stupid, too, and vulnerable: just how I liked him.

"I'm just thinking about work," I said. This seemed to satisfy him. But really I was thinking, haven't so many people died already that one more body wouldn't hurt? If anything, the Chief's death would be payback for all the blood spilled in his name.

The Chief blew circles of smoke into the clammy room. The ceiling fan shuddered above us, pushing heavy air from one side to the other. A fly, befuddled by the heat, crawled up the burglar bars that blocked the open window. I stretched out in the bed and listened to the sound of his heavy, smoky exhalations. I counted the breaths, and I fantasised about stepping into the shower in just a few hours' time to wash every trace of this man off me. Blood and all, if it came to it.

He started talking, as he often did, about his police work. He was unguarded and voluble in my presence, sharing stories he really should have kept to himself about his operations and the mischief he had got up to. I tried to absorb as much of his chatter as I could in case there was anything worth reporting back, but I was wary of his moods; they could shift in an instant. In the corner of my eye, I saw a wink of gunmetal in the setting sun.

After a while, the Chief switched to his second-favourite subject: an unrequited love affair with a hostess on an intercity coach. She had cheated on him, and he still wasn't over it. It had come out of nowhere and stained his masculinity. The Chief was the kind of man who left women ... women didn't leave him.

The whole saga—which I had already heard countless times before—made for tedious listening. When the Chief and I first met, he had been between marriages, although he was engaged to the next woman with a wedding date already set. She either didn't know or didn't care that I came up to see him every fortnight or so, using my work as a journalist as pretext for my frequent trips to northern Namibia.

The evening shadows grew long and gathered in the corners of the bedroom. My rambling, lovesick, murderous police Chief slowed in his speech. Around him I tended to listen much more than I spoke. I was forever feeling out his moods, wary of his capriciousness. Besides, he liked his women best when they were sitting still and looking pretty. Now, as he slipped towards sleep, I offered ever fewer comments to sustain him, letting him drift away from consciousness until he was snoring gracelessly beside me.

He lay naked and foetal, his body slim, tanned, and exposed. His dark hair was curled against the white of the pillow, with one damp tendril glistening like an unwound spring in the nape of his neck. I studied his body closely, setting my eyes on the dark thatch of hair that covered his arms, creeping all the way down towards his hands. He wore a gold signet ring on his ring finger, a common sight among Afrikaner men. The ring caught the last of the sun, casting patterns like spectral figures, apparitions from another world, onto the wall opposite. He smiled in his sleep. A slow, narrow, sidelong smile whose meaning I often questioned.

Slowly, quietly, I pulled myself out of bed. He didn't even stir as I crept around to his side of the room, my bare feet delicate on the refreshing cold of the floor. My eyes flicked like a switchblade between his naked body, that fragile expanse of skin and blood and organs, and the revolver on the bedside table. The gun winked at me, and I obeyed.

The handle fit so perfectly in my hand it felt like an extension of myself. Its heft was familiar, and in that moment I felt the echoes of my time in the Soviet

Union, where I had been trained in espionage and intelligence gathering, and where I had been taught to shoot—and kill, if necessary. The feel of a gun in my hands brought me right back to the range just outside Moscow: my fingers almost frozen solid, the trees heavy with snow and more of it still falling. I heard the voice of my instructor telling me to fire, and as I pointed the gun towards the sleeping police chief I weighed in my other hand the eternal cost of taking a life, balancing this cold accounting against the weight of the revolver gleaming like a treasure in the low light of Namibia's desperate sun.

A WHITE MAN'S CHILD, 1964

MY MOTHER PERCHED on the edge of the heavy wooden chair in the doctor's consulting room. She pulled her miniskirt towards her knees, patted her beehive hairdo, and took a deep drag of her Peter Stuyvesant, red lipstick staining the filter. She looked like a woman who could do with a gin.

We had spent the past two hours queuing my for pre-nursery school vaccinations in a shabby waiting room of the Railway Sick Fund. The chairs were scuffed and uncomfortable, and the walls behind them were marked with greasy stains, phantom imprints from the succession of heads that had lolled against the dull paint in boredom or despair. A sign above the door read *Slegs Blankes*, "Whites Only." The air was thick with stale sweat and cigarette smoke, and flies buzzed lazily around a broken ceiling fan. The only reading material was an Afrikaans Bible.

A woman in the throes of early labour moaned, a sickly man blew his nose, a baby cried, a smoker coughed, and someone retched over a sick-bowl. Such was the glory and the privilege of belonging to the Railway Sick Fund—a perk of my father's job—and having to wait to see the railway doctor at his surgery in central Pretoria.

The nurse, a recent arrival from Portuguese East Africa (now Mozambique), struggled with English and was even more lost with Afrikaans. She seemed to be trying her best to drown out the noise by clattering away in the nurses' room, where she was busy sorting out packages of that new-fangled contraceptive pill, then available only to married ladies.

Abortion was illegal and sinful in the South Africa of my youth, and the wretched women who survived backstreet abortions were often driven to suicide by guilt and shame. At family planning clinics, which were few, the pill was kept in a locked box. Women were interviewed to determine the appropriateness of them being given contraception. Often, the verdict was that the woman in question was just promiscuous, in which case she would be threatened with God's wrath and sent packing.

Premarital sex was a heinous sin, and society at the time considered anything to do with sexuality to be *sies*—an Afrikaans expression for objects of unadulterated, stomach-turning disgust. It was more than just a judgmental exclamation; if you were *sies,* you were beyond the pale, a non-person who would do well to disappear into your shame. It was a wonder any Afrikaner babies were born at all, considering that the human body, nudity, sex, and all bodily functions were considered dirty and profane, unworthy of discussion. When television made its debut in South Africa in 1976, conservative Afrikaners expressed outrage at the shortness of the tutus worn by ballerinas performing classical ballet.

Contraception was also frowned upon by the Nationalist government as a policy. South Africa's White supremacist leaders wanted the White minority to reproduce, while Black women were secretly sterilised at the overcrowded and filthy state hospitals where they came to give birth. It emerged years later that the government had even funded development of a vaccine that made Black women infertile. The vaccine was the brainchild of Dr. Wouter Basson, a cardiologist who in the later years of Apartheid was also the head of Project Coast, South Africa's secret chemical and biological warfare programme.

I was due to get some shots of my own. But because I was White, the state was on my side. I had nothing to worry about.

This was Pretoria, 1964. This was a place where race was a consideration even among the seriously ill, where White doctors would walk past a dying Black patient as if they were an animal at the side of the road. It was the law. Your race was not something inherited from your parents; it was something assigned to you by the state, something so important it deserved to be capitalised.

In our Whites-only waiting room, the Portuguese nurse was back from sorting through her contraceptives. Now she was tutting and clucking around a crying woman who was having a funny turn.

"Oh dear," the nurse said, over and over again in accented Afrikaans as she patted the patient's hand.

"Ag, shame, man," my mother said, looking over with a mixture of pity and disgust. "Here, have a tissue." She passed the tissue to the poor woman and muttered under her breath, "This place is an absolute disgrace ... like a bleddy cattle market."

The toilet ("Whites Only") in the corridor flushed for the umpteenth time and my health-obsessed mother grimaced, imagining malevolent faecal microbes drifting across the room and landing on my outstretched hands or, worse, in my mouth. She rubbed at me vigorously with her hanky, as if that would save me from disease.

My mother had seen her fair share of illness when she worked as a midwife and nursing sister in the Black provincial hospitals of the Eastern Cape in the 1950s. She still believed sickness lurked around every corner, even—and perhaps especially—in doctors' waiting rooms.

This place was like a hothouse for my mother's neuroses, and simply being there put her in a foul mood. Moments earlier she had glared at an Afrikaner member of the Blou Rokke, who had sniffed and glowered back in turn. She didn't even lose her place in her prayer book. The Blou Rokke (Blue Dresses), formally the Latter Rain Mission, was a conservative religious cult striving towards holiness and spiritual rebirth. This particular zealot must have felt far from God as she grappled with the realities of wearing a nylon and crimplene three-piece suit ensemble (well below the knee, of course), black tights, a pillbox hat, and black lace-up shoes in the heat of a Pretoria day.

A long queue snaked down the corridor outside the waiting room. Black railway employees could see their (Black) doctor that day too, but there were no seats in their designated waiting room, and the very ill were left lying on the floor or in the corridor. Pregnant women and nursing mothers had nowhere to rest and had to queue standing for several hours. There were no toilets for anyone who wasn't White.

Earlier that morning we waited under the waxy, purple blossoms of the jacaranda trees at the bus stop near our flat in Sunny-side. My mother battled her way with me and my pushchair onto the red-and-white bus that arrived to take us the few miles to the doctor's office. We did not share transport with Black South Africans; we had our own bus service with a White driver. Blacks had to wait for squat, ugly, green buses, which were slower and dirtier and belched diesel fumes through the streets. Likewise, Black train passengers were forced into their own third-class coaches with sealed windows and no toilets.

Every morning, Black commuters waited in long queues in the Black townships around the city to catch Black buses, which took them to the White areas in which they worked. The Group Areas Act, passed in 1950, assigned different racial groups to distinct residential areas outside the city centre. This act would be cited during the forced removals of the 1960s, 70s and 80s, when South Africa's second- and third-class citizens were required to pack up their lives at short notice and relocate to these designated areas of racial homogeneity. Nearly 600,000 people—Black, Coloured, and Asian—were displaced under this legislation.

Of course, the Black areas consisted of forgotten townships outside of the city, where there was no proper housing. Nor was there running water, sewage systems, or electricity. Entire communities relied on a single cold tap at the end of their un-tarred road for water. If you were Black, tuberculosis, hepatitis, measles, and polio were facts of life. Disease was rife in the townships, and it was treated at inferior, ill-equipped clinics—if at all. White people, meanwhile, had access to modern medicine and the latest drugs.

The psychology of "separate development," as it was then called, was already entrenched in the national psyche. Throughout my life, it only became further entrenched in legislation. This system came to be known as "apartheid," meaning "apartness" in Afrikaans. It should come as no surprise that under apartheid, Black life expectancy (estimated at fifty-five years in 1980) was considerably lower than White (seventy years).

The Group Areas Act also meant many Black workers had to commute long distances, since those employed in White houses weren't allowed to reside anywhere near the neighbourhoods in which they worked. When the unreliable Black buses broke down in the morning, those most aggravated and inconvenienced were the White suburban "Madams" whose helpers did all their housework, prepared their meals, and looked after their children.

Blacks were only allowed to reside in White areas if they were employed as live-in helpers, and it was not uncommon for a family's "maid" to go several months without seeing her husband or children. She was fortunate if she could bring a baby to live with her in her spartan domestic quarters. Most families did not allow this and would force their maid to pass her children into the care of relatives, if she had any.

Blacks could only enter White areas with the correct documentation in their much-despised Pass book. Pass books documented the holder's work status and official racial classification. Even if you had permission to leave your own area for work, your Pass would confine you to a specific town or district only, and you could bet you would be harassed by the police the moment you strayed into the wrong part of the city. Spouses and children had to be left behind in the *bantustans*, the Black territories.

The Pass Laws segregated the population, limited the freedoms of Black people, and gave the state total control over the movement of labour. The Pass book, or "*dom Pass*" ("stupid Pass" or "accursed Pass"), as it was derisively known, was one of the most insidious and enduring symbols of apartheid. Whites, of course, didn't have to carry one. But if you were Black and you were found to be travelling without a Pass, you would be deported back to the *bantustan* where you belonged. If you were lucky. Otherwise, you faced arrest and imprisonment. Throughout my childhood, it was common to see police vans patrolling the streets of Pretoria, hunting for Pass offenders. The *dom* Pass Laws were only repealed in 1986.

In the South Africa of my youth, apartheid was all-encompassing and enforced with zeal. It touched every aspect of life: public beaches, swimming pools, graveyards, drive-in cinemas, car parks, and public toilets were all segregated. Blacks could not run businesses or professional practices in White areas unless they had a permit. Neither were Blacks allowed to buy hard liquor, although they could buy cheap beer. Blacks were also technically prohibited from attending church under the Churches Native Laws Amendment Act of 1957, but this was an exception to the rule of apartheid in that the policy was not always enforced. As such, churches were one of the few places where races could mix.

Bizarrely, for a regime that held one's racial classification above all else, racial designation was a subjective matter. Everyone had a race, and this was something officially assigned at birth along with your name. Your racial classification determined where you could live, who you could marry, your access to healthcare and education, and ultimately your life expectancy. It was important that the government got your classification right.

These classifications were serious things. You could be White, Coloured (mixed race), Asian (Indian), or Black. These races were all legal classifications, and they all sat on a hierarchy; Coloured people had more rights than Blacks, but fewer than Whites, for example.

However, not every case was, literally, so Black and White. There exist several intermediate shades of humanity, which is where confusion frequently came. If questioned, certain unofficial and arbitrary tests would be used by the Office for Race Classification to determine someone's race.

The most disturbing of these was the pencil test. A pencil would be slipped into your hair, and you would "pass" or "fail" the test based on how readily the pencil fell out. If the pencil wouldn't stay in your hair, you were White. If the pencil stuck, but fell out when you shook your head, you were Coloured. If the pencil stayed in your hair, you were Black.

The state also subjected individuals to examinations of the palms of their hands, the soles of their feet, their fingernails, the shape of their buttocks, and the colour of their genitals. Babies were undressed to look for Mongolian blue spots—dark patches over the lower back that were said to prove the presence of Coloured blood.

These tests were as immoral as they were shallow. Families were divided on the basis of these facile and racist examinations; if one family member had a lighter or darker complexion than the others (despite being born to the same parents) they risked being classified differently. And a family split along racial lines couldn't live together, as the Group Areas Act decreed that the distinct races had to live in their distinct areas.

Sandra Laing, who was born in 1955 to White Afrikaner parents, was a high-profile example of this insane policy in action. By chance, Sandra had a darker complexion than her parents and brothers. Sandra's slightly darker skin went unnoticed throughout her early childhood until, one day, two policemen arrived at her Whites-only school to take her home. The parents of one of her school friends had objected to her complexion and she was duly expelled.

The state went even further, and Sandra—the daughter of two White Afrikaners—was officially reclassified as Coloured. Her grandparents and great-grandparents were also White. The family's White friends, family, church, and community shunned the Laing family. Sandra's father insisted on a paternity test.

Sandra's parents protested this sudden change in their fortunes. The paternity test proved beyond any doubt that Sandra was her parents' daughter, and ultimately she was officially reclassified, again, as White. However, the damage was done, and the family had already been marked by racial stigma. Things were never the same: the Laings' neighbors didn't look at them the same way, and the family no longer felt welcome at the church where they had unwittingly introduced their "Coloured" daughter to the all-White congregation.

Shunned all her life by the White community—even though she was legally one of them—Sandra eventually married a Black man. The resulting children from the marriage were, this time, classified at birth as Coloured. Sandra asked to be reclassified as Coloured—otherwise she wouldn't be allowed to live in the same part of town as her children. This process reawakened old wounds, and Sandra's parents cast her out of the family. She never reconciled with her father, who threatened to kill her because of the shame she had brought, but she later salvaged the remains of a relationship with her mother. Sandra's family was just one of many destroyed by apartheid.

Never mind the horrors of racial classification, God help you if you fell for someone of a different race. Some of the first apartheid laws passed by the National Party, following its rise to power in 1948, were the hated Prohibition of Mixed Marriages Act and the Immorality Act. These racist laws prohibited marriage and sexual relationships between White people and people of other racial groups. The former also nullified interracial marriages of South Africans that had taken place outside the country. Interracial sexual relationships between those classified as Coloured, Black, or Asian were allowed, so long as no Whites were involved.

A breach of the Immorality Act incurred a penalty of five years in prison for a man and four years for a woman. A prototype version of the act, passed all the way back in 1927, prohibited sex between Blacks and Whites. The amended Act of 1950 went further to forbid "unmarried sexual intercourse" between Europeans and any other race.

If you were discovered to be in a mixed marriage, you could expect to be arrested and imprisoned. If you officiated at such a union, you would receive a fine. If you lied to the celebrant about your racial classification, you risked charges of perjury. And outside of the legal ramifications, you would almost certainly be ostracised by your community and probably cut off by your friends and family. This was nothing new. Racial segregation and White dominance existed in South Africa long before apartheid, although it wasn't until the rise of the apartheid regime that racism was formalised, legalised, and expanded to cover every sphere of life.

South Africa has a bloody history, and wars have long been waged for her land, natural resources, and minerals. The first Dutch settlers, from whom the Afrikaners are descended, arrived in the seventeenth century. The appearance of the Dutch heralded greater conflicts to come, and in time an increasing number of foreign powers became entwined in our nation's story. All subsequent European colonialists played a part in the subjugation of South Africa's indigenous peoples, usually through military repression.

But it wasn't until the 1913 Land Act that the foundations for apartheid were formally laid. This law forced Black South Africans into reserves and made it illegal for them to work as sharecroppers. Opponents of the Land Act formed the South African National Native Congress, which eventually grew into the African National Congress (ANC)—the party of Nelson Mandela—and the best-known of all the anti-apartheid forces. The Depression and the Second World War brought increasing economic difficulties in South Africa, and Whites as well as Blacks felt this pain, although it was always the latter group that bore the greatest brunt of any hardship.

My origins are working class, and both my grandfathers worked for South African Railways. My maternal grandfather, Bill Griffin, was a train driver and a stationmaster in the Eastern Cape Cookhouse area, while my paternal grand-father, Frank Eagarr Millson, began work as a train conductor in the Western Cape.

My father's mother, Irene Winifred, stoically endured life with Frank and was renowned for her poise, endurance, and her ivory cigarette holder. She raised the children while Frank worked his way through night school to become a draughtsman. Meanwhile, my maternal grandmother, a battle-hard-ened, sturdy woman by the name of Hilda Gertrude, took in lodgers to boost the family income while Bill moved restlessly between towns.

In short, neither family was a stranger to poverty. My mother looked to nursing and midwifery to escape the trap, while my father—a dashing ladies' man in his youth—graduated from the University of the Witwatersrand (Wits) in Johannesburg before working on the Copperbelt in Northern Rhodesia (now Zambia) and Congo (now Democratic Republic of the Congo) as an engi-neer. He returned to South Africa in the late 1950s, when he met my mother. They married in 1960. I am their only child.

As a White South African, I was born a beneficiary of a system of institu-tionalised racism, as far as such a system can be said to benefit anyone at all. Apartheid was the backdrop to much of my life; it shaped me and my experi-ences, and if you speak to any South African of my age—Black, White, Colored, or Asian—they will tell you it shaped them too. When people ask me where I am from, I want to say apartheid. That's how all-encompassing it was.

Apartheid tore at South Africa and South West Africa (now Namibia) for almost fifty years. The culture of apartheid ensured the White minority, then around eighteen per cent of the population, dominated South Africa politically, economically, and socially. "Petty apartheid" was the term used to refer to the segregation of facilities, whilst "grand apartheid" referred to structural segregation in housing, education, and employment. Considering the devastating effect apartheid had on so many lives, none of it was very petty to my mind.

Apartheid officially started after the (all-White) Afrikaner National Party won the 1948 general election, strengthening its already explicit policies of racial division. The party was dominated by members of the far-right *Afrikaner Broederbond*, a secretive and deeply conservative organisation dedicated to advancing the well-being of Afrikaners at the expense of everyone else. Most of the Afrikaans-speaking members of successive Nationalist governments, and all apartheid leaders, have been members of this "brotherhood."

When the much-hated Hendrik Verwoerd became prime minister in 1958, his priority was to move the Black population to the newly created *bantustans*, literally, "homelands," where there was little farmland, poor infrastructure, and few amenities—with little scope for economic development. Schools and hospitals were virtually non-existent. He called this "separate development." Black exiles would become legal citizens of their independent "homelands," sacrificing their South African citizenship in the process. If they wanted to continue working in South Africa, the country of their birth, they would have to register as migrant workers, and even then they would only be granted temporary permits.

Large swathes of South Africa's majority Black population were moved to ten tribal homelands, four of which became nominally independent states: Transkei (1976), Bophuthatswana (1977), Venda (1979), and Ciskei (1981). These were South Africa's puppet states, ruled by apartheid stooges. Farcically, South Africa was the only country to recognise their independence.

This was the South Africa I was born into. This was the South Africa of unequal health provision, wildly varied life expectancies, and White-only doctor's surgeries.

It was here where one of my first memories is rooted. I can still picture my mother sitting dead still as she surveyed the consulting room, my vaccinations having finally been administered after all that waiting. The doctor was a chain-smoking, sweaty man with a thick moustache and Brylcreemed hair, which had been radically parted just above his left ear. Behind him was a flyblown South African flag, curled at the edges and stained with nicotine, and on his desk sat framed photographs of a succession of Nationalist Prime Ministers.

Pride of place was Dr. Hendrik Verwoerd, the godfather of the *bantustans*. He was smiling manically, his ludicrous blond quiff standing upright like the crest of an angry bird. My mother, worn down by the long wait, ground her teeth.

The doctor leaned forward and sighed. He stared at me. I was very pale, a small girl lost in a mass of blonde curls that my mother could never comb. He reached forward and ran a nicotine-stained finger up my arm, where he had pricked me just moments before. His dentures were loose, and he whistled as he spoke.

"Hell," he said in Afrikaans. "That's a White man's child if ever I saw one."

My mother got up and, with as much dignity as her tiny five-foot frame could muster, swept me into her arms.

"I should bleddy hope so!" she said, as she flounced out the door.

"THE ROK," 1965

THE SLAP ECHOED ACROSS THE BACK of my bare thigh. I had been looking the other way, and the blow came as a surprise.

I remember the burn and the sting of his open hand, the sharp intake of breath that left me choking, sobbing, gasping for air. I stumbled to the edge of the sandpit, the grey sand sticking to my bare feet. I sat down hard to blot out the pain and hide the perfect handprint throbbing red against my pale skin.

I turned to stare at the man who had hit me, and my three-year-old heart filled with shame, rage, and indignation. It was my first betrayal. My bottom lip trembled and a tear rolled down my cheek, cutting a warm channel through the dust and dirt that clung to my sweat. I refused to blink, my stare distorted by the lens of wet anger brimming in my eyes.

My father glared back, a loose, blond curl falling over his forehead. I hoped his hand hurt, and I hated him then and forever with a childish purity of feeling.

"Don't you ever do that again," he said. "You do not throw sand at people's eyes!"

Through my sobs I tried to explain "the rok" had started it.

My father worked then at an office in central Pretoria, where there were no English-speaking nurseries. That was how I ended up at an Afrikaans one, where I spent the first few days in a corner crying for my mother. At first, the staff took pity on me. They tried to include me with their broken English, since I spoke no Afrikaans. But they soon got bored of me. It didn't take long before they forgot I was there. I only got through the days by copying the other children, but I always felt perplexed and disturbed by an unease lurking beneath the surface of my every interaction. The other children didn't like me. I wasn't one of them.

It seemed the Boer Wars—a series of conflicts between British colonists and the descendants of earlier Dutch arrivals—was still being fought in the nursery playground. The Afrikaners, the Boers, called me a "pom" and a "limey" because of my English ancestry. They also liked "*rooinek,*" literally "redneck"—a name that stuck because of the vicious sunburn exhibited by British soldiers whose pith helmets had failed to protect their necks. I understood none of these names at the time, although I already possessed an arsenal of derogatory terms to throw back at them. I learned from my parents that Afrikaners were "roks," "ropes," "jaaps," or "planks." If they called me names, then I could call them names right back.

The "rok" in the sandpit was at least two years older than me and twice my size. Pale, flabby, and brimming with spite, he couldn't keep his hands off me. Every day I returned home having been pinched, punched, and called names I had never heard before. I did not understand why this child hated me so much. In time, my sadness turned to anger, and then to hatred.

Then, one day, he kicked me hard in the shin.

"*Engelse kont,*" he hissed in my ear. Although I didn't know at that age that he was calling me an "English cunt," the words still stung. His vitriol hit me like sand in the wind. My heart hurt because a stranger hated me.

This fat little bully feasted on my pain and confusion. He waited to see what I would say in response. As he waited, he wiped his sleeve across his nose, staring me down. As soon as his guard was lowered, I dropped to my haunches, scooped up a fistful of dirty sand, and in one motion flung a blinding cloud of grit into his stupid, smug face. Most of it went in his piggy eyes.

He reeled back, howling and clutching his face. I noted with satisfaction that he had wet himself. Savouring my victory, I watched the stream of urine run down his legs, pooling in the grubby sand at his feet. Of course, that was the precise moment my father happened to arrive to pick me up. He delivered his slap and left me crying, gasping, in the sand.

Now, still smarting from my punishment for a fight I hadn't even started, anger seeped from me like sweat. Every pore oozed hatred, some directed at my father but most reserved for the flat-footed dullard who had called me a name I didn't understand in a language I couldn't speak. I watched his cropped head in the distance as he pushed over another child and grabbed a toy, the rolls of fat on his neck wobbling as he ran away.

As if things couldn't get any worse, another parent, a photographer, had also witnessed the altercation and the disciplining that came after. He took a photograph of me sobbing in the sandpit and gave my father a copy of it the next day.

My father duly presented the photograph to my mother, whose first instinct was to frame it. It sat, in its frame, on her dressing table for the next fifty years.

My humiliation was complete and felt like it would never end.

MY FRIEND APRIL, 1969

THE BABY BLUE RENAULT DAUPHINE was parked like a squat bullfrog outside the school gates. My father, who loved his cars, was waiting in the driver's seat, polishing the dashboard with a shammy. My mother sat beside him, adjusting her hair in the rearview mirror as a fresh Peter Stuyvesant burned between her fingers. This was Cape Town, 1969, and the summer term had just finished.

I clambered into the back seat, my bare legs sticking to the fawnish leather in the heat. I couldn't wait to hand them two brown envelopes: one containing my report card, the other containing my class photograph.

These end-of-term afternoons were what life was all about. We always marked the start of the holidays with a trip to the Foresters Arms, where I would be permitted an Appletiser while my parents quaffed a bottle of Grunberger Stein with lunch. If I was lucky, I'd get to run barefoot on the beach afterwards.

My father fished out my report card and read aloud the contents. "Susan has worked hard this term ... Susan continues to improve ..." The usual remarks. I watched him intently as he read. He laughed and threw the card towards my mother, who caught it eagerly.

Now my father lit his own cigarette and opened the envelope containing the school photo. I hoped he would comment on how pretty I looked or offer an indication of any kind that he was proud of me, that he loved me. He held the photo up to the light. He grunted and passed it to my mother, who studied it for a moment.

Then, she asked, "Who's that?" She was pointing at my friend April, a girl who had always treated me with kindness.

"That's April," I said. "She sits next to me."

My mother's fingernail hovered over April's head as my father strained in his seat for a second glance.

"Hells bells, luvvy," my mother said. "Look at that one. Black as the bleddy ace of spades."

"Christ," my father said. He sounded shocked. "There's a touch of the tar brush, if ever I saw it." He turned to me, met my eyes. "Sue, is that kid Black?"

I truly didn't know and said as much. Even if I had known, I wouldn't have understood why it mattered.

"Well," my father said, "you don't go near her, okay?"

"And don't hold her bleddy hand," my mother added. "You don't know where it's been!"

My parents laughed over the sound of the ignition. My mother passed me the photo, and as we made for the Foresters I looked at it again.

A class of twenty seven-year-old White girls smiled up at me. My beloved teacher, Miss Burn, stood proudly to one side, her long hair loose around her shoulders, as was the fashion of the day. But I was more interested in my friend, April. It was true that she was darker than the rest of us. I wondered if Black washed off in the rain.

JACARANDA CITY, 1970

A YEAR LATER, thanks to my father's work, the three of us would move from cosmopolitan Cape Town—a place of beaches, oak trees, and south-easterly gusts that blew you off your feet—back to Pretoria, the drab, conservative Afrikaner capital. Table Mountain watches over Cape Town; whereas it's the hideous Voortrekker Monument that guards Pretoria on a hill to the south of the city. This granite monstrosity glorifies the bloodthirsty battles between the indigenous peoples and the Boers. It was typical of Pretorian sensibilities that the senseless fighting over indigenous land should be commemorated in such a tasteless way.

The only thing I liked about Pretoria was the jacaranda trees, whose purple blossoms erupted each spring to wash the city in vibrancy and colour. These trees are so beloved and so numerous that Pretoria is also known as Jacaranda City.

As part of my father's transfer, we moved to the leafy, well-to-do eastern suburb of Waterkloof Ridge. Our house sat right under the flight path from Waterkloof Military Air Base, from which Mirage fighter jets patrolled South Africa's northern borders. Giant Hercules troop carriers took off from the base as well, making sounds like thunder as they churned the air between their huge propellors. Another sound I associate with my childhood is the frequent screech of air-raid sirens. Whenever the sirens started—always a false alarm, or a drill, or a test—my mother would run screaming to the door to call me inside, convinced that the Black hordes from the north were about to attack us. Only the Russians cultivated more fear and paranoia in her damaged mind.

My mother had worked her way up from the deprivation of the *dorps*, the small towns, where her father had lived while he was working on the railways. Determined to escape her impoverished background, she studied hard at school and trained to become a district nurse and midwife. Her vocation saw her travel around Black townships, working in underfunded hospitals and delivering babies in the community. Health and sanitary conditions in the *dorps* were poor, and in the course of this work she knew she was risking her own well-being. She ultimately contracted tuberculosis, one of many conditions with a high incidence rate among the neglected and impoverished Black rural population.

After her recovery she moved to Pretoria, where she met my father. It was 1958, and he was a dashing, hard-drinking, and quick-tempered young engineer. A party girl, blessed with good looks and several male admirers, my mother would have been something of a catch. Despite his shyness, and a degree of social ineptitude, my father eventually managed to win her over. They bonded over their shared railway heritage and fell in love. They got married in 1960, and I was born just two years later.

My father followed the family vocation, albeit in a more distinguished capacity. At the time of our move to Pretoria, he was a senior mechanical engineer at South African Railways, in charge of rolling stock for all of Southern Africa. The title was impressive, but my father never liked his job. His was a staunchly Afrikaans and conservative department. Many of his colleagues belonged to the right-wing *Broederbond*. Needless to say, most of them were also outspoken supporters of apartheid.

My father hated his colleagues, and they hated him. It was difficult to know who he despised more in South Africa: the Blacks or the Afrikaners. The only time he would ever mellow out was after a few glasses of whisky. Blunted by the alcohol, he would grow nostalgic, regaling me with stories of his life as a younger man on the Copperbelt. His work had taken him as far north as present-day Democratic Republic of the Congo, and he had also lived and worked in what was formerly Nyasaland (Malawi) and Northern Rhodesia (Zambia). He was a small-minded racist, but it was undeniable that my father understood Africa as a continent. Rightly, in my opinion, he blamed the greed of European colonialists for most of her troubles.

My father's exciting, whisky-fueled tales of Africa fermented something in me. I was already interested in the wider world, and I would grow up to be an inquisitive and open-minded child. My parents were neglectful and dysfunctional, but at least my father gave me his passion for Africa. I'm grateful for that. In almost every other regard, I was jealous of my classmates, many of whom barely saw their parents.

Back then, many White children were raised by Black nannies who also served domestically as maids. If you worked in a White household as a live-in maid, you could expect long hours and pitiful wages, in addition to the inevitable pain of being separated from your family.

Many domestic workers lived in rudimentary outbuildings, often without hot water or electricity. They would never eat with the family, and they were forbidden to use their facilities inside the house—the same facilities they cleaned and tended around the clock. Most worked a seven-day week, with only a few hours off on a Thursday afternoon. They went several weeks at a time without seeing their own children, who were left in rural areas in the care of poverty-stricken and infirm older relatives.

Black women—adults—working in White homes would often be called "the girl," a status-reducing term that was used to remind everyone, both worker and employer, who was the boss. A man employed to look after the well-groomed gardens of the suburbs would be referred to as "the garden boy." In response, I was used to hearing Black people call White women "Madam" and White men "Boss."

None of these terms were accidental, and neither were they used flippantly. They were just one of a million ways in which White people diminished and undermined Black people. In this way, the language of apartheid was similar to the parlance of the American South at that time.

As a White child, I was supposed to live a life of peaceful and ignorant oblivion, unaware or unbothered by all the ways (both subtle and not-so-subtle) in which the regime of White supremacy was exerted and maintained. Little girls like me were told not to interact with Black people—with the exception, perhaps, of the nanny.

My mother was unusual in that, at first, she flatly refused to have a maid in the house. She had heard one unlikely horror story too many about domestic workers entertaining male friends in their cold, dark accommodation and blowing their noses on the dishtowels. In later years she relented and allowed my father to employ Andries, a Black cleaner they had known when they first started living together. All went well for several years until unfortunate Andries contracted tuberculosis and languished in a filthy hospital on the outskirts of town.

My mother went to visit him, which was unheard of in those days. She wanted to talk to his doctor, to check if he was still infectious, and to get a sense of when he could safely return to work.

Andries recovered, and all went well for a week or two. Then, one day, my mother caught him blowing crumbs out of the toaster. And that, they say, was that.

ENDLESS SUMMER, 1971

THE GRASS WAS WET beneath my bare feet, its lush shades of green mirrored in the grasping leaves of the peach tree overhead. The Pretorian sun was warm against the back of my neck as I stretched for a peach, feather-veined leaves brushing against my arm. I bit into the peach, and its sweet juice erupted around my teeth, spilling down my fingers and into my palm.

It was a crisp morning, and the dew was cool underfoot, the breeze soft against my skin. The smell of wet grass hung in the air, so clean you could taste it. It blended with the scent of jasmine from the night before. The sky was threaded through with the pinks and yellows of sunrise, a rainbow enriched by the vibrant plumes of the loerie birds that were chattering away in the trees nearby. The early sun made the peaches shine like gold. South Africa always had been a gift for the senses.

It was my secret that each morning, before the household stirred, I would run into this garden, this pocket of paradise, to check if the buds had opened on the climbing rose. The lizards and skinks, with their tails like yellow whips, were my company in these early-morning excursions. They soaked up the first rays with me and shared my interest in the tiny insects scurrying among the petals. We listened together to the kaleidoscopic choir of birdsong.

This was Africa, my Africa. This was my home—a place I would have died for, and almost did. But this is also a place where the most vibrant creatures are the most dangerous, and where red is the most pertinent shade in the rainbow, in the flag. This was a place where Black and White were the essential designations that determined your rights as a citizen. A place where the immutable facts of your birth decided whether you could use public bathrooms, whether your children would receive an education, and whether you could access healthcare when you got sick. It was the lottery of race that determined whether you could move freely around your own country, whether you could go to the cinema or drink alcohol. Your colour determined whether you could look to the police for protection or persecution or whether you could walk down the street without being attacked for no reason other than the pigmentation of your skin.

Today, South Africa is still known as the Rainbow Nation. But in the South Africa of my childhood, Black and White were the colours that mattered most. Even then, as a little girl in Pretoria, I was taught to hate those who were different to me. But as far as I was concerned, the only colours worth paying attention to were those in my beloved garden.

I was nine years old, at home in this oasis brimming with beautiful and exotic plants: green aloes, the flame-red kaffirboom, a rare silver oak tree, and the waxy white moonflowers whose beauty belied their poison. The sun shone on the strelitzia, the orange-and-blue flower known as the "bird of paradise" that can be seen throughout the gardens of the Cape. Mousebirds sang in the trees by the house and the lawn was busy with a belligerent flock of hadedas, sub-Saharan ibises with hooked beaks and a penchant for rifling through bins—named for the distinctive "*ha-de-da*" sound of the cries they made.

In summer the heat would accumulate through the sultry afternoon until the sky filled with thick cumulous clouds. Then, with a sudden clap of thunder, the sky would burst like a ruptured piñata, rain and lightning spilling from the clouds' seams. These summer storms would set me dancing barefoot on the grass, face turned towards the sky as I tried to catch the raindrops in my open mouth.

As a solitary, only child, that garden was the only place I never felt alone. There were always new sensations to enjoy, new experiences to be had. It was a world filled with wonders: from birds and bugs to the bright flowers and heaving fruit trees. Fat mulberries fed pet silkworms; the juice from those berries stained my fingers a deep purple.

I walked through the wet grass to the house, forcing myself to retreat from my refuge, my paradise. The top half of the stable door was already open, golden sun streaming into the dark interior like a spotlight. The furniture in the hall was dull with a layer of fine dust, which mixed in the rays of sunlight with a raised finger of cigarette smoke. The smoke was stirred through with dust motes, turning and twisting in gentle whorls. She was already sitting in the rocking chair overlooking the garden, a freshly lit Peter Stuyvesant in her hand. My mother looked up and regarded me with pale blue eyes. She took a drag and stared at me for several seconds, wide-eyed and without blinking.

Her dentures rested on her bottom lip in a warped and cartoonish parody of a grimace. I ran from the room.

A familiar fear rose like bile in my throat. It was the beginning of the long, six-week summer holiday, and time yawned before me, stretching from December through to the New Year.

I was to spend the holiday as I spent all my holidays: abandoned in a quiet house, alone save for a mother too busy consorting with her demons to find time for me. I would stand rooted to the spot as I heard snatches of conversation through the walls, knowing full well that nobody else was home. There was laughter, and shouting, and tears. I couldn't see the pageant of characters that paraded in front of my mother in the dark and filthy front room. Much of my childhood was spent listening, trying to make sense of it all. I was hostage to her deep desperation, and I wasted many hours wishing that my mother would come back.

In the past handful of years, she had changed a great deal. She was haunted daily by the pain of an earlier car accident, and she had already surrendered to a mania and delirium that was only getting worse with time. Getting older didn't agree with her either, and losing her looks (as she saw it) affected her mental health, contributing further to the depression that hounded her throughout this period.

I had long since given up asking for food and drink while I was alone with her. There was nothing in the house, and at her worst she would not have been able to make a drink for herself, let alone cook dinner for me. I waited each day to see if she would move from her chair and get dressed, but the furthest she ever travelled was back to her unmade bed.

My mother had no interest in the sun. She had no time for the feel of dew beneath her feet, and she was blind to the beauty of budding flowers. She wouldn't even stir for the taste of freshly picked peaches. Instead she would sit all day in the greasy floral rocking chair that had become her throne, surveying a dreary kingdom of dust and delirium. She had long stopped bathing and washing, and she lived in a tatty blue dressing gown that she pinned over her frame with one precarious button. She was oblivious to me and to all that a child needed, and I relied on my father for meals and clean underwear. He would get me out of bed before leaving for work in the morning, and we would eat our cereal in silence as my mother slept. He would be on his way to work by seven each morning, leaving me alone with my mother, but in his rush he often failed to notice that my school uniform or shoes had grown too tight or that I had no other clothes because my mother was incapable of taking me to buy any. I spent that particular summer holiday wearing the same ghastly grey hand-me-down dress, a rare gift from my mother. She did not wash it once in six weeks.

One day my mother decided, amid her madness, that she would benefit from a creative outlet, a way to drown out the delirium. She settled on the organ, and an annoying little man who looked like a bible salesman duly arrived later that week to install the huge instrument. He set it up in the back room, usually my father's domain, and began to give lessons.

I hated that organ. The hideous brown beast, with its fake squat wooden casing, looked ridiculous next to my father's exquisite Japanese oak bar. He had fondly designed the bar himself, fashioned as it was with barley twist carved columns, brass fittings, and a copper bell that he had screwed to the side to ring for last orders.

Organ music became the soundtrack to my endless summer. My mother embraced her new hobby wholeheartedly; the organ provided her with yet another emotional outlet as she sobbed and chain-smoked over the hideous contraption. She thumped out Engelbert Humperdinck's "Please Release Me Let Me Go" with violence and sang the lyrics lustily, artlessly, between drags of her cigarette.

Such obsessions were typical accompaniments to my mother's depression and melancholia. She became obsessed with my health and developed a crippling fear of anything she perceived to be unclean. Her greatest fear was that she would infect me with some unknowable contaminant and that, once infected, I would die because of her. Her neuroses prompted an endless monologue of, "Is it fresh?" as she sniffed her way through the contents of the fridge. "Is this clean?" she would ask, thrusting crockery under my father's nose as he tried to read the newspaper after work. Her harassment often drove him out of the house.

"Pull yourself together, for fuck's sake," he would say as he rose to his feet, his dining chair scraping hideously against the floor. My position in this awful tableau was usually behind the kitchen door, where I stood wordlessly, watching my parents argue. Both my father and I retreated to the garden when we had had enough. He was most content in the company of our dogs, who my mother largely ignored, while I was happiest in my lush world of plants, flowers, birds, and insects.

That summer, thanks to the arrival of the organ, the house changed from a place of near silence—punctuated by Mother's conversations with those she alone could see—to a kind of amateur music hall, driving me to seek comfort in my "study." This was really a drab spare bedroom with a creaking bookcase, a divan, and a large table (made by my father) above which was taped a vast map of Africa. I had recently found some posters I liked in Pretoria's only art shop, and I livened the dull magnolia paintwork with the beauty of Henri de Toulouse-Lautrec, Alphonse Mucha, Alfred Sisley and Pierre-Auguste Renoir. Mucha was, and still is, my favourite: a mysterious mixture of sensuality, beauty, confidence, and romance.

On the windowsill, pride of place, was my tiny transistor radio, which served as a gateway to another world. At the turn of its dial my little radio brought colour, excitement, humour, and comfort. It told of a world outside myself and outside the house's oppressive atmosphere of mental illness, fear, and anxiety. The radio distracted me and made me feel there was a future, that my life could and would improve as I lurched towards adolescence.

Back then, the English radio service of the South African Broadcasting Corporation (SABC) was hardly an impartial and factual source. I enjoyed *The Goon Show*, *The Men from the Ministry*, *Just a minute*, Anthony LeJeune's *London Letter*, *The Navy Lark*, and many more. Through my radio, I became curious about a world outside South Africa—a world I was yet to know.

My shows took me everywhere, but I most cherished my journeys else-where in Africa. This was the origin of my lifelong interest in the continent and her people. I listened to news broadcasts every hour and learned about liberation movements and political struggles. Even SABC as a state-controlled mouthpiece couldn't censor everything about the independence mania that was gestating and would, in a few years' time, lead to a clutch of new African states being born.

Sometimes my curiosity got the better of me, at which point I would attempt to talk with my father about morsels I had heard on the news. I surprised him with my interest in politics and amused him with my increasing fear, brought about by state propaganda, that the Russians were desperate to seize the Cape sea route and all South Africa's gold and diamonds. This was why the Soviet Union backed the liberation movements in Angola, Mozambique, Zimbabwe (then known as Rhodesia), and South Africa. According to SABC, the Russians wanted to bring our government to its knees ... the Russians wanted to steal the farmland from its White custodians and give it all to the Blacks ... the Russians were evil ... the Russians were everywhere, and South Africa's days were numbered. I lapped this up, at first, and my childish prayers at the time centered on keeping my family safe during the Russian invasion that was surely imminent. Thus my youthful terror embraced not only the very real fear of what was happening under my roof, but also the imagined horrors of the outside world. It was a fearful existence.

In time, however, my views changed. As I grew and learned, Russia stopped terrifying me and started to intrigue me instead. I was drawn by a kind of intellectual magnetism towards this superpower that was constantly vilified in biased news broadcasts, and which I soon learned—through my own research—was nothing like it had been made out to be. I immersed myself in the history of the Russian Revolution; I listened and learned and gradually developed a greater awareness of the world.

My politics, too, would in time take on a distinctly Soviet flavour. I became a great believer in socialism, which I saw as a solution to South Africa's own problems.

As a precocious teenager, I longed to travel to Moscow, to see St Basil's Cathedral, and to take part in the glorious November Parade in Red Square. In my imagination the bravery of Lenin and the Bolsheviks fused with my popular Russian folk tales of love, death, and suffering. It seemed that to be Russian was to be truly alive. The only problem was that I was a South African, which—according to SABC—meant the Russians were my mortal enemies.

In time, my radio also evoked a crucial revelation that struck much closer to home. I learned that the rest of the species was not quite so obsessed with race and politics as we South Africans were. In other countries, your skin colour wasn't the be all and end all, and even as a child it was obvious to me that there were better ways to organize society than by racial classification. My radio taught me how, in other countries, Black and White people had found ways to live alongside each other, peacefully and happily. Of course, racism was still rife throughout the world, although in more developed countries there was much less of it, and what racism there was already less overt and enthusiastic than the explicit campaigns of division waged here in South Africa. I could see, thanks to my growing interest in the wider world, that racial equality was a value to be cherished, something that made life better for everyone. I was unusual, and fortunate, among White South Africans to have learned this lesson at such a young age. Many of my countrymen would never learn it at all.

No school friends ever visited my unharmonious family home. I was too worried that anyone I invited over would take one look at my delirious, organ-obsessed mother and run the other way. Not that I had many friends to invite. I was viewed at school as an oddball and a nerd, in part because of my obsession with the radio. My rebellious streak, and my growing awareness of politics and injustice, made me stand out even more. I carried this reputation with me through my school years. The lack of friends didn't bother me, however, because even at that age I found my classmates' discrimination repugnant.

I was also teased and bullied for being different, for being an only child, for wearing glasses, and for having a crazy mother. And on the rare occasions when said mother was lucid enough to attend school open evenings, she always embarrassed me with her unwashed hair and dirty clothes (something I feel awful about these days, as I know somewhere in her disordered mind she was only doing her best). I would always creep into school the day after one of her disastrous cameos, trying to avoid the looks of pity from my teachers and the glares of disgust from my peers.

My friends then were my Barbie dolls. They were modeled on fashion icons like Jackie Onassis, Audrey Hepburn, and other famous women of the era. My own ragged, hand-me-down wardrobe was a world away from the elegance and opulence of my dolls' outfits, and to my mind they were all members of a happy, well-balanced family. I envied my worldly Barbies for their joyful outings, scarcely believing that the women they had been modelled on could be so fortunate as to travel the world. It seemed an almost impossible luxury that anyone should be able to go wherever and whenever they wanted. I collected stamps and fantasized about exciting far-away countries I had read about in my history books. And, as the summer dragged on, I read, played with my Barbies, and cranked up the radio, trying to drown out the cacophony of suicidal organ music from the opposite end of the house.

Throughout this troubled childhood, I found solace in music, too. I adored Bob Dylan, Joan Baez, and Leonard Cohen, all of whom stood, in my mind, for political change and liberation. These icons of mine advocated for personal freedoms that most South Africans could only dream of. I loved Dylan's prophetic, angry growl in "The Times They Are A-Changin'" and "Masters of War." My sadness and loneliness echoed that of Baez and Cohen as they sung of alienation, corruption, and injustice, all of which touched me passionately. During term time, I longed for the end of each school day so I could escape to listen to them; Dylan and Co. gave me a sense of hope that all was not in vain and that one day, during my lifetime, I would taste for myself the freedom evoked by their songs. In the process, I dreamed I would see my country change, and that said freedom would be extended to everyone under the vibrant South African flag, regardless of race or status.

This is how it all began: with a lonely, only child, terrified by the madness surrounding her yet unable to speak out about the fear and neglect that constituted her everyday life. Although he wasn't always much help, things were better when my father was home. I dreaded the moment every morning when he left for work, leaving me with my mother's galloping madness and my own catalogue of anxieties about the state of the world. Whenever she slept, I worried my mother wouldn't wake up. Whenever my father shut the front door, I worried he would never open it again. Whenever I heard shuffling in the hallway, I worried my own mother would try to hurt me. There was no love in her vacant stare. I had no idea what she was capable of.

She did attack me, once, during one of her angrier episodes. She hit me in the face with a Mason Pearson hairbrush, a hefty weapon. To both our surprise, I grabbed the brush and whacked her right back, knowing that I faced a hiding from my father when he returned from work. At least my stand put a stop to any further violence.

Social stigma didn't help our dysfunctional family situation. Mental illness was something South Africans just didn't talk about. My father knew how unwell my mother was, yet he never spoke openly about what was going on. I never received an explanation from anybody as to the nature and origins of my mother's afflictions, and neither did I receive any reassurance that she would, or even could, get better. I had to figure it all out for myself, and that left room for dark thoughts of my own.

Among my many worries, my greatest was that I had caused her madness by being a bad or disappointing child. Ironically, even as she was terrified of killing me with one of her invisible contaminants, I was fretting that by driving her mad I had condemned her to her own death. As much as I feared her, I was more worried that her death would bring total abandonment.

The summer days, despite the bright southern-hemisphere sun, were dark and hazy. The holiday eventually ended, and the daily distraction of school started up again, but that didn't mean my family's troubles were over. All the time, things were happening around me that my young brain just couldn't process. Looking back, I often wonder if my mother tried to take her life during that period. It would explain why, one morning, she was transported without anyone telling me to the Astrid Clinic, a mental hospital in downtown Pretoria. She was kept there for several weeks while a detached and bespectacled psychiatrist named Dr. Plomp took over her care. I came home from school on that first day, and she was just gone. I worried it was because of something I had done.

My father, however, must have known in advance that my mother was going away.

"Be nice to your mother," he had growled as a parting shot that morning, as he was leaving for work. I tried to question which of us should be the one being nice to the other, but I was met with a stony stare. "Susan," he said. "If I had to choose between your mother and you, I'd choose your mother. You're spoilt and selfish. This is your fault because you won't listen to her!" That was the moment my nine-year-old heart was crushed. I knew then without a doubt that I was unloved.

Dr. Plomp was there when I visited my mother that evening. She had been prescribed shock therapy to jolt her out of her depression, and the doctor cautioned me she might not recognize me at first—a temporary side effect of having 120 volts of electricity pumped directly through her skull. As he delivered this news, Dr. Plomp made a point of examining his shiny, black shoes. My mother, who had dribbled down her nightdress and was without her dentures, opened her eyes and stared at me with a blank look and a slack mouth. I wondered if it was possible to shock her into loving me.

Dr. Plomp presided over a series of shock therapy sessions, and we all waited patiently for the improvement that was supposedly just around the corner. My mother celebrated the triumph of her barbaric therapy by crying continuously. She developed anxieties about the end of the world, which she insisted was imminent, and she was slow in recovering her short-term memory. When we visited, she often did not know who we were, and at times she convinced herself she was a child again in the dusty, poverty-stricken railway camp at Cookhouse.

Sometimes she surfaced from her fantasies, but only briefly, and only when plied with drugs to take the edge off her nightmare world. She was never with us for long, however, because the nurses feared she would develop an addiction to the pills. So she was left to wander back to her own private universe, and the cycle of madness would begin again. It was impossible to trust her, or even to know her.

As her outpatient shock therapy continued, she wrestled with various obsessions, compulsions, and intrusive thoughts. She developed a claustrophobia that prevented her from closing the toilet door, using a lift, or travelling in a car with electric windows. She still thought she would infect me with a deadly illness and scrubbed her hands throughout the day, refusing to touch me or my clothing in fear of contamination. If we went anywhere, we could not leave the house until she had counted her way through endless rituals to make sure we turned every electrical appliance off, in case lightning struck the house and burned it all down.

Eventually my mother improved with a controlled (but addictive) drug regime and with weekly sessions with Dr. Plomp. That was until he moved away, at which point the wheels fell off. My mother took his departure personally, thinking he had rejected her, and through the tears and cigarette smoke I braced myself for more organ music. Fortunately for my father and I (but not for God), my mother discovered religion and threw herself into it wholeheartedly. She became a staunch member of the Women's Auxiliary at the local Methodist Church, which helped keep her distracted and focused.

Dr. Plomp had diagnosed her with Generalised Anxiety Disorder and depression, but the roots of my mother's illness were as physical as they were neurological. The origin of her disorders could be tracked back to a childhood of poverty and deprivation in the railway camps of the northern Cape. As a girl, she had sacrificed her education to nurse her mother through inoperable uterine cancer. Then, after she had trained as a nurse, she found herself caring for her terminally ill father as he died at the local hospital in Port Elizabeth. A childhood garnished with death must have had an effect in uprooting her psyche.

Thanks to the drugs, my mother eventually found some measure of peace and stability. But even in the not-so-bad times, we knew madness was never very far away. Each time she tried to change or come off her medication, she would have a wobble so seismic my father would roar, "For Christ's sake, keep taking the tablets! You're unbearable!"

Dementia exacerbated her madness in later life—so much so that after a harrowing visit to a residential home some years before her death, I said my final face-to-face goodbye. I promised we would still speak on the phone each week, and we did. But I could not bring myself to look into those pale, hateful eyes. Every time I saw her face she reduced me to that frightened nine-year-old girl.

Despite everything, I hold no grudges against my parents. Instead, I try to see how they attempted to do their best at raising a child even as they fought their own fragile psyches. And despite the challenges of growing up in such a dysfunctional family and doing so in a society that was embarrassed by mental illness and did not acknowledge it, I remained resilient and determined to live a life unlike my mother's. I was also determined to one day be a better parent than my father had been to me. Even if he rarely acknowledged it, he knew all along that my mother was very ill, a danger to herself and to me. He knew she was incapable of caring for me and that she often scared me. Yet he still left me alone with her almost every day. Truth be told, she frightened him too, but what frightened him more was the thought that people would find out about her mental illness and strange behavior. It was easier for him to lock her away in the house and escape each day to work than it was to confront the problem or to protect me.

CHILDREN OF THE REVOLUTION, 1976

THE FAMILIAR SOUND of ice cubes clacking against the glass was followed by the equally familiar sound of my father's sigh.

"Well, that's it," he said, walking in from the next room. He shook his head as he swirled his glass, whisky churning like an ocean. I caught the smell of peat. "Now we're going the same way as the rest of Africa. It's only a matter of time."

My father, never one for optimism, stared glumly at the small television. On the screen, in black-and-white, a hysterical teenage girl ran towards us. She was holding the body of her brother in her arms. He had been killed by police bullets.

This was one of the images that, for me, defined the Soweto Uprising. The massacre was the lead item on the evening news and the source of my father's concern. We sat quietly, transfixed by the shrill indignation of the newsreader, his monologue delivered over pictures of Black schoolchildren, no older than myself, marching towards the camera, column after column. These children had rage in their eyes, hatred on their faces, and even from where I was sitting their outrage seemed so tangible I feared the screen would shatter with the force of it.

My mother, wringing her hands, checked once more that the front door was locked. She had banished the dogs to the garden, the first line of defence against the "marauding mobs." Never mind that the demonstrators were mostly school-age children. White South African homeowners feared nothing more than a Black uprising—after all, the Blacks had numbers on their side—and whenever racial tensions threatened to bubble over, hysteria gripped the suburbs.

I stood behind my parents as they stared at the screen.

"They bloody brought it on themselves," my father muttered between sips of whisky. He was talking about the "Nats," the ruling Afrikaner National Party. He was cross at the Nationalists for provoking the Blacks, and he was cross at the Blacks for threatening the system of racial division from which he benefited. "They've gone too far—no wonder these kids are rioting. Bloody Nationalists." The veins in his neck bulged above his collar, and his cheeks grew hot with alcohol and indignation. "The best thing you can do, Susan, is to bugger off. Leave. Get away from here. This is just the beginning. There is no place for the White man in this country!" He slammed down his whisky glass, and I flinched, fearing it would shatter.

"Don't say that!" my mother said. The phone rang, and she rushed off to answer it. Her church friends had been calling all afternoon to share their fears about the beginning of the revolution. The Soweto Uprising was all anyone would talk about. It seemed a seismic event, a turning point. "Let's hope they stop them before they march to Pretoria," my mother called over her shoulder, before picking up the phone and launching into a concerned clucking. "Ag, I know ... it's awful."

The TV showed police officers and soldiers swarming through the streets of Soweto, a township in Johannesburg, as they tried to suppress the uprising. They set dogs on schoolchildren and fired live ammunition into the crowds. Coils of tear gas reached upwards from ruptured canisters. Anyone who got too close would be beaten back with *sjamboks*, heavy leather whips used in close-quarters crowd control. Many children were shot in the back as they tried to run. Officially, 176 people died that day. However, this may be an underestimate, and some believe as many as 700 students were killed in the fighting.

I was fourteen. The same age as many of the children who were bleeding and dying on the TV. Sobbing parents combed the streets of clotted sand, searching for their children. Footage showed adults cradling small, broken bodies. The implication conveyed by the newsreader was that these people deserved this for opposing the state and threatening to upset the system.

Those children had little enough, and not much left to lose. The flashpoint for the uprising was a new rule that would displace English as the official primary language of South Africa, changing it instead to Afrikaans. Afrikaans was the language of the Nationalist Party, the chief oppressor, and this outrage was the final straw for a generation of young people who had never enjoyed the rights and dignity afforded to their Afrikaner peers.

At schools in the townships, only basic literacy and numeracy were taught, and national history was imparted from the White man's perspective. The Nationalist government wanted to keep the Black population under-educated and ill-informed. In the eyes of the government, the Blacks were there only to serve the Whites, and it was considered dangerous to arm the Black masses with an education. But now the Nationalists were learning that it was just as dangerous to inflict needless humiliations upon an already desperate population. Because of the new primary language law, townships all over the country seethed with anger. Footage of the Soweto Uprising only stoked the fires. Survivors of the massacre fled the country in large numbers to join ANC training camps elsewhere in Southern Africa.

My parents had a schizophrenic attitude towards the whole situation. They feared the Black masses yet they hated the Afrikaners, who they believed were liable for most of the country's problems. They generally avoided talking about race in polite company, but I grew up with political conversations during the weekly Sunday roast, when, after a few drinks, they voiced their true opinions.

By now, I had grown out of my childhood fears concerning the "Red Peril." My parents, however, still believed the fiction that Soviet communists were set on destroying South Africa. The government's radio propaganda still insisted the Soviets were after our gold, diamonds, raw materials, and the Cape Sea Route.

Worse still, in the 1960s and 70s we were told that the Soviets were backing liberation movements throughout Africa, as country after country cast off the shackles of colonialism and achieved independence, usually through guerilla warfare. This, at least, was true. Even then, senior ANC members in South Africa were closely watching developments in other African countries and learning how to wage an armed struggle against a powerful and organised colonial state. We were told in biased broadcasts that the revolutionary wave sweeping Africa would result in Whites being killed or driven into the sea.

By the time of the Soweto Uprising in June 1976, I had long developed my own views about our nation, the continent, and the wider world. I didn't share my parents' fear of the poor Black children who were being gunned down on the other side of the country. I remember sitting calmly in the bath on the night of the uprising, looking at my white legs, magnified by the water. The well-lit bathroom and the white tiles completed the entire glaring image of Whiteness before me. How could it all be about colour? Why was I different to the children of Soweto? We all bled just the same.

The image of the broken boy lying in his sister's arms flashed before me again. Where was she taking him? Where were their parents? Who would help them? Something awful had happened, and nobody was there to comfort them or make it right. It could never be right.

And yet the children on the screen did not seem like children to me. Their expressions were like nothing I had ever seen in the blue eyes and pale faces of my classmates. The children of Soweto looked more like adults, their bearing and expressions revealing a depth of emotion I was yet to develop. They had known suffering and they had known pain in ways no child should. They weren't really children because they had never been permitted a childhood. Instead, their innocence had been ripped from them and crushed into the blood-stained dust of the township by a policeman's boot.

Over the following days, I reflected on the images I had seen on the television and on the narrative pushed by the state-controlled media. I felt a strange mixture of feelings, but among the general malaise I was able to unpick strands of fear, sadness, anger, horror, and, above all, outrage. It was an outrage that any of this could be allowed to happen. I was particularly disgusted that so much private suffering—that girl with the boy in her arms—had been splashed across our TV screens for us to gawp at and discuss, as if it were a weather or traffic report.

While many of the Whites I grew up with chose to ignore—or even endorse—the system that made this so, it didn't take me long to realize the essential truth that apartheid was humanity at its very worst. This was a truth that billions of people all over the world would come to see, evidenced by the numerous campaigns to sanction and boycott South Africa. There were no winners under apartheid, of course. But not everyone had as much to lose.

This was the South Africa I knew, a country whose surface-level beauty belied a deep ugliness. As a White girl, my South Africa should have been a country of sweet peaches and birdsong. But for the Black majority this was the furthest place from paradise. I wasn't blind to that fact, and I remain aware today that my upbringing couldn't have been more divorced from the experiences of most South Africans. I don't claim to have felt firsthand the horrors of apartheid or to have known the suffering of my Black countrymen. The story of apartheid and the toppling of the regime that instituted it is a predominantly Black story. But there was a shared humanity in our opposition to the regime, and that day I made a choice to wield the privilege of my birth against the system that had taken power from my Black countrymen and invested it in me.

In deciding that I wanted to do something about the world, to change the way things were but didn't have to be, I felt a new and forbidden excitement. Above all, I wanted to have been there in Soweto, among those impossibly brave students who had seen the world as it was and decided to stand up against the injustice of it—even if that meant facing down bullets and *sjamboks*. It became my most closely guarded secret that I wished to be there marching with those children, even if it was the barrel of gun I was marching towards.

Ending apartheid was the work of years and the work of millions. I was just one in this huge, human movement. But even then, I knew I would be content to be just one tile in the ever-growing mosaic that would one day depict freedom and dignity for all South Africans.

BEER AND SUNBURN, 1979

LAUGHTER CUT THROUGH THE NIGHT. The atmosphere was heavy, smoke and sweat mixing with the odours of charred meat and spilled beer. The sour stench of fresh vomit rose from a nearby flower bed. That won't do the roses much good, I thought, as I peered through the gloom. I had to breathe through my mouth so I didn't gag. It was a typical Friday night in the wealthy suburb of Waterkloof.

Our neighbours were all professionals: all rich and all White. There were three American diplomatic families among the Waterkloof set and, with the benefit of hindsight, I can see now that these were most likely CIA employees: the organization took a very keen interest in South African politics during the 1970s. I found these foreigners intriguing, and I listened closely whenever they spoke of the world beyond my narrow horizons. Many evenings were spent on their manicured lawns—*braais* and beers amid the safe, leafy surroundings of the suburbs. At such times, I couldn't help but imagine life in the townships. The decadence and indulgence of my neighbours' lawn parties was excessive enough. But to live so well in an enclave surrounded by abject poverty, hunger, and sickness was obscene.

Tonight I didn't even have the benefit of the Americans and their stories to pass the time. Instead, sprawled on the patio, their meaty faces burned red, were White South Africa's finest. A pack of young men, all in varying states of undress and inebriation, lounged on the concrete patio beside the swimming pool. A few Castle Lager bottles bobbed in the water; the sun reflected off them and bounced prisms of light back onto the white walls of the immense house. "You Ain't Seen Nothing Yet" by Bachman-Turner Overdrive blared from the record player, and some of my scantily clad school friends, sporting big hair and bigger heels, danced unsteadily in a corner of the garden. We were at that age where we thought looking cool was a matter of clutching a beer can in one hand and a cigarette in the other.

The guffaws reached a crescendo, as if the men by the pool had heard nothing funnier in their lives. Their laughter was like the braying of donkeys or—more appropriately—the "hee-haws" of jackasses.

The object of their amusement was Steve Biko, the leader of the anti-apartheid South African Black Consciousness Movement. This was a group that sprung up to fill the vacuum left by the crackdown on ANC leadership after the 1960 Sharpeville Massacre—a slaughter that saw hundreds of peaceful protestors gunned down by the apartheid state for demonstrating against the Pass Laws. Like at Soweto, many demonstrators were shot in the back by the police as they ran for safety. In total, there were 249 casualties, including 29 children. As a result of the disorder, the state came down hard on the ANC leaders who were viewed as agitators and, wrongly, held responsible for the violence.

After the massacre, Steve Biko became a senior anti-apartheid figure and a thorn in the government's side. He had died of brain damage in 1977 after being severely beaten by the Security Police whilst in detention. News of his death, initially denied by the apartheid regime, led to protests around the world and a United Nations-imposed arms embargo against South Africa.

At the time, the mean-spirited and pig-eyed Minister of Justice and Police, Jimmy Kruger, told the world that Biko had died whilst on a hunger strike. However, the truth had since emerged.

Biko had been arrested for his anti-apartheid activities in Port Elizabeth. He was tortured at the hands of police officers before being transported some 700 miles to Pretoria Central Prison. He spent the whole journey in the back of a police van, nursing critical injuries. In Pretoria, he was left chained on the floor of a filthy hospital cell, and it was here that he died. Despite a post-mortem that revealed five major injuries to his brain, and other injuries caused by beating and assault, the judgement at the inquest was that "no one was to blame" for Biko's death. Some (White) commentators even suggested Biko had committed suicide—by beating out his own brains on the urine-soaked floor of the hospital at Pretoria Central Prison.

As a fifteen-year-old, I followed the lies published in the wake of his death with a rising anger and hatred. Meanwhile, my school friends were more interested in who had groped who at last weekend's party. My classmates rarely read newspapers, listened to the radio, or watched news bulletins. They were oblivious to the existence of a world outside their own in a way that only the privileged could be. They couldn't understand why I cared so much about anything that mattered.

Once, after a heated classroom debate on human rights, my teacher took me aside and told me to calm myself down because my views were "upsetting" my conservative classmates. The isolation and friendlessness I faced as a result made me all the more determined to break out of the cocoon of unknowing that surrounded me.

We know now that Steve Biko was officially the forty-sixth victim of torture and death under the apartheid government's State Security Laws, which were instituted to crack down and repress opposition groups. At the time, Minister Kruger went on record to say that Biko's death "left [him] cold." But this state-sanctioned murder did not leave me "cold." It left me furious. And I was even more furious when I saw—egged on by the laughter of his friends—a drunken ass enacting the scene of Steve Biko's "suicide" by the pool of a luxurious house in one of Pretoria's most exclusive White suburbs.

The ass in question mimicked how Biko was supposed to have repeatedly smashed his head against the concrete floor. The audience of White suburbanites loved it. They howled and brayed with laughter, and shouts of "stupid *kaffir*" came from the inebriated crowd.

Bile rose in my throat as the pinpricks of hot tears burned in my eyes. The red flower of rage that bloomed across my chest made it hard for me to catch my breath. I turned and walked away from the scene as fast as I could.

MOSCOW BY THE MINES, 1979

In 1979 I FINISHED HIGH SCHOOL and entered university, which took me away from Pretoria. I chose to study in Johannesburg, at the University of the Witwatersrand—Wits, as everyone called it. Along with the University of Cape Town, Wits had a reputation for being one of the most liberal and left-wing universities in the country. The two institutions were cynically known in the press as "Moscow by the Mines" (Wits) and "Moscow by the Sea" (UCT). This didn't put off a teenaged rebel who was obsessed with the Soviet Union, increasingly convinced that only communism could save South Africa.

Because of their use of English, both Wits and UCT were viewed with suspicion by Afrikaners. They were thought of as hotbeds of rebellion and revolutionary thought, a reputation they both deserved. Students from Wits and UCT often fell foul of apartheid legislation that censored speech and inhibited political association. Outspoken meetings and incendiary student newspaper articles often attracted the attention of the police, and many young revolutionaries were detained, tortured, or imprisoned over the years. I had absolute admiration for those who paid such a price, but I realised even then that they would always be watched closely after their release. This would limit what they could achieve in politics and prevented them from operating outside of suspicion. I thought it was far better and more effective to keep my head down—for now, at least.

I enrolled for a social sciences degree and became engaged to a fellow ANC supporter. But even as I was signing up for my course of study, I was desperate to sign up for something bigger, something better. I wanted to join the ANC.

By now, the ANC had already been banned for twenty years; its supporters were routinely persecuted, and many of its leaders had been imprisoned or exiled. Chapters of the ANC still existed at home and overseas, with an official headquarters operating out of Zambia, but rather than functioning as a political party, it was now forced to operate as an underground resistance movement. It was known that the ANC employed undercover agents tasked with destabilizing the South African regime from within, while the direct action of its armed wing, uMkhonto we Sizwe (MK), known as "The Spear of the Nation," was more overt. Throughout White South Africa, and in the eyes of the government's international allies—including those in America and Britain—the ANC was a terrorist organization. MK was even worse.

"The time comes in the life of any nation when there remain only two choices—submit or fight," reads MK's manifesto. "That time has now come to South Africa. We shall not submit and we have no choice but to hit back by all means in our power in defence of our people, our future, and our freedom."

The ANC was the natural rallying point for serious opponents of the government. And through my new sister-in-law, Joan—an exile living in Zambia—I was able to make contact with the banned organisation.

Joan Brickhill had worked as a journalist until, a few years earlier, the Security Police came calling to investigate one of her stories. She refused to reveal her sources and was forced to flee South Africa, which is how she ended up in Zambia. There, she found work at the ANC's headquarters and became directly engaged in the struggle for a free and equal South Africa. Her husband, Jeremy, was a senior military intelligence officer in the Zimbabwe People's Revolutionary Army, the military wing of the Zimbabwe African People's Union (ZAPU). Joan and Jeremy were staunch ANC supporters, and they were friendly with a senior ANC member and MK military intelligence officer by the name of Ronnie Kasrils.

Finally I saw how I could help shape the new, democratic South Africa I had always hoped to see. I wanted to join the ANC and become involved in the armed struggle. All I cared about, even as I embarked on my university career, was leaving South Africa at last and joining the resistance. I wanted to live in a better world, and I was prepared to die if my blood would help forge one.

I wanted to know the smallest details about Joan and Jeremy and the mysterious Ronnie Kasrils. I learned that Ronnie and his wife Eleanor were regular guests at Joan and Jeremy's dilapidated second home in London. It turned out that this venue was a favorite haunt of political activists in both ZAPU and the ANC. Joan and Jeremy's life was peopled with an exciting cast of communists, socialists, and radicals. Their address book read like a who's who of the various liberation struggles of Southern Africa.

Theirs was a world I longed to inhabit, an existence that couldn't have been further from my conservative upbringing. I had been raised with a front-row seat to apartheid, and all my life I had been a spectator of injustice without seeing how I could possibly prevent it. But now I had a chance to tear up my ticket and storm the field. I wanted to meet these shadowy ANC cadres in exile; I was sure the organization needed all the help it could get and would jump at the chance to recruit another idealistic young revolutionary. As a White girl from the suburbs, the struggle for Black rights may not have been mine. But as a South African—as a human being—I was fully invested in the fight for equality.

I would be breaking the law and risking social exile just by associating with these cadres from a banned organization. In the eyes of my family and community, I would be betraying my race and my country. I was all in.

LIVING A LEGEND, 1981

IN THE SUMMER OF 1981, I made my first trip to London to make contact with the ANC. I was wide-eyed and overawed, and although I was there to meet Joan and Jeremy's ANC associates, I couldn't help but indulge in a flurry of sightseeing first.

Once I had seen enough of Big Ben and the Houses of Parliament, I was introduced to Aziz Pahad, a member of the National Executive Council (NEC) of the ANC. Once a political prisoner and now subject to a banning order, Aziz had left South Africa for London after the Rivonia Treason Trial sentenced Nelson Mandela to life imprisonment in 1964. Aziz was busy in his exile; he helped establish the Anti-Apartheid Movement (AAM) in the UK and Europe and was already an important figure in the ANC diaspora. He would later become even more important: in 1994 Nelson Mandela made him Deputy Minister of Foreign Affairs.

When I met Aziz I was pleased enough to be face-to-face with an ANC organiser and recruiter, although my excitement didn't last long. Our meeting took place at a pub in Paddington, our conversation hushed beneath the chatter of punters and a patter of rain against the windows.

Aziz was not what I had expected. He looked miserable, his eyes expressionless above a thick beard and moustache that made him seem like he was all hair. When I told him I wanted to join the ANC, he looked at me like I was a mutant. Perhaps he had not had many young, White South African women approach him before, but Aziz seemed to avoid my eyes. He made me feel invisible and clearly didn't take me as seriously as I took myself back then. But perhaps he was right to be guarded.

The South African newspapers at the time were full of stories about spies and informants, many of whom were embedded among the left-wing student population. Espionage had become something of an obsession for the paranoid apartheid government, and puppet journalists filled their pages with photos of ANC spies whose covers had been blown. In response to the hysteria they themselves had whipped up, the government ensured every university intake was populated with a handful of its own agents to flush out the ANC's recruits. There were so many exposés about student spies and counter-spies at the time that it seemed every campus had two informants for every genuine student. When I met Aziz, the student movement was a viper's nest of agents and double-agents, hence his wariness towards me.

Years before, in 1973, the Student Representative Council (SRC) at Wits had had several spies elected on to it, including Craig Williamson, an under-cover Security Policeman. Other notable names included Special Branch officer Heston de Bruin, whom I would later encounter in Namibia, and Paul Sarbutt and Arthur McGivern, both agents of the Bureau of State Security, the state intelligence agency established in the sixties under General Hendrik van den Berg.

The apartheid State viewed Wits as a hotbed of communist depravity and had installed Williamson as a so-called "lightning conductor," an intelligence term for someone who draws attention away from real—and much more subtle—spies placed to gather significant information. In this case, the role of intelligence gathering fell to de Bruin, Sarbutt, and McGivern. Williamson was brash, gauche, and pushy, which made him perfect for the role.

The government's infiltration of the student movement yielded awful results. Throughout the seventies and eighties, several prominent student leaders were arrested and imprisoned after they were caught out by government spies posing as fellow ANC supporters. On release they told of torture and interrogation, and many young detainees were utterly broken in their captivity. Anxiety, depression, and Post-Traumatic Stress Disorder (PTSD) were common among the victims of the apartheid state's brutality.

Some student radicals, like Ahmed Timol, never made it out alive. The police detained Timol under the Terrorism Act and charged him with being a member of the ANC and the South African Communist Party (SACP). He fell to his death from a window on the tenth floor of the police headquarters in John Vorster Square, Johannesburg. The police claimed he committed suicide, and in 1972 an official inquest ruled no one was guilty for his death. But I didn't believe it for a second, and a judicial review in 2017 found Timol had indeed been tortured and murdered by the police.

The stakes were high, then, as Aziz Pahad tried to work out if I was really the person I claimed to be. For all he knew, I could have been working for the government. For all he knew, I could have just been a dumb and unserious kid who would abandon ship at the first sign of trouble.

Aziz asked, in a detached and perfunctory way, what I planned to do with myself when I was finished in London. When I told him I was going to go back to South Africa I thought I detected a flicker of interest, a spark of life in those dead eyes.

"Here's what you should do," he said, flapping his large hands gracelessly over his pint glass. "Go back to South Africa and create a legend for yourself. Make this legend and stick to it religiously. And then come back to us when you're living the lie."

This advice would later prove to be among the best I was ever given. At the time, however, I was dejected at being essentially told to go away and try again in a few years. Really, it was in that moment that my espionage training started.

I left London feeling like a failure. My hope had been that Aziz would recommend me to another ANC higher-up, perhaps Joan's associate Ronnie Kasrils, or that I would be asked to join the resistance straight away. Instead I was instructed to go back home and blend in with everyone else. Only then, once I was beyond reproach—a good and wholesome member of White society— would I be useful to the ANC.

I wanted to join more than anything, so I did as I was told. I went back to South Africa and tried something I had never done before: I tried to blend in. I created a legend for myself, and I made a commitment to living it.

REPUBLIC DAY, 1981

"FUCK YOU, you fucking *kaffir* lover! You communist cunt! Fuck you!"

The Afrikaner thug in the blue uniform was close enough that I could taste the nicotine and onion breath that stuck to his words. His mouth was creased in anger and his eyes bulged with hatred. I winced, fearing a blow, but at that moment the sounds of commotion came from elsewhere in the crowd and the policeman hurried off, brandishing his *sjambok*.

It was May 31st, Republic Day, a national holiday to mark the date in 1961 when South Africa officially broke free from the British Empire and became an independent country. The nation's twentieth birthday would also be the day I first saw police brutality with my own eyes. What we experienced was nothing like the barbarism that had been unleashed against the student protesters of Soweto in 1976 or during the Sharpeville Massacre of 1960. But it was enough to politicise—there and then—those White, sheltered, middle-class students who witnessed it.

It was a frosty morning on the Wits campus, and a large group of students had gathered early on the grass to smoke roll ups and drink coffee ahead of a protest that was due to start at lunchtime. Most Wits students would take any chance to demonstrate against the government, and Republic Day provided the perfect backdrop. Someone had brought a massive South African flag. Its colours were bright against the cloudless cornflower-blue sky.

I had already decided to avoid the political gatherings and marches that seemed to take place constantly around me. I believed living a legend meant living apolitically, feigning detachment to the radical cause that obsessed so many of my peers. It was frustrating to watch these mass actions from the sidelines when all I wanted to do was get stuck in, but I reminded myself often why I had made this choice. I wanted to work undercover for the ANC, where I could do the most good. Missing out would be worth it if it meant I stayed unknown to the police, with no photos of me on any of their files.

It proved hard to resist the lure of student politics, but I managed. Subjects that had been so mindfully ignored in the staid comfort of suburban sitting rooms and on the *stoeps* (verandas) of the eastern suburbs of Pretoria swirled around me at Wits. My past seemed to have disintegrated, floated away like Transvaal dust on the wind. In its place was left a red, raw anger that seethed somewhere beneath my breastbone. A year later, this anger would force me to make an exception to my no-protests rule—but only once.

On February 5, 1982, Dr. Neil Aggett, a White trade unionist, was found dead in his cell after being detained without trial for seventy days. Aggett, a physician who practiced in Black hospitals in Soweto and elsewhere, had been interrogated and tortured at the police headquarters at John Vorster Square. I was among the 15,000—including Desmond Tutu (Bishop)—who attended his funeral, and I joined a march across Johannesburg afterwards.

Police officers had allegedly stripped Aggett naked and suspended him upside-down from the ceiling (a technique referred to as "the helicopter" by security police), before placing a wet sack over his head and attaching electrodes to his genitals. When he was found hanged in his cell, the official line was that he had killed himself, although it was clear to me that his awful treatment was what drove him to look for respite in death. I had heard of so many atrocities carried out under apartheid, but the torture of this principled trade unionist was not something I could ignore.

The inquest into Aggett's death attracted global attention. Former detainees testified they had also been tortured by the police—the first time such a claim had been heard in a South African court. Aggett himself had lodged a complaint of torture against his chief interrogator, Lieutenant Steve Whitehead, the day before his death. The magistrate's ruling? It was a simple suicide, and the police weren't at fault.

In 2020, at the re-opened inquest, former security branch officer Nick Deetlefs stood accused with other former police officers of torturing scores of political activists, including Neil Aggett, on the notorious tenth floor of John Vorster Square. Throughout the apartheid years, eighty-nine political detainees died in custody without a single police officer being found guilty.

Growing up in a country where these atrocities were a regular occurrence fortified my resolve. I wanted to be part of the generation that would change South Africa forever, and as a first-year student at Wits I was unspeakably envious of those who had left the country to take up arms for the ANC. Growing up drenched in obscene White middle-class privilege was like being blinkered. It was like being trapped in a conservative world of narrow horizons, exposed every day to a microcosm of the suffering that was taking place throughout the country on an unimaginable scale but unable to do anything to change it.

In a way, I was looking for freedom too, albeit a different kind to the freedom sought by the Black masses. I wanted to be free from my past; free from the constraints of my world; free from being sent to university only so I could meet a professional husband; free from expectations; and free to make the choice to fight, and die, for a new South Africa. The anger seethed and bubbled. But I never let it show.

Many of my fellow students were overt and unashamed in their outspoken opposition to the government. I admired them for it, of course, but it did arouse suspicion. I took care not to even associate with the loudest radicals, in case my reputation was tainted by my proximity to rebellion.

Time proved some of my peers to be devoted contributors to a democratic South Africa. From my student days I knew figures who would become distinct in academia, like Dawid van Wyk, Eric Itzkin, and Mike Sarakinsky. Others, like eventual ANC spokesman Carl Niehaus, were less subtle, lurching from one messy public crisis to another. I always gave Niehaus a wide berth at university.

Naturally, feelings on campus were running high on that tinderbox Republic Day in 1981. I had just emerged from the social sciences block after an early lecture, and I was about to head to the library when I saw a group of students arguing around the oversized flag. One man lit a match and held it to the cheap nylon fabric. The flag took instantly; the whole thing went up with a whoosh of flame as acrid smoke bled into the air.

Most of the group looked horrified. The destruction of the flag was supposed to have taken place later that afternoon as part of the demonstration. Now they would have to find another one.

The blazing flag served to catch the attention of everyone nearby, its glow like the sweeping signal of a lighthouse. I saw a warning reflected in the flames, but most of my peers were drawn moth-like to the fire. Representatives from the Black Students' Society gathered around the flag and raised their fists in salute. Others joined in, and a cry of *"Amandla Awethu"* or "Power to the people" rose from the crowd. Moments later, the demonstrators broke into a rousing chorus of *"Nkosi Sikelel' iAfrika,"* the banned anthem of the ANC. Originally a church hymn ("Lord Bless Africa") composed in 1897 by Enoch Sontoga, a

Xhosa clergyman at a Methodist mission school, the song had since became associated with political defiance against apartheid.

A cohort of Security Policemen had been stationed near the campus in advance of the trouble expected that afternoon. They had many informants among the student body who would have warned them to expect something big to mark Republic Day. Campus would have been crawling with plainclothes police before the demonstrations even started, although so far the officers had been content to bide their time. But at the strains of the resistance anthem—a song that struck most White conservatives as a provocation—the police sprung into action.

As the plainclothes officers called for back-up, a small group of Black students began to perform the *toyi-toyi*, a war dance supposed to instill fear into the enemy—usually the police—during demonstrations and riots. Before long, hundreds of students were stomping their feet and chanting, turning their anger into a weapon and a bulwark. I had seen footage before of mass toyi-toyis, demonstrators wielding the power of the chant to stand their ground against police and soldiers armed with tear gas, rubber bullets, and live ammunition. And now a small army of students was performing it on the grass of the Wits campus to voice their disgust at commemorating the formation of a "republic" that oppressed the majority of its population. From my position nearby I could appreciate, for the first time, the war dance's true power. It was terrifying and awe-inspiring and galvanising all at once—not something you want to be on the wrong side of.

The toyi-toyi gathered momentum as students threw away their cigarettes and coffees and rose from the grass to join in. As the throng moved around the smouldering remains of the flag I heard again the strains of *"Nkosi Sikelel' iAfrika,"* the cries of "Power to the people!" There was applause and then the group started to drift towards the steps of the Great Hall, where the organisers of the protest were addressing the crowd.

It didn't take long for uniformed Security Police to arrive en masse, armed with dogs, photographers, and their trusty *sjamboks*. I suspect they had parked their vans on one of the roads near campus with enough officers and equipment to invade a small nation. It was one thing for Black students to be demonstrating, but the crowd that gathered was racially mixed. The police worked themselves into a frenzy at the sight of White protestors arm-in-arm with their Black friends and peers, joining the shouts that rang like a call to arms across the campus. To betray one's race was the ultimate transgression.

The Security Police first fanned out among those of us on the sidelines, establishing a perimeter around the steps of the Great Hall. Students shrunk away from raised *sjamboks*, and the crack of hard leather against soft flesh threatened anyone who stood their ground. Then the police formed a line, bristling with whips and clubs, and charged the mass of demonstrators by the steps. The students braced themselves for the onslaught, many of them linking arms.

Police photographers circled the crowd, randomly snapping anyone who got in their way. A few of the more brazen students swore at the photographers or tried to push their cameras out of their hands, but any and all resistance was met with a hard slap across the face—if you were lucky—or the biting sting of leather—if you weren't.

"We shall overcome, we shall overcome, we shall overcome one day ..." sang the students as the police charged towards them, bent on inflicting maximum damage in the shortest amount of time. Then came the screams and the barking of dogs, the smell of sweat and vomit, and the relentless whistle of *sjamboks* swishing through the air and, in almost the same moment, the crack of whips against Black and White flesh. There were tears and howls of pain and everywhere an all-encompassing panic, like someone had picked up the world and shook it and now it wasn't obvious which way was up or which direction gravity operated in.

The attack didn't last long, but the protestors had been routed and it was clear who had won. The police withdrew to their vans, which were parked nearby, and the arrival of the local press and TV crews filled the void they created. All around me discarded shoes sat in ones and twos on the grass, and bloodied ribbons of torn clothing flapped like streamers in the breeze. Here and there were protestors lying on the ground in pain and disbelief, cradling wounded limbs and calling out the names of their missing friends. Tiny fragments of the burned flag drifted through the air like black snow. The police had swept in with the sudden force of a tidal wave, and their withdrawal had left the ragged ephemera of humanity scattered across the lawns like debris on a beach.

Stunned and sickened, I made my way to the Great Hall, trying to see through tears of rage. Students were sitting on the steps, gathered into small groups for comfort and security. A kind of magnetism had pulled them together after the assault. Some were bleeding; others were crying. Above all hung an eerie quiet, and the day turned colder. It was as if the birds had stopped singing, and the sky that had seemed so bright just an hour ago now appeared leaden and charmless. The bare branches of the trees dotted around the lawns were dead and skeletal.

"How bad must this get before we do something?" I said to no one in particular. When I got closer, I saw the steps of the Great Hall were spotted with blood, the red sticky and incongruous against the white stone.

GIRLIE, 1982

BLOOD AND VOMIT was drying on the wooden floor in dots and dashes.

My hands shook as I gripped the mop, the bucket of disinfectant broiling at my feet. I scrubbed at the stains through tears of rage and sorrow, trying not to look at the reddish-brown swirls that pulled like threads through the soapy water. I cleaned up the worst of the mess and piled the clothes in a corner, ready for burning now that the district surgeon had taken away the underwear for testing.

The toilet seat was ringed with blood and shit, and I tried not to retch as I wiped off and flushed away the worst of it. There was so much blood, more than it seemed one person could possibly contain. Great clots of it swirled around the bowl of the toilet, the loud flush drowning—just for a moment—the sobs that came from the adjoining bathroom. There Janie sat in a tub filled with Dettol, the bathwater thick with the strawberries-and-cream froth of blood and disinfectant. She was shivering despite the heat of the water. I could only watch as she drew her knees to her chin and groaned in agony at the latest spasm to tear through her body. When the water started to cool from scalding to merely hot, she leaned over—despite the pain—and opened the hot tap all the way. Movement made the wounds start weeping anew.

When the water got too bloody, Debs and I lifted Janie out so we could clean and refill the bath. I held Janie, her body shaking in my arms, and wrapped her in a thick towel as Debs saw to the tub. More Dettol and more hot water.

We had tried to help Janie wash herself, but the pain was too intense and she couldn't stand us touching her, however gently. We could only offer her aspirin, which was all we could find in the kitchen cupboard. All the while, David paced up and down, shouting to himself. He was raging about how even rapists were victims of apartheid, how we were all fucked up by it. I tried to ignore him as I mixed the aspirin, but I had an overwhelming desire just to hit

71

him in the mouth—anything to stop the whine of his voice. He had to be the centre of attention, even now.

We were third-year students. I thought this sort of thing only happened to other people—to adults, not to us. I couldn't grasp the strangeness and brutality of it. It was like a slow, gut-churning nightmare that wouldn't end, however hard I tried to wake.

We did not know when Janie would stop bleeding or the extent of her injuries. After cutting off her clothes and performing the necessary vaginal and rectal swabs, the police had called the district surgeon, but he had shown little interest in treating or examining her properly. He stitched the worst of the cuts and gave her a tetanus shot, but he could do nothing for the bruises that were blooming all over her body. The bitemarks on her face and neck were still bleeding, and her skin was turning blue around her wounds. She had cried for hours already and showed no sign of stopping.

I thought my heart would break. I didn't know what I was feeling exactly, but I could identify some of the emotions that pulsed through me like toxins: anger, grief, disbelief, and the sheer horror that human beings could do this to another. Janie had been vaginally, orally, and anally raped. Then she was thrown out of a moving car onto a dirt road in the darkness as her drunk-and-high attackers laughed and sped off into the night.

She had stumbled in shock and agony, bleeding and sobbing, to the nearest farmhouse. She walked barefoot down a gravel track, a road studded with broken glass and thorns. At the farmhouse, the terrified occupants wrapped her in an old dog blanket and called the police. All the while they fretted that the people who had done this to her would come back and do the same to them.

The police arrived, but that wasn't the end of it. This was South Africa, after all, and no story of South African brutality can be told without the issue of race rearing its ugly head. Janie's race was mixed. This shouldn't have mattered, but it did.

The cops (all White) shoved Janie (Coloured) into the back of their van like she was a piece of luggage. The district surgeon (also White) swore at her for being the reason he was dragged out of bed in the middle of the night. When Janie threw up on the floor of his examination room, the doctor cursed and complained, and he was perfunctory in cleaning her up and stopping the worst of the bleeding. The policeman who took her statement was uninterested (because he was White and she wasn't). Janie called David (one of our mostly-White friendship group) to pick her up, and while she was waiting for him the (White) sergeant on duty stared at her with unconcealed disgust. He was even more outraged when David turned up: *a White man was friends with this hysterical Coloured girl? What was the country coming to?*

Janie arrived back at our place wrapped in a blanket and still bleeding profusely. Her teeth chattered from cold and shock, and Debs and I had to take extraordinary care in undressing and cleaning her. Every touch was like an aftershock of her attack. She begged us to run the bath as hot as we could get it, to pour in all the disinfectant we had. She cleaned her teeth over and over and only realised as the bristles emerged bloody that one of her attackers had chipped her teeth when he punched her in the face. Her eyes and nose kept swelling, and her hair was matted. Our first instinct was to hug her, but she recoiled through raw sobs.

I didn't know Janie that well back then; she wasn't the closest of my friends. But in that moment I knew her completely. Hers was the face of every woman in South Africa who was beaten and raped. She would bear the scars of that night forever. In the months to come she would crawl into the darkest recesses of her mind, start cutting her wrists, and search for oblivion on the cold tiles of the bathroom floor.

Debs cried without making a sound. She had been with Janie as they strolled through the *veld*, the bush, around the farm that balmy autumn afternoon. The two young women had walked together along a narrow track and Debs had listened as Janie confessed she had developed feelings for David. She was confused and worried; she didn't know what it would mean if she, as a Coloured woman, became involved with a White man.

Out of nowhere, a battered car carrying several young Coloured men appeared on the road. The car stopped, and the men eyed Janie and Debs through the dust-dulled windows. Both women had a bad feeling. They tried to run, stumbling over the uneven ground, but the men were quicker and stronger. They overpowered both of them and dragged them into the car, which reeked of booze and cannabis.

As the men drove away, they conducted a hurried conference, the girls screaming and struggling in their hands. Some of the men thought it was too risky to abduct a White woman. They knew the police would be immediately mobilised to hunt down a pack of Coloured men who had taken a White girl captive, and they knew they would be beaten and jailed—and possibly killed—if they were caught. The scenario fit a common narrative, at the time, of the dark-skinned barbarians desperate to defile any pure White girl they could get their hands on. An agreement was reached, and the car stopped abruptly, skidding to a halt in a cloud of grit and gravel.

Debs was thrown out of the car, landing heavily on the dusty track. The men decided it was too risky to take her, but Janie was fair game. If the police ever got involved in the abduction of a Coloured girl, they wouldn't pursue her attackers with anything like the same level of zealous fury as if a White girl had been taken. Everyone knew that if you raped a Black girl, you'd get away with a slap on the wrist—and that was assuming anyone believed the girl's story in the first place. Janie wasn't officially Black, in the eyes of those men, she was close enough to being Black that *she* didn't matter.

This was South Africa, and this was apartheid.

NEWSHOUND, 1983–1985

I GRADUATED IN 1983 into a society that seemed as broken and unjust as it had ever been. Apartheid still raged like fire, threatening to consume everything good and hopeful in this country of beauty and hatred, a land of inherent contradictions. If anything, the political situation was getting worse, and with each passing day I was increasingly committed to joining the struggle, to making good on my plans to live the legend of the apathetic White girl from the suburbs. I would make myself like a moonflower, become beautiful and benign and let everyone think I was nothing more than a pretty White rose. Only I knew my true nature, the hidden poison that was growing inside of me. I would make my burning rage felt when the world least expected it.

Now that I had graduated, I needed a job. What could be better cover, I thought, than working for one of the biased newspapers that served as mouthpieces for the apartheid government? So I donned a pencil skirt and kitten heels, straightened my shoulder pads, fluffed up my spiral perm, and went for an interview at *The Citizen*.

Founded in 1976, *The Citizen* was one of many pro-apartheid tabloids, although it was the only major English-language newspaper to support the ruling Afrikaner National Party. It seemed an excellent place to cut my journalistic teeth and make some government contacts, all while establishing an image of neutrality and indifference. The main man in those days of hard copy and clunky typewriters was Johnny Johnson, an old-school hack and a harddrinking, hard-working, foul-mouthed stereotype of an editor. He used to prowl the newsroom in shirt sleeves and baggy trousers with a pencil stuck behind his ear, shouting abuse at anyone who split an infinitive or missed the best news angle in a story.

I was shown into Johnny's office by Cecily, his wife. The room was powdered with cigarette ash, and we spoke through a haze of smoke. He looked me up and down and rose from behind his desk to get a better perspective. He was only five-foot-tall, and his huge personality seemed out of keeping with his tiny stature. After surveying me in his office, he asked me to turn around, which I duly did, spiral perm trailing behind me.

"So you wanna be a journalist?" he growled.

"Yes, please," I said. I gave him my widest eyes and brightest smile.

"Start tomorrow, nine a.m."

"Thank you, sir."

I spent the next few months wrestling with hideously boring copy and fighting off my lecherous colleagues, who seemed to think it was okay to play with my hair and touch my backside without my permission. They gave me the nickname "Fluffy," but I didn't mind, as it conveyed perfectly the vacuous character I had been trying to play.

At first, Johnny only ever assigned me to write pulp articles of no real significance. While the country burned and battles raged in the townships, I covered dog shows and drum majorettes.

Once, after a booze-soaked Christmas party, Johnny offered me a lift home. I was horribly naïve, and I didn't realise at the time that this was a euphemism for something else. He was way over the drink-drive limit and it didn't help that he was barely tall enough to see over the steering wheel. We wove our way through Doornfontein to my home in Yeoville, spluttering through every red light we encountered along the way. Outside the house he stopped, blocking both lanes of traffic, and turned to me.

"So," he slurred. "Do you want me to fuck you?"

It wasn't lost on me that the car door was locked.

"No," I said, after a moment's hesitation. "Thank you."

He visibly soured. "Go on then," he said. "Bugger off. I only gave you the job because you had nice tits."

He unlocked the door, and I scrambled out.

"Thank you, sir."

Things were never the same after that, and from then on Johnny growled and grunted through most of our interactions. I endured his scorn and tried to smile through the exoduses to the pub that occurred at every opportunity.

A few months later, a better vacancy arose, and I left *The Citizen* to work as a news writer at SABC—the horrendously biased broadcaster whose radio shows had ignited my obsession with the Soviet Union all those years ago.

It seemed posts in newspaper or broadcast journalism were easy to come by for anyone who was White, plugged-in, and fluent in English. It was common practice to start out on a local newspaper, affectionately known as "knock and drops" because they were delivered free to the doorsteps of households in White suburbia. Many of my colleagues had started their careers this way, while a handful like myself had been to university first. As a rule, specialised journalism degrees were frowned upon, as the embattled, deadline-obsessed newshounds who ran the papers believed the only way to grow into a competent reporter was to learn on the job—preferably after being thrown in at the deep end. I came to agree with this attitude; the only way to dig deeper into a story—and get closer to the truth—was to speak with people on the ground and get to grips with their reality.

To my surprise, the SABC interview went well. It was the first step towards true undercover work—work that demanded I convey a particular image and not allow myself to deviate from it. It was also the beginning of a life of control and discipline, one in which my true self and feelings had to stay hidden.

I enjoyed exploring this quality of self-control. It was good to know my legend was convincing, and this gave me the confidence to meld myself into who I needed to be. It encouraged me to watch, to listen, and to wait, always conscious of who or what was around me.

Working at SABC certainly fit the conservative, apolitical, airhead persona I strove for. However, positioning myself at the heart of the state broadcast media compromised my patience and my integrity. My first post was as a translator and writer on regional radio news, overseen by a boring middle-aged editor called Dick. He turned out to be a prime example of nominative determinism in action.

I translated reams and reams of rubbish from local news correspondents about the cherry crop in Vicksburg and the state of the roads in one-horse towns better suited to donkey carts than motor vehicles. At times, I thought I would genuinely go mad as Dick by name and by nature debated precisely which verb suited best the mood of each sentence.

Most of my colleagues were graduates from Afrikaans universities. As a rule, they were tight-lipped and conservative, and downright disapproving when they learned I had a degree from Wits, commie hotbed that it was. The editors I worked under regarded me with distaste and thought of me as something of a fallen woman. I once had a stand-up row with an unpleasant man who told me I was wasting my time at the SABC and that I would be better off staying at home and having children. The pent-up fury of several months unleashed itself as I launched into a tirade about small-minded provincial Boers who drank too much and harassed young women. He never bothered me again after that.

I begged anyone who would listen to transfer me to the news desk, where the stories were more serious and impactful. I passed the necessary security clearance for such a post by virtue of having no criminal record, and before long I was knee deep in bulletins and headlines, working shifts to feed a news machine that never slept. The stories we reported on were heavily censored, with most of the bulletin content coming from watered-down reports from the South African Press Association. We essentially served up news bulletins without the news.

The work was hard, but it was better than listening to Dick and his relentless, round-the-clock conjugating. I stuck it out for a year and half before I left for a job with better pay and career prospects, a decision that led me to *The Star*, a middle-of-the-road, liberal, White publication. The year, by then, was 1985, a time of growing disquiet in the townships. My work put me in the thick of the action, and every state of emergency was a new story. They kept coming thick and fast, and we kept writing about them. I was employed as a reporter and feature writer, but in time I found myself taking a growing interest in the crime reporters who sat near me. Most of them were on the payroll of the police.

They disliked me intensely at *The Star* because of my reluctance to talk about politics, from which they inferred I was a right-winger. They were wrong, of course, but I was cheered to know I was achieving the effect I had been aiming for. I also knew now how it felt to *really* not fit in: hated at one place for being an English-speaking liberal and then hated at another for being a Boerish reactionary. Such is the dilemma of working in plain sight. Nobody likes you, and you shouldn't care.

Thankfully, I didn't.

I thrived on shallow friendships, not giving much of myself away and making a rule never to express a political opinion. I felt, occasionally, that I had sold my soul to the devil. The result was a creeping exhaustion by the end of the working week, and as soon as Monday came round again—always too soon—I found myself longing for Friday evening when I would be free to remove the mask I had been wearing. Throughout this time I found comfort in the outdoors and distraction in the escapism of films. And whenever living a lie felt like too much, I reminded myself of the choice I had made. There was more at stake than my own well-being, and if it was a sacrifice the cause demanded, then it was a sacrifice I would endure.

RONNIE KASRILS, 1986

HE WAS DARK AND SWARTHY. And hairy. Very hairy. I was mesmerised, I remember, by his shaped nails and the black hairs growing in thickets up his fingers. He smelled of sweat, and his hands were shaking, the right more than the left. I wondered which of us was more nervous.

It was a humid summer evening in Golders Green, North London. Although the restaurant was busy, only his presence filled the room. At first glance he looked like any other balding, middle-aged man, but to those of us who knew him, he was so much more.

He had a dark, reptilian look. His eyes darted, taking in the diners and the door, and he never stopped watching. I learned later that he always chose to sit where he could see the entrance, and he always planned his escape upon entering a room for the first time. It's a habit familiar to anyone in our line of work, and one I still maintain myself. His little sideways glances reminded me of a chameleon, a creature I had admired all those years ago in the garden of my childhood. The comparison was apt; here was a man renowned for his ability to blend in with his surroundings. He flitted from country to country, and even among his allies he was notoriously difficult to pin down. He had a knack for avoiding surveillance that was close to magic.

His voice was deep, and he still retained a thick South African accent, which was surprising given he had spent so long away from his homeland. When he spoke, small drops of saliva gathered in the corners of his mouth and glistened for a few seconds before drying. I tried not to stare at Ronnie Kasrils, the most senior member of the ANC I had ever met.

Our meeting that summer evening in 1986 had taken years to arrange. He had heard about the White girl who was desperate to join the ANC, who had made contact with the organization years earlier but had been sent back home to master the art of blending in. I wanted to be a chameleon too, and already I was getting good at it. I just needed Ronnie to see that.

Ronnie Kasrils, Comrade Chameleon, had been involved in the struggle for most of his life. He had joined the South African Communist Party (SACP) all the way back in 1961, and soon after became involved in the then-fledgling ANC. The organisation sent him, along with 200 Black cadres, to the USSR in 1964 for military training. He worked his way up the ANC's ranks and by 1983 he was Chief of Intelligence in MK and a member of the armed resistance group's high command. Now his job included personally selecting promising recruits for military training in the USSR, where young idealists were tempered into battle-ready soldiers. I was desperate to be chosen.

From the early 1980s, international sanctions had started to weaken the apartheid regime. Government ministers in pork pie hats grudgingly made minor concessions and reforms to the system, but almost all injustices and inequalities remained, and any token reforms were nothing more than crumbs on the table. The people's anger was palpable, and they wanted more, so much more. But despite the anti-apartheid campaigns and concerts of the 1980s, the impassioned calls to release Nelson Mandela, and all that made South Africa a fashionable cause, we were still at war. A new, democratic South Africa would not be won without a fight, and there was no time for niceties. This was my chance to enlist for real. If Ronnie liked me, I would be given my uniform and sent to join the fight.

News of me had reached Ronnie through his wife, Eleanor. She was friends with Joan, my well-connected sister-in-law. Eleanor was a small, angular, bird-like woman with wild grey hair and little time for small talk. Like so many others, she had been detained and imprisoned by the apartheid state, and it showed in her demeanor, as if she was the victim of a haunting. She vetted me and reported back to Ronnie, and he decided he wanted to meet me to see for himself.

At our meeting Ronnie asked what I had been doing since my last contact with the ANC, testing how committed I was to living the legend I had built for myself. His questioning did not bother me, nor his chameleon stare. He saw all of me, and I let him. He saw my anger, my White guilt, my frustration at the walls that hemmed me in. I felt only relief at being seen so completely.

Then Ronnie changed tack and spoke of an "interlude," something that would be vastly different to anything I had experienced before. He described a journey to Eastern Europe and an education far from ordinary. He spoke of lessons in politics, intelligence gathering, radio work, reconnaissance, surveillance and counter-surveillance, explosives, and firearms. This "interlude" was to be my military training at officer rank as a cadre for uMkhonto we Sizwe, the Spear of the Nation. A new feeling flooded my chest. I felt I belonged.

Ronnie said MK would fly me to Moscow, where we would spend around a year in training. I now had to create a new legend, telling family and friends that I would spend the next twelve months or so backpacking through Europe before I planned to finally settle down for good in South Africa.

Because of our position at the tip of the African continent, thousands of miles away from Europe and the Americas, South Africans tend to harbor a great curiosity about the rest of the world. But the White suburban hunger for international gossip, the interest in foreign sports stars and celebrities, had always bemused me. Our darker-skinned countrymen and women, the majority of South Africans, struggled just to make it from one day to the next, while the White elite chose to direct their focus and their interest anywhere else.

The White population's fascination with the world beyond the glass was partly a symptom of our pariah status. The wider world had recoiled in horror at footage of the Sharpeville and Soweto massacres, and by now South Africa had largely been cut off from the world family. In the 1960s through to the 1990s, whenever South Africa was given its moment on the international stage it was usually because of a new round of sanctions.

As a result, we viewed all things European and cosmopolitan with awe, and overseas travel was a sign that you were doing rather well for yourself. Backpacking around Europe was becoming an exciting and fashionable thing for upwardly mobile twenty- and thirty-somethings to do. It was the perfect cover for a young professional woman who wanted to see the world and make wonderful memories before settling down to a domestic life back home. It was the perfect lie.

Under Ronnie's instruction, I would first travel—for real—to the UK, France, Switzerland, Holland, Austria, Germany, and Italy. During this whistle-stop tour (replete with phone calls from each country to family and friends) I would collect my travel documents, plane tickets, and ultimately a new identity from the Soviet mission in Rome. From Rome, I would fly to Moscow, where I would meet my minder and interpreter, who would take me to where I would be living.

My fake jaunt around Europe was to be self-financed. Ronnie was always coy about money. He rarely talked about it—let alone offered me any—which made me wonder if he saw me as a spoilt White South African princess with deep pockets. I didn't mind either way. The ANC never paid me for anything, and I would have felt compromised and cheapened if I had been. I received a small military wage during the course of my training, but that was all I earned in service of a cause I believed in. I would be paid in the knowledge that I was doing my own small bit to change the world. That was enough for me.

Ronnie's dark eyes searched my face as I absorbed all this information. His hand flew to my neck, where I wore a gold cross as a prop—part of my conservative persona. He pulled at it, flicking the cross between a stubby thumb and forefinger.

"Get rid of this," he said. "They don't like things like that. They'll start asking questions. Too awkward."

I didn't move. I held my hands in my lap to stop them shaking. Perhaps because of my subconscious desire to emulate Ronnie and become a chameleon, I even stopped blinking. All my energy was channeled into listening intently to all he said, scarcely daring to breathe in case I missed an important word. I stared at him, taking in every detail of his face: the way his mouth moved, the way he breathed. My own reflection stared back from within dark eyes framed by black and bushy eyebrows. I felt I had been absorbed into his soul.

At no time during our conversation did Ronnie mention exactly what he wanted me to do in the future, once I had completed my training and redeployed to South Africa. I suppose I was too in awe of him to ask—either that, or it simply didn't occur to me to find out how I fitted into Ronnie and the ANC's long-term plans.

I know now that there was a good chance Ronnie never told me his plan because he didn't have one. It's quite possible the ANC never knew quite how to use me, but just thought I would be a good asset to have and hoped I would prove useful someday. From what I discovered later, Ronnie liked to have people on the ground. His operatives might not have any clear role or instruction, but they would receive a full course of military training, disappear back into South African society, and wait. One day they might be called into action, or else they might glide forever under the radar— forgotten or not noticed by those on either side of the war they had signed up to fight. Many people would languish in "deep cover" in this way, waiting for Ronnie's call to arms. Even for a paramilitary operation, it was all a bit ad hoc. I would learn this in time.

When it was time to say goodbye, Ronnie promised he would visit me regularly in Moscow. I left first and made my way to a dark, piss-soaked phone booth outside Golders Green tube station, where I pretended to make a call. The phone booth offered a vantage point over the High Street and the walkway leading to the station. If anyone was following me, I would be able to see them through the glass.

I heard his footsteps and heavy tread before I saw him. Those dark chameleon eyes flitted in every direction as he came towards the booth. He was displaying the pre-agreed "all clear and safe" signal—a newspaper folded under his arm. This meant we hadn't been followed, our meeting had been successfully conducted in private. Our eyes met for an instant. There was no flicker of recognition from Ronnie Kasrils as he walked towards the tube station.

I waited for a moment longer and watched the leaves swaying in the evening breeze. A street light flickered. A blackbird sang above the traffic noise, and I knew in my heart that my life would never be the same.

GOLDEN AUTUMN, 1986

THE PLANE CIRCLED Sheremetyevo Airport, and from my window seat I saw the onion domes of cathedrals glistening in the late sunshine. The city below was ablaze with the colours of autumn leaves: russet, gold, and orange.

The half-empty plane descended, shuddered against the runway for what felt like a very long time, and then lurched to a halt. My fellow passengers and I disembarked into a grim concrete building, its doorway flanked by hatchet-faced armed guards. At our approach, one of these guards nodded to someone inside.

A tall, thickset man in an ill-fitting blue suit and scuffed shoes stepped forward, and in a rich and endearing Russian accent introduced himself as Igor Olegivich. He was to be my translator, bodyguard, and companion.

Igor was a little awkward, ungainly even. He had a habit of walking on his toes, so much so that he always seemed a stiff breeze away from overbalancing and falling to the ground. He had closely cropped brown hair and large, soulful eyes, and he usually smelt of garlic (because of a penchant for garlic sausage). But his smile was as broad as they came, and for a long time I would find it hard to believe Igor was capable of being anything other than warm and friendly. It was only later that I discovered another side to him—the side that sent his minions scurrying in every direction to appease him, all while he shouted in loud and vitriolic Russian. But this was an Igor I never knew. From our first encounter in that spartan terminal building, he was always kind to me, and I felt safe with Igor by my side. He was one of the good ones, and I took a liking to him immediately.

Like many Russians I would meet, Igor was prone to bouts of sudden melancholia. He was genuinely concerned about the state of the world, derisively mocking the then-American president Ronald Reagan and the Star Wars policies the USA was pursuing at the time. He also found the permissiveness and morality of the West deeply offensive, and he viewed the USSR's enemies, those in the blue corner, with suspicion and distaste. This attitude was typified by his response to a question I asked a few days after I met him.

During the 1980s, AIDS and HIV were very much in the news in the West, and not long after my arrival I innocently asked what was the Soviet Union's stance on the issue. He met me with a stony stare.

"Such things do not exist here. There is nothing like that in the Soviet Union. It occurs only in the West. If you have heard that we have such a problem, then it is Western propaganda." Bang. End of conversation. Igor sulked for the rest of the afternoon.

Now, in the airport, Igor ushered me out of the terminal through a side door. Outside, a shiny, black government Volga—the USSR's executive car of choice—was waiting for us. The engine was already running, and the driver made a show of drumming his fingers against the steering wheel. We got in the back, and Igor barked his instructions to the driver, who stamped on the accelerator to send the huge car shooting forwards into the afternoon traffic.

I stared out of the window as we drove through the outskirts of Moscow. Apartment blocks and parks flew by, a blur of golden trees in the September sunshine. It surprised me to see so many statues of heroes and workers, poets and musicians. There was culture in every corner of the city. We passed the entrances to underground stations, works of art in themselves, while red and white streetcars rattled across the wide streets, dodging the tide of Ladas and heavy trucks that rumbled down the road.

Couples walked hand-in-hand down the wide boulevards, and proud mamas pushed their plump babies in large prams. There was a brisk trade in newspapers at the kiosks on every corner as the afternoon edition of *Pravda* hit the streets. There were long queues, and few shops. The sun streamed through the car windows, and I rolled up my shirt sleeves, commenting on how toasty it was.

"It is what we call 'golden autumn,'" Igor said. "It is exquisite. I will take you to the Park of Culture and Leisure and show you how it looks. We will collect mushrooms. It is what Russians do in autumn." I caught a glint of gold between his teeth as he smiled his slow, gentle smile.

It took me longer than it should have to notice that both Igor and the driver were constantly shifting their attention between the side and rearview mirrors. Not only were we speeding, I realised, but the driver was weaving in and out of traffic to avoid being followed.

As if he had read my thoughts, Igor said, "We must take precautions, as you are … what do you say … special passenger." He watched me intently, then gathered his thoughts. "I am surprised to see that you come from Africa and are White. We have not had a White woman comrade from the ANC. I was expecting you to be Black. We have had Black male cadres for training here. Also, we must agree on your new name. This is the last time I will use your proper name. I will forget it. Maybe you like the English princess, Lady Diana? We will call you Deana."

And just like that, I was no longer Sue Dobson. I was Comrade Deana.

ASSAULT RIFLES AND ICE CREAM, 1986

MY EARS ACHED and my eyes streamed from the cold as I aimed down the scope. Before me was a desolate landscape, a white expanse of nothingness unlike anything I had ever seen. The trees were heavy with snow from a recent fall, and crows cawed in the branches above me, disturbing the powder as they hopped between boughs. Their feathers were coal black against the flat and pale winter sky.

I was wearing a greatcoat and a *shapka*, a Russian fur hat favoured by soldiers. I had tied it tightly beneath my chin, its fur tickling my ears and muffling the instructions Igor was shouting from just a few yards away. I nestled the AK-47 into my shoulder, where it fit so comfortably it felt like an extension of my own body. I understood why these mass-manufactured assault rifles were so popular; they were easy to use, easy to clean, and easy to maintain. It was my favourite out of all the weapons I had handled already.

Igor and his colleagues had taken me to this firing range outside Moscow on a raw January day to try out a variety of weapons, detonators, and explosives, with the promise of an outing to the ice cream parlour afterwards. Admittedly, this didn't make a great deal of sense, given the weather. It already felt like I had already been on the range for a very long time. The cold numbed my hands, making it hard to work the triggers beneath throbbing fingertips.

Pytor, a sweet grandfatherly soul who also happened to be a professional sniper instructor, took great delight in telling me how my earlobes and the tip of my nose would fall off when we reached minus thirty-five degrees. We weren't far from that, and the cold and the military kit was already making it impossible to move in drifts of snow over three feet thick. My mentors didn't seem to notice the chill, and Igor cheerily told me, "There is no such thing as bad weather, Deana, only bad clothing!" He and Pytor flashed wide, gold-tipped smiles.

I felt a tingling sensation handling these weapons. My nerve endings buzzed as I stroked the cold, smooth metal forms of the rifles. Their power made itself felt through the wool of my military-issue winter gloves, a terrifying mixture of beauty and destruction. The difference between life and death rested in my hands, and the responsibility was huge.

These weapons had been designed to end lives, which was in itself an ugly *raison d'etre*, and yet their purity and functionality didn't escape me. In the line of work I hoped to enter, they were simple instruments of survival. There was no room for sentimentality. If I was going to spy for the ANC, I needed to know how to use these things, and their power demanded my respect. I couldn't dither and have second thoughts in a them-or-me situation. I had to make damn sure that I would be the one to walk away from any firefight, and these objects would help me do that.

I thrust any doubts, fears, and feelings of conscience as far away as possible and focused on the task at hand. Snowflakes swirled softly around me, parachuting onto my fingers even as I pulled the trigger, the rifle bucking against my shoulder in the same moment the bullet cracked against a target downrange. The smell of metal and gunpowder rose into the crisp and clean air.

Much to Igor's anxiety, I tried out a variety of weaponry that day, from a bolt-action Browning to the standard-issue Belgian-manufactured R1 and R4 battle rifles used by the SADF and police. I was also given a go with mortars, rocket launchers, and limpet mines, tools designed to be attached magnetically to the hulls of ships. My firm favourites for big bangs and pyrotechnics, however, were rocket-propelled grenades (RPGs). Nothing lit up a snow-covered landscape like an RPG, a weapon designed for use against tanks and other heavy armour.

Igor watched on as I pulled the trigger, the force of the RPG knocking me into the bank of snow behind me. My shoulder throbbed from the recoil. The explosives were flashy, but it was obvious to everyone that they wouldn't be my strong point.

I also became acquainted with the RGD-5 hand grenade, a nasty bit of post-World War 2 kit. It was a weapon used by many of the Soviet Union's allies, often with a booby trap firing device. The explosives instructor, Sergei Sergeiovich, knelt beside me in the snow to show me how to connect a trip wire between two trees. We activated it and stayed well back to watch it detonate.

I was also given a grenade to throw, but my frozen fingers and heavy uniform made it impossible to launch it far enough—ideally one hundred feet—before it exploded. Sergei, Igor, and I ran for cover as the subsequent explosion, like the sudden throb of a bass drum, thumped the snow from nearby boughs. Again, explosives were not my forte.

Other weapons included an anti-tank rifle and PMN landmines packed with enough explosives to disable tanks. We also worked with anti-personnel mines that could blow off a victim's leg and significantly damage at least one other limb. I found these evil things terrifying enough at the time, but now I deeply regret that I so much as touched them. I have since seen the injuries anti-personnel mines have caused civilians, especially children, in the Angolan Civil War. They were used by both sides in the conflict: UNITA (National Union for the Total Independence of Angola) forces using mines manufactured in South Africa or the United States, whilst the MPLA (Popular Movement for the Liberation of Angola) used those produced in the USSR. The South Africans also left areas of northern Namibia severely mined when they withdrew prior to Namibian independence in 1990.

Ironically, South Africa these days has banned the use, production, and trade of mines after previously having been their largest producer in Africa. Even so, several types of South African landmines have been discovered in neighbouring countries as well as further afield, in places as far away as Cambodia. There are even reports of mines being advertised in the classifieds of a South African newspaper as a deterrent for burglary. Only in South Africa ...

Landmines and anti-personnel mines are devastating anywhere, but in Africa their impact has been particularly awful. A blast will not only blow off a limb but will also pummel the body with dirt and debris, creating a high chance of infection. The force of the blast can also damage blood vessels, connective tissue, and muscles so badly that amputation often has to take place higher up the limb to remove the damaged tissue. In countries with less advanced health-care systems, the outlook tends to be poor. Victims often end up permanently disfigured and disabled, ostracised by communities where disability is still stigmatised and where there is little help available for those unable to support themselves.

The horror of mines, of course, is that they are indiscriminate. They do not discern between the soldier fighting for the apartheid regime and the village child searching for firewood. Both individuals face the same chance of being maimed or killed by a mine, and many mines lie dormant for years after the end of a conflict.

Sadly, such moral issues were not discussed when I was undergoing my military training, and it was only much later that I came to regret holding these killers in my hands—and placing them in the frozen ground of the Moscow firing range. Perhaps the snow had numbed my heart as well as my fingers, freezing any feelings about the impact of these weapons, or perhaps I was just too ideologically blinded, too young and naïve, to know any better.

I fared better with the sniper rifles and pistols I was taught to use by "Uncle" Pytor. Here was a man who firmly believed that a woman's place was on the front lines, and as a sniper, no less. He idolised the women who had joined the Red Army in their thousands during the Great Patriotic War—as Russians proudly called World War Two. His idol was Lyudmila Pavlichenko, who had killed over 300 Nazis to earn the nickname "Lady Death." He wanted to make a new Lady Death out of me. I just hoped I would be able to live up to the high ideals of the old soldiers—lions with the hearts of lambs—who had taken me under their wing and continued to invest so much care and kindness in me.

***

My Russian hosts put me up in an apartment on Gorky Street, where I lived with two housekeepers. These colourful characters were employed by the Soviet military and instructed to take care of me.

Nina, an attractive, brown-haired woman in her mid-thirties, spoke no English but was always welcoming. From time to time I saw her big, brown eyes red-rimmed from crying, but I never asked why. I later heard, through Igor, that the Mujahideen had tortured and killed her husband, a casualty of the Soviet campaign in Afghanistan. His death left her to care for their son, Maxim, on a meagre military pension. The instructors genuinely cared for Nina, as her husband had been one of their colleagues, and they did their best to support her.

The other housekeeper, Irina, was less of an open book. A red-haired lover of cheap cosmetics, Irina was also kind and obliging. She didn't speak English either, although I came to suspect that she and Nina both understood it and would have reported back to the Soviet military if I ever said anything suspicious. Irina was sharp and watchful, and I learned that in a past life she had been something of a good-time girl, with quite a few husbands on the scene. I remember having a conversation with her where I was horrified to learn she had had nine abortions. Back then, abortion was the only contraceptive available in the USSR, and she told me frankly there had been no question of her keeping any of the babies. It went to show that as much as the Soviet Union seemed like paradise to a young and idealistic communist like me, life could still be tough without the modern luxuries we were used to in the West.

Every Thursday afternoon, Pytor and Igor would show up at the apartment with gun cases in tow for a few hours of firearms lessons. If it was too cold to go to the range, we would attempt target practice in the front room, although the usefulness of this was limited because there was no way Nina or Irina would let us use live ammunition indoors. Pytor taught me to focus, concentrate, and follow his precise instructions. A steady hand came later.

The housekeepers received these visitors with glee and saw Pytor as a most eligible widower. For them, Thursday afternoons meant a flurry of baking, with the samovar gurgling away in the corner and the finest linen and crockery laid out for the veteran gun-nut, our esteemed guest.

Part of my training was to learn the difference between Western- and Eastern-bloc weapons and to become acquainted with both. Often, weaponry had to be adapted for African conditions, and the use and care of these firearms was time-consuming and messy. I was also taught military topography and navigation, and I was trained in basic tactics: how best to attack a certain target or where best to hide arms caches. As an intelligence officer it was unlikely that I would ever need these skills, but the theatre of war is fluid, and knowledge is the greatest weapon any soldier can have.

As I looked down at my boot print in the snow one day on the range, it occurred to me that I could not have been further from Africa, my Africa, with its heat and dust and cornflower blue winter skies. I knew then that there are many beauties in the world and that Russia, with its tendrils of frost and snow, was just as glorious as the hot and stormy Highveld. Africa's beauty was brash and immediate, while Russia's was as delicate and precious as the history of the sorrowful land itself. I loved them both.

Our trips to the ice cream parlour after explosives and weapons training grounded me. The tingly sensation of ice cream on a long metal spoon was a comfort. The sweet taste stirred up homely memories stored somewhere in the recesses of my past: end-of-term family outings to seafront hotels in Cape Town. With each savoured mouthful, each exotic taste, I became more relaxed.

The ice cream parlour was the place to be seen in downtown Moscow. Here, ice cream was consumed in all colours and flavours and in all kinds of weather. We regularly went there after a day on the firing range: Igor, Sergei, and me, in our full military uniform, noses and fingers red from the cold. We would sit solemnly and savour each mouthful of garish ice cream, served in stainless steel dishes with long spoons. I looked like the group mascot, seated between the two enormous men. I was always drowning in my military greatcoat and my *shapka* was so big it fell over my eyes. My boots, too, chafed like mad, but none of that mattered. There were no differences and no disagreements, only contentment as we sat together in a companionable silence on the fake leather seats. Ice cream was shorthand for a moment of unadulterated happiness shared among friends.

Soon after my arrival in the USSR, a military doctor, Sasha Alexandrovich, thoroughly examined me to check my suitability for becoming a soldier. After a range of blood tests (one of which was to determine if I had HIV or AIDS), I was taken to see a dentist and then to a specialist military hospital that dealt with rheumatological diseases. I had seen many such specialists already: for years I had suffered with a litany of joint problems and autoimmune diseases, including arthritis and ankylosing spondylitis, which had been wreaking havoc on my spine for most of my life. When I told Ronnie about these problems, fearing they may preclude my recruitment into the ANC, he was adamant that I get the best medical care available. Left unchecked, these genetic problems would cause increasingly unbearable pain and, eventually, cripple me.

Sasha confided that many Black ANC cadres often arrived for training in very poor health, and hepatitis, HIV, and AIDS were increasingly a problem. Many trainees had never seen a doctor or dentist in their lives, and tuberculosis was common among new arrivals. I was assured that I would be looked after throughout my time in the USSR, and I did indeed receive proper medical care to beat back the autoimmune problems that were threatening to become an even bigger issue.

Not only was I being well looked after, but the first time in my life I was also surrounded by people who took me seriously, people whose ideals and goals were aligned with my own. I was especially taken with the civic pride on display everywhere I went; in the USSR, a love for the concept of community—and everyone in it—was something worn on one's sleeve. More than once, I saw a pedestrian litter in the street, only for the person behind them to pick the rubbish up, tap the litterer on the shoulder, and inform them, "Excuse me, Comrade, you mistakenly dropped this."

The sheer enthusiasm of the man in the street was something to behold. I would walk through downtown Moscow—a place studded with beautiful parks—and I would see workers on their lunch breaks protesting for world peace. It may have been naïve, but to me this proved that things could—and, one day, would—be different.

I was already terribly idealistic, and ever since my adolescence I had been rooting for the USSR and its grand communist experiment. My experiences in the country only entrenched my beliefs. The wonderful people I met convinced me I had picked the right side, and I was struck almost immediately by a greater sense of shared humanity than I had ever experienced. The people were patriotic—nationalistic in many cases—but I understood why. It was inconceivable to me that the politics of the USSR should be so unpopular back home in South Africa and in the wider world. Time has since blunted my enthusiasm for communism, but back then I couldn't see that Soviet politics only worked on paper; to my eyes, its success was evident in every interaction I had with the smiling and proud Russian masses who loved their country and loved their countrymen even more. Every Russian I met made me feel like I was one of them, like I belonged. It probably helped that I looked the part, having been kitted out in full Soviet military uniform shortly after my arrival.

Prior to our trip to the outfitters, Igor and I had an awkward conversation about "vimmins' ondervear"—as he called it—and sanitary products. The USSR was still a man's world, and back then sanitary products had to be bought from a special "paper" shop across town, where purchases would be wrapped in brown paper for discretion. I learned later that recycled rags were the more affordable option for most Soviet women, even in the eighties.

I tried to explain to Igor my need for several pairs of cotton pants and a few bras, having arrived with only the basics in my rucksack. Igor blushed, a slow, agonising, and all-encompassing tide of redness that made his face glow beneath his stubble. I was wracked with embarrassment and Igor disappeared for the day, only to join me later in the army supplies room with a broad smile and a tightly wrapped package clutched to his breast.

He waited until we were alone before beckoning me over. I was told to open the package, and there, beneath Igor's affectionate and proud smile, was a set of seven garish nylon bloomers with the Russian days of the week emblazoned on them. And so, Comrade Deana waddled off in her days-of-the-week "vimmins ondervear" to wage war against the racists.

Later, Igor and one of his assistants, a young woman armed with a measuring tape and stick of chalk, ushered me into a military store room and cleared everyone else out. The assistant and I eyed each other as Igor discreetly withdrew to an adjoining room. After a flurry of tape and pins and bust and hip measurements, I was presented with garment after garment: fatigues, military boots, a Red Army greatcoat, and my *shapka*, which to my horror, as a strict vegetarian, was made from the finest sable fur. I had to explain, as respectfully as possible, that whilst I was touched that my hosts wanted to give me their finest, I could neither accept nor wear it as a matter of principle. We had several such delicate conversations over a winter coat. My hosts wanted to give me a fur one, but I was determined not to take it. An almost tearful Igor told me such articles were much valued and longed-for by Russian women, and my hosts would take offence if I did not accept one. We compromised on the *shapka* and a fur collar that haunted me on every outing to the ballet. I was, however, proud to wear the uniform of the Soviet military, even if doing so meant betraying the country where I had grown up. I would side with whoever was willing to fight against racism, and in this case the enemy of my enemy was my friend.

MILITARY COMBAT WORK, 1986

"CONGRATULATIONS, Comrade Deana!" sang Valery Pavlovich in his soft, accented voice, his gold teeth and oiled hair shining in the half light. I had just dragged myself into the apartment after a marathon surveillance session, and from the smile on my mentor's face I assumed I had passed muster.

I peeled off my *shapka* and coat and picked at the laces of my oversized boots. He watched me and softly wrung his hands, his gold wristwatch and onyx signet ring glinting. He stepped forward and shook my hand. The skin of his palms was cool and dry, as I would imagine the belly of a snake to be. He whispered when he spoke and accented the "s" in words, lending his speech a serpentine hiss. In this way he reminded me of a black mamba, one of South Africa's deadliest native species, always poised and ready to strike.

I loved Valery, his butchery of the English language, and his craft. He was devilishly intelligent and funny, with coal-black eyes that were forever darting back and forth, and he taught me his craft with patience and precision. Valery was my intelligence instructor, and he was as determined as I that I should succeed. He made it clear that failure was not an option, and I owe my survival to his lectures, diagrams, and field work exercises.

It was not appropriate to ask personal questions of my instructors, but they often volunteered information about their lives. I learned Valery was from the Krasnodar region, near the Black Sea, and loved fishing. He was proud of his Cossack origins and had a wife and two sons, the eldest of whom was training to be a cosmonaut. The family had recently adopted a small, runtish kitten, whom they christened "Barsic," the Russian name for a snarling, strapping snow leopard. Valery was a great lover of irony.

"Frankly, the matter is that you have succeeded in exposing six of the eight agents tailing you ... excellent work, Comrade, excellent work."

Nina and Irina appeared from behind him and took my snow-covered clothing, tutting at how cold I was. They bustled off to make tea and serve *blinis*, a warming Russian pancake.

I sat down opposite my instructor at the table, which had been set for afternoon tea. It was resplendent with the best silver and crockery, laid on the best white tablecloth, the one Nina regularly ironed in the dark back bedroom. The centerpiece of the table was a spluttering samovar. It was all very Russian.

Valery bit into a piece of black rye bread with blackcurrant jam and wiped a manicured finger on the linen napkin in front of him. He raised his teacup with a poised little finger and studied me above its rim. He lifted a dyed-black, plucked eyebrow. Flushed with success and hot tea, I waited for him to speak.

"Quite frankly, the matter is that we must clearly work on picking up the surveillance of vehicles and defensive driving, but your work on foot is very good and you have expert attention to detail." He flashed a gold smile, and I traded him a smile right back.

I had set off that morning on a wide-ranging surveillance exercise that took me all through the centre of Moscow. My mission: head from Gorky Street to Mayakovsky Square, past Mayakovsky's statue and the neat flower beds covered in fresh snow, and into the Mayakovskaya Metro. I would then make my way into the beautiful depths of the city's ornate underground system. After changing lines, I was to surface at Ploshchad Revolyutsii (Revolution Square) and work my way through the streets to the Pushkinskaya Metro Station and back on to the trains, changing lines until I found myself back on Gorky Street in the Tverskoy District.

My route would also take me near Red Square and the Kremlin, the iconic St Basil's Cathedral, the Bolshoi Theatre where Igor and I would go to the opera or ballet on a weekend evening (laughing unashamedly when the male soloist unceremoniously dropped his partner during a *pas de deux*), and Lenin's Mausoleum, where the great man lies in state while crowds of solemn citizens shuffle round his pale, waxen face to piped patriotic music in the half light. One can purchase red carnations (always in odd numbers, for good luck, according to Igor) and set them by the leader's tomb.

Valery and I had worked out the route in great detail. This exercise would be the first of several opportunities to put theory into practice and to prove I had been listening during the lessons he gave me on covert surveillance and how to evade it. Two teams of four, roleplaying as hostile agents, would place me under surveillance in crowded downtown Moscow. My task was to identify and "out" them before I made it back to the apartment. It was never going to be easy, and Valery had laughed and wrung his manicured hands at the thought of catching me out. Success would require constant, intense concentration, an awareness of my surroundings and of those around me on foot, on the metro, and in heavy traffic. To slip the noose of surveillance you needed eyes in the back of your head.

I set off at the arranged time and made my way down Gorky Street, towards the towering statue of the tragic revolutionary poet and playwright Vladimir Mayakovsky, who had killed himself after suffering the agonies of unrequited love. Gorky Street's busy crowds and the narrow alleys between its buildings lent me the chance to throw off the agents on my tail. It also helped that Moscow's public telephone booths were made of clear glass, which made it easy to duck into a booth—on the pretext of making a call—and get a look at who was behind you. That was how I flushed out the first agent.

The man in question did not have time to slow down before I slipped into a booth, spun around, and caught his eyes fixed on me. He hurried past and disappeared into the crowds ahead as if nothing had happened, but I had already got a clear look at him. Bingo. It occurred to me that Valery's team would carry the props so useful in these kinds of scenarios: changes of clothing, disguises like hats, newspapers, and glasses to hide behind and cast off when it was opportune to do so. I knew why Valery had been so excited for me to try my hand at such a large team, whose operatives could shed their skins like the lizards of my sun-soaked childhood. He didn't miss a trick.

The exercise continued on the metro, where the crowds were thicker. My adversaries were working in teams, so I kept my eyes open for any suspicious characters who were carrying walkie talkies or who appeared to be mumbling into a lapel or wristwatch. I studied faces on the escalators of the beautiful metro stations I passed through. These places were like museums, their cavernous spaces decorated with frescoes, statues, marble, and crystal chandeliers, and it took all my focus not to be blinded by the beauty of my surroundings. I kept a watch out for anyone who sidled too close, and I regarded with suspicion anyone who hopped into carriages as late as I did. I moved just as the doors started closing, so anyone who seemed to board the train as a sudden reaction to my movement would stand out. I flushed out another agent in this way.

The Moscow Metro truly boasts some of the most beautiful stations in the world. The inside of Mayakovskaya station was my favourite, with its arches and domes, its mosaics and ornate lamps. Other stations featured stained-glass decorations and golden arches. Each was different, and each was place of wonder.

Built by Stalin as "People's Palaces," depicting the history and achievements of the Soviet Union, each station has a unique history, complete with artworks from the time of its construction. But now the beauty was a distraction, the living past of a country I loved.

The exercise continued above ground as I wove down busy pavements and crossed roads to duck through traffic. I asked a stranger the time, giving me the opportunity to halt suddenly and look behind me. The man following me almost tripped himself up—another one down. The thick sleeves of my greatcoat were stuffed with tricks passed down by Valery: reflections in shop windows and the compact mirror I used to check my make-up served as the additional eyes I needed.

Another valuable trick was to cross the road swiftly, giving yourself the opportunity to look in both directions and to see who slows down when you do. Many of these tactics can be hampered by the weather, which can make the whole exercise considerably more complicated. This was something I discovered that day when the snow started to fall in thick flurries, drifting through the air on a cold wind that whipped at my eyes. I had to be smart to counteract the blinding effects of the Russian climate. My next prize came when I ducked into an alleyway and turned to watch the man following me stop dead and look around. He caught my eye, laughed, and raised his hands in mock surrender before heading off.

The most difficult facet of this test was to out pursuers in cars or on motor-bikes. Surveillance drivers have the advantage of speed if their prey is on foot, and the ability of bikes to weave in and out of traffic make them essential tools in the spy's arsenal. Often, a team of agents will travel together in one car, with the driver dropping off team members at strategic points, from which they can continue the chase on foot. If you're too busy scanning faces in the crowds of pedestrians around you, it's easy to forget that danger can also come from the road.

Timing is critical in surveillance and, as I had expected, my pursuers often altered disguises on the move. But while it's easy to slip in our out of a coat or jumper, or to pop on or take off a cap, in the field there's never time to change one's shoes. As such, a pursuer's shoes are often a dead giveaway, and during the course of my career I have been served well by paying attention to the footwear of those around me. During the course of Valery's big test, I nullified an operative's change of outfit by looking down and recognizing the boots he had on. By the time I got back to the apartment, I had outed all but two of the pursuers. It was far from a perfect score, but for a girl with no prior training, still fairly fresh off the plane, it wasn't bad. We celebrated my success with hot tea, and I listened intently as Valery reminded me of the importance of checking the roads as well as the pavements. Thankfully, I was a quick learner.

My training continued in other disciplines essential to espionage. I was instructed in photography and the handling a variety of Soviet and East German camera equipment. Such lessons concentrated on photographing documents, in case I ever found myself alone in a room with just a stack of sensitive paperwork for company. Unfortunately, very few South Africans had cameras, so this aspect of my training proved to be less useful than Valery's surveillance classes. Back home, carrying a camera around would have drawn too much attention, so when it came to a time when I would have to copy sensitive paperwork, I would have to let my memory do the heavy lifting. My profession as a journalist had taught me to be attentive to detail, which certainly helped.

Still, we made an impromptu darkroom in the bathroom back at Gorky Street, negatives arrayed over the antiquated shower and basin, photographs perched on enamel bowls and buckets as they developed. I plastered my efforts to the walls and pegged them on the washing line, much to the irritation of Nina and Irina, whose washboard and carbolic soap were among their most commonly used possessions.

I was also taught how to make and write with invisible inks, concocted from everyday substances like lemon juice. This work demanded a light touch, as any damage to a piece of paper, or even a change in texture or smell, could be a giveaway. A sad-eyed specialist by the name of Pavel Andreiovich completed my communication lessons with instruction in Morse Code. I paid close attention throughout this crash-course in the dark arts of undercover work, never knowing which skills I would need and when I would need to use them.

A dashing lieutenant colonel by the name of Vasily Sergeiovich was tasked with handling the political aspects of my instruction. With his blond hair, high cheekbones, and firm jaw, he looked every inch the Hero of the Soviet Union and resembled the traditional image of Soviet manhood depicted in the statues across town. Highly decorated from campaigns in Afghanistan, he wore his medals proudly on his tailored winter coat. He had known Nina's late husband and often chatted to her in the kitchen. In my company he had a habit of striking a pose in the front of the classroom as he delivered his lectures on Marxist theory.

He was a man with a deep and broad knowledge of his country. But while he knew Siberia and the far eastern republics well, it was not their politics or systems of government that interested him so much as the fish he caught on the frequent winter expeditions to Vladivostok. He was happiest sitting on a plastic bucket on the ice of Amur Bay, bundled in his sheepskin coat with an ample supply of vodka, waiting for the arctic Rainbow smelt or flounder to bite.

After class I would devote myself to exploring the streets of Moscow, always with Igor in tow. We spent evenings at the opera, and I whiled away my quiet moments in the sparse but homely surrounds of the apartment. Nina and Irina were forced to live frugally; communism's promise had not yet delivered a bounty of modern conveniences to the citizens of the USSR.

There was very little available in the way of soaps and detergents, and we washed dishes with wire wool and boiling water over the Belfast sink in the cold, draughty kitchen, beneath pipes that clanked and sputtered around the clock. The fastidious housekeepers only used the vacuum cleaner, an unwieldy and voluble beast, when we had important visitors, and even then they filled the air with Russian expletives as they hauled the contraption from room to room. Their preferred cleaning tools were an antiquated carpet sweeper that spewed out dust wherever it went, a dustpan and brush, and a feather duster full of cobwebs. They waged a constant battle against the army of bed bugs, moths, and cockroaches that called the old, creaking, pre-war building home. The apartment also accommodated several mice, who scuttled over the parquet flooring and ageing linoleum at night, nibbling the bags of flour and rice in the pantry—to the housekeepers' fury.

The furniture was old and drab, but the apartment was generally warm and comfortable, with rugs on the walls and colourful carpets on the floors. Display cabinets heaved with cut glass, and the finest Bohemian crystal was proudly displayed with the best silverware and linen whenever visiting generals came to tea. Such events occurred every few weeks, and the mere mention of visitors would send Nina and Irina into meltdown as they cleaned the apartment until it shone. They made sure the table resembled a spread fit for royalty, complete with champagne, the best vodka, and caviar: both the black Siberian variety and the bright orange of salmon, served on little bits of toast. Igor, too, approached these visits with dread, as it meant that he had to translate interminable Russian speeches and toasts into English for me.

I was so swept up living the Soviet life, and so busy with my classes, that news of a visit from my handler, the elusive Ronnie Kasrils, caught me by surprise and resulted in a further frenzy of deep cleaning in the apartment. The ANC's very own chameleon would be joined, we were told, by a group of generals who were sympathetic to the cause.

Honoured that we were going play host to both a clutch of generals *and* a foreign guest, and rather taken by Ronnie's charm and toothy smile, Irina arrived for work on the special day with her eyelashes coated in thick mascara, her cheeks rouged, her red hair coloured and curled, and sporting a thick lipstick pout. All of her paintwork dissolved into a colourful smudge as she laboured in the steam of the kitchen. Nina looked at her, raised her eyebrows, and tutted over the cabbage.

Ronnie and I had established systems of communication that we would use while I was in the USSR, and then later after I had redeployed to South Africa. We spoke through coded postcards sent through a safe UK address, by highlighting certain words or phrases in a particular library book, or by placing cryptic ads in local newspapers. This all sounds very impressive, but in truth this was a painfully inefficient way for my handler and me to exchange information and for him to pass on orders. This was one of many ways in which the whole ANC operation could seem slapdash and ad hoc. A breakdown in communication would eventually place me in grave danger. But I didn't know that then. I was just happy to be in the USSR, training to be the spy I had always wanted to be.

***

Military Combat Work (MCW) featured in the education of all ANC cadres, to a greater or lesser extent, and formed the backbone of my personal training program. It focused on building our movement and establishing a political and revolutionary army as the armed wing of a socialist state. Politics classes included the teaching of South African history, the history of the ANC, international history, and the foundational principles of Marxism-Leninism.

Literacy was often a problem for cadres arriving to study in the Soviet Union from South Africa, especially those whose education had been interrupted by the Soweto Uprisings of 1976. By necessity, lessons included basic literacy, as many cadres could not read very well or were not used to studying in English. This concerned the instructors, who always felt they were wasting too much time teaching the basics before they could get to the nitty gritty of MCW.

There are no published figures about the exact strength of uMkhonto we Sizwe, and Soviet archives remain closed on the number of cadres from southern Africa who trained in the USSR. It has been estimated that only 10,000 to 12,000 cadres formally trained outside South Africa from the 1960s to 1990. Most of these recruits, both male and female, were Black and were taught in groups, either at the Perevalnoye Military Training Centre on the Crimean Peninsula or the Northern Training Camp on the outskirts of Moscow, or else at other secret locations, as I was. Very few White women trained in Moscow, and even fewer deployed back into South Africa after their training. I was one of a very small and very select cohort.

I felt, and still feel, privileged to have been selected and thought worthy of such training. That summer evening in Golders Green, when Ronnie chose me, the door to a different world was opened. What Ronnie's Russian comrades taught would save my life and keep me alive in the years to come, when the apartheid government's own agents were snapping at my heels back in the heat and dust of South Africa.

My family, meanwhile, and everyone I knew back home, believed I was still jollying it up on a gap year around Europe. They had no idea that I was really learning how to fight, undergoing training that would turn me into a soldier in MK.

For my training to be successful, I knew I would have to lie to everyone I knew. And how I lied. I had already lied through my teeth by telling everyone what a wonderful year it was going to be. I had promised to send postcards from Europe and write regularly. My family and friends, in turn, sent their letters to me to Poste Restante in each European capital, where local Soviet embassy staff collected them and sent them on to me in Moscow.

In order to reply to these missives from home, my Soviet hosts kept me stocked with a pile of postcards depicting dreary European tourist attractions. I would sit at the table in the apartment nibbling the end of my pen and writing platitudes. I often found myself wondering what the places I was writing about were really like. I hadn't seen most of them, and doubtless never would. But at least I had seen the Soviet Union, the country that had fascinated me ever since I was a child.

One autumn evening, as I stood next to Igor on the steps of the Bolshoi Theatre, my thoughts slipped in time until I could see myself back then. I pictured a frightened nine-year-old, alone in the house with only the fruit trees in the garden and the voices on the radio for company. As the Kremlin clock above the gates to Red Square offered a tuneful chime, I remembered how I had once longed to see the golden domes of St Basil's Cathedral and stand before the statues of the Soviet revolutionaries who watched over the streets of Moscow. And here I was.

At the time, the USSR was supplying financial and military aid to various liberation movements throughout Africa. The Soviet Union's support was born from its opposition to colonialism and racism, and the Communist Party of the USSR showed solidarity with the South African Communist Party (SACP) and the ANC. Of course, there were also geopolitical concerns at play, as there always were when the great powers deigned to involve themselves in the proxy wars that took place in their satellites.

The countries varied, but the revolutionary tactics were broadly the same. Foreign training gave cadres the opportunity to gain military skills and a better education, and on leaving the USSR many cadres were redeployed to training camps in southern African countries such as Angola, Mozambique, Tanzania, and Zambia, where they in turn trained other recruits. Limited operations also took place in Swaziland and Lesotho.

Meanwhile, an exile community of South African freedom fighters became well established in London from the 1960s onward, later leading to the establishment of an ANC "HQ" there. An organisational system sprung up around it, with unit groups and other structures growing to support the ever-larger exile community. The ANC forged strong links with anti-apartheid factions back home on the ground and sought to influence South African affairs as much as they could from without.

The Soweto Uprising of 1976 fueled the anger of millions of young South Africans (mostly Black, but also some White) and it was at this point that MK's ranks swelled. Camps in Angola and Zambia suddenly faced an influx of idealistic would-be freedom fighters, who had been radicalised by their own government's violent and merciless response to peaceful protesters. Most of the ANC general training occurred in Angola from 1976 to 1988. This basic training lasted six months and was usually followed by specialisation courses that took another three to four months. Some took longer, depending on the discipline. Instruction was in English, usually provided by fluent Soviet veterans who visited the camps to pass on their knowledge.

Although the USSR was responsible for most of MK's training, China, Algeria, and Yugoslavia were among the nations to offer military and intelligence assistance to the anti-apartheid cause. Cuba and German Democratic Republic (GDR) also provided intelligence training to cadres from the African camps. Cuba's involvement included the training of special forces, as well as air force, anti-aircraft, and tank training for conventional warfare. This specialised training took place in the Angolan camps, where there was always a real chance of aerial bombardment by South Africa. Subjects taught in the larger African camps included military drill, battle strategy, hand-to-hand combat, and military first aid.

The changes that rang through Eastern Europe in the late 1980s meant that much of the training moved to African countries such as Tanzania, Uganda, Zimbabwe, Zambia, and Ghana, and at this time the MK leadership switched to the training of a conventional army that would one day form the core of a future defence force for a new, liberated South Africa. Later, as part of the complex negotiated terms for Namibian independence, MK was forced to move out of Angola, but training continued in other sympathetic countries until the 1990s.

Thirty years after my training, after considerable research and having become close to my instructors, I still do not know the exact name of the organisation that trained me. I have a shrewd idea as to who they were and the name of the establishment, but I could not confirm it with any certainty ... and so it should be. All I can say for sure is that I was trained by the USSR with a view to being redeployed into deep cover in South Africa. What came next would be up to Ronnie and the ANC.

I regard the mystery of who exactly trained me as I regard many things in the espionage world: best left unknown. It simply does not matter. Names and details were always on a need-to-know basis, and I didn't. If I didn't know, then I would betray no one—even if I was detained and tortured, as so many ANC cadres were.

Things are better this way. This way it will always remain a secret.

MALEN'KAYA MYSH, 1986

I LAY STILL—my head turned to the window, my forehead resting against the frigid steel of the cot—and waited. I drank in the stillness. The moonlight played upon the thick snow outside and the northern wind moved the bare trees, setting shadows dancing across the floor.

He came like a thief in the night when the dark was at its thickest and those in the building were long asleep. I knew he was there, waiting for the right moment to reveal himself. He was announced by the patter of his soft footfall.

A tiny, pinched face turned towards me. Bright eyes regarded me through the blackness. His whiskers twitched and his fingers, elongated by the dancing shadows, reached out for the biscuit crumbs I had spread across the windowsill. The large, velvety ears trembled as the snores from the next bed rose and fell and then reached a vibrato crescendo.

The mouse stopped to look directly at me, as if for reassurance. I blinked. He blinked back and picked up a crumb between his front paws, chewing a mouthful as fast as he could; he knew the risks of visiting me each night. Then he left, as quickly and quietly as he had come. It was just me and the darkness again.

After all the companionship and solidarity of the past months, I was as lonely as I had ever been in my life, the long days of my solitary childhood included. And now I didn't even have the lush surrounds of the garden to comfort me. There was nothing good about being here, in Military Hospital Number 1, as it was known to me. It was probably the Burdenko Hospital in Moscow, which specialises in neurological diseases and treats members of the armed forces and their families.

The seizures, or blackouts, as they sometimes manifested themselves, had started in a familiar enough way. As a sufferer of migraines since my early teens, I knew the unexplainable aura, the strange metallic taste in my mouth, and the shimmering of my vision could only mean one thing. All my life I had been wary of these symptoms, and at the first sign of their onset I would reach for the migraine medication.

By then it was usually too late, and the horror of a hemiplegic migraine was soon upon me, complete with nausea and auditory and visual distortions and an increasing numbness in my limbs. Without fail, a headache followed, mostly on the opposite side to the numb extremities. While I was in the throes of an attack, I could not walk or talk, my fingers and face became rubbery, and my tongue would stick to the roof of my mouth.

I learned to identify the triggers, including bright, fluorescent light, eating meat (in my pre-vegetarian days), the smell of chlorine (I've always hated swimming pools), and long flights. I usually spent the first day of any holiday in a darkened room lying dead still because any movement, however slight, hurt.

My arrival in the Soviet Union, many months ago, had been no different. To my hosts' alarm I retired to bed soon after our introductions, clutching my head, which felt it could burst open at any second. An increasingly concerned Igor duly summoned Dr. Sasha, the military doctor, who checked I was still breathing every fifteen minutes. He prescribed a hearty dose of the herb valerian, which rendered me nearly unconscious but did little to ease the pain.

Back then, Dr. Sasha had shaken his handsome head and regarded me with sad, china-blue eyes. He spoke English with a heavy accent, the voice of a million Russian stereotypes.

"Deana," he said. "This is because you will eat no meat. You must eat meat to be healthy, especially in this climate. We have very good meat here!"

Igor was inconsolable, and spent the afternoon pacing, yelling down the phone and screaming at the housekeepers. His repeated volleys of Russian profanity did nothing to soothe my thumping head.

To my horror, and everyone else's, the migraines worsened during my time in Moscow until they became more like seizures or blackouts. It's well-documented that hemiplegic migraine sufferers can experience seizures, and it seemed my condition had evolved into something even more vindictive. It was unclear what new trigger preceded these vicious attacks, but whatever it was, it must have been everywhere.

The familiar migraine aura would descend and soon after I would start to shake uncontrollably. I would develop a thundering headache, and with my limbs numb and quivering I would feel completely spaced out. The seizures could last for hours, occasionally consuming an entire day. I had few memories of the episodes, which wasn't helped by increasingly hefty doses of valerian root and the lithium injections that Dr. Sasha tenderly produced from his battered leather bag. It was clear that these strange and unexplained neurological blips were a growing problem, and they dogged me throughout my time in the Soviet Union.

My hosts were concerned I either had a brain tumour or extreme anxiety and decided after one prolonged and particularly hideous attack that I should go to hospital and be thoroughly investigated from top to toe. A proper check-up did seem in order, as it hadn't been long since I was formally diagnosed with ankylosing spondylitis, the rheumatological problem that had dogged me throughout my life but that was only now being taken seriously by doctors. Igor bundled me into an ambulance that freezing night and sat with me as we bucked and jived across the potholed streets of Moscow to a facility where I was assured senior military officers and diplomats were treated. It was the best hospital in the city, and there I would receive excellent care and a proper neurological diagnosis.

I know it was a good place, staffed by compassionate and competent professionals, but the hospital was bleak, spartan, and desolate in a brutal and Dickensian way. The ancient building creaked as it settled, and the long corridors of peeling paint and polished floors—lovingly cleaned by growling, black-clad *babushkas*—all seemed to lead to unknowable and undesirable destinations. The plumbing in my ward's decrepit bathroom groaned and shrieked, and the boiling water that poured from the shower left me pink and scalded. My insistence on showering every day puzzled the staff, as they felt a weekly wipe down with a rag or flannel was sufficient in the cold Russian climate.

Although they were kind, and although they understood it, the staff did not—or would not—speak English, and communication was non-existent. The hospital diet was comprised of hearty, meaty meals, most of which I couldn't eat. I quietly starved and nibbled on the cabbage leaves and beets, supplementing my diet with whatever food my visitors brought me. My ward-mate would implore me in Russian to eat as she shovelled down helpings of the rich and sickly food, cabbage pasted to her gold teeth.

The doctors, meanwhile, were stumped as to what was wrong with me. Clearly there was a cause behind my seizures, but whatever it was it can't have been obvious. Physicians bombarded me with patronising questions: *Are you anxious? Are you homesick? Are you unhappy? Do you think it's your diet?* Their questions made me furious—I wanted less interrogating, and more diagnosing—but in hindsight they may have had a point about my diet. Some of my problems were probably nutritional, and the doctors' vehement rejection of my vegetarianism did make sense. Still, I was a stubborn young idealist, and I wasn't about to give up my principles because of a few blackouts.

***

I had arrived in the hospital amid a confused frenzy of activity. Orderlies wheeled me, still shaking uncontrollably, into a chilled, white-walled room and helped me into a steel cot. Behind me was a large window through which I could just make out the shapes of barren trees in the moonlight. Nobody would speak English, and my conversational Russian was rudimentary. I did not have my beloved Igor with me to translate, and the doctors and I could only conduct our jilted conversation with the help of an English/Russian dictionary.

The place reeked of herbal compounds and disinfectant. Despite this, rats and mice thrived in the crevices and corners and danced quadrilles loudly into the night, their toenails scraping the polished floors. Sometimes, as I lay awake watching the moonlight sweep over the snowy grounds, I thought I could hear them squeaking as they sang the song of their people. They were my confidants and my friends.

My ward-mate, Ludmilla, was a strapping lady in her seventies, a veteran of the "Great Patriotic War." She had fought off invading Nazis at Stalingrad and wore the medals on her nylon nightie to prove it. She had blazing red hair and a mouthful of gold teeth that clattered when she spoke. Ludmilla also had severe gastritis that caused her to belch uncontrollably, day and night. She taught me that it was possible to belch loudly in one's sleep, even between snores.

Over a three-week period I was prodded, poked, scanned, and X-rayed by neurosurgeons wearing what appeared to be tall chef hats, the standard uniform for clinicians in Russia. They took copious amounts of blood from me with long and blunt-seeming needles, and more than once I had to endure the added indignity of being woken at midnight and dragged to the sluice room to be given a compulsory enema, which the beaming nurse assured me was "otli-chno" —"very good"—both for my intestines and my neurological and mental health. But despite many investigations, cheerfully administered weekly enemas, homeopathic compounds, and increasing doses of lithium and valerian, my migraines continued unabated, complete with exhausting episodes of shaking that went on for hours.

I felt as I had years before when I was the only English-speaking child in the Afrikaans nursery; once again, I was in a place where nobody spoke my language, and I had no way of making my feelings known. I regressed back to a little mouse of a girl.

While I was indisposed, Igor was sent away by his commanders to welcome a new group of (Black) South African recruits for military and explosives training. Sadly, he was too busy to visit me in hospital and they sent another translator, Viktor Alexseiovich, in his place. Viktor grumbled about the weather, the West, Ronald Reagan, and having to come and see me. We didn't hit it off.

One time he arrived clutching a bunch of flowers he had bought outside the Metro station and handed me my longed-for English newspaper, the communist *Morning Star*. That day, October 19, 1986, the front page showed a downed plane, still smouldering. My heart turned to lead when I read the caption: the South Africans had killed one of my heroes, Mozambican president Samora Machel, a devoted Marxist-Leninist. His presidential plane had crashed near the Mozambique-South Africa border. The president had been at a summit in Zambia, but on his way home he overruled instructions (for his own safety) not to travel at night. Investigators believed the South Africans lured the jet off-course, causing it to crash into a hillside at Mbuzini, just inside South Africa. President Machel and thirty-three others died.

To Viktor's acute embarrassment, I burst into tears and ordered him out of the room. Ludmilla rushed over and embraced me as I gestured towards the picture of the wrecked plane. She clucked gently through her gold teeth as she stroked my hair. That night I waited for my *Malen'kaya Mysh,* my "little mouse." His bright eyes and soft fur comforted me as he ate from my palm in the darkness. I named him Samora in honour of a fallen comrade.

LIVING THE SOVIET LIFE, 1986–1987

THE SOPRANO, staggering under the weight of her jewelled headdress, clutched her ample bosom and took a deep breath before hitting the high C. The notes, pure and clear, rose to fill every corner of the auditorium. They danced on stage—so fine, so precise, so delicate. I visualised them as they filled the plush red-gold opulence of the Bolshoi Theatre in Moscow ... filled it to the rafters so the ancient building seemed to brim with glorious music. In that moment, the music was all that mattered.

After a few weeks of observation I had been discharged from the hospital, undiagnosed yet—purely by chance—feeling much better. Incidentally, it would take years before I got a diagnosis for my neurological problems; there is still some uncertainty but I suspect now that my seizures were caused by secondary lupus. But I have never been a picture of perfect health, and there are other possible culprits that could have been at the root of my problems. Either way, the Russians weren't sure what was wrong with me, and upon my discharge the ANC arranged for me to see a specialist in England. It was a fairly fruitless trip in the end, but at least the doctor was able to confirm that I was broadly fighting fit and unlikely to suffer from any more protracted bouts of whatever it was that had lain me up in that awful hospital.

But as I soaked my battered body in the music of the opera, I cared for nothing outside of the moment. I was drunk with sights and sounds and feeling, and I willingly surrendered myself to a new but ancient world. Here I was in the country I had read and fantasised about for so long. I was living my dream in a nation of ideals and aspirations, a place of tragedy, history, and sorrow.

I stole a furtive sideways glance at Igor, who was sitting next to me. I liked having him back at my side, and I liked even more the gentle smile, a hint of happiness, which rose at the corners of his lips. He was sitting at a slight angle in the hope that I wouldn't see the tear glinting in his eye. Through a small opening in his suit jacket came the wink of the revolver strapped to his body, a reminder of who he was and why we were there.

I ran my hand across the soft, red velvet of the armrest and wondered who had sat in this seat before me, delighting in this stunning building filled with history and purpose. Here was where Mikhail Glinka's patriotic opera *Ivan Susanin*, known also as *A Life For The Tsar,* had been performed many times. It first premiered in the Bolshoi's sister theatre, the Bolshoi Kamenny in St Petersburg, in 1836, in front of the Tsar Nicholas I himself. The great man loved the performance and rewarded Glinka with a huge diamond-encrusted ring for his trouble.

The Bolshoi—meaning "big"—Theatre is a beautiful, historic building, with its neoclassical frontage and a hammer and sickle above its heavy velvet curtains. It was now accessible to the common man, who, for the price of a few rubles, could enjoy music, dance, and culture. Culture for everyone, anytime, as it should be. Having opened in 1825, and subsequently been renovated several times, the theatre was home to the Bolshoi Opera and the 200-strong Bolshoi Ballet: the world's biggest ballet company.

Igor had taken me to the Bolshoi Theatre that Saturday night to see the famous *Ivan Susanin.* It proved to be a very Russian opera, with four acts, many crowd sequences, a ballet, and many choruses. It is an eye-watering four hours long.

We arrived at the theatre looking like any Russian couple, having paid a fare of a few kopeks (a few pennies) on the streetcar that clattered and clanked down Gorky Street towards Red Square. Before boarding the streetcar Igor had treated me to a glass of *kvass* from a street vending machine. A traditional Russian beverage, *kvass* tasted of berries, honey, and fermented rye bread—a mouthful of Soviet autumn.

Igor was smart in his blue suit and autumn coat, finished neatly with his Trilby—his "spy hat," as we called it. He encouraged me to dress like a Russian woman so that I would blend into the crowd. It worked to some extent, and my black autumn boots and itchy polyester dress, partially hidden beneath the hated autumn coat and its fur collar, looked Russian enough. However, try as I might, I couldn't tame my hair, and my spiral perm—a style unavailable in the USSR—gave me away as a Westerner. The Muscovite women around me were all well-dressed and well-groomed, many with dyed hair, rouged cheeks, and painted lips. Nail polish, like sanitary wear and tights, was hard to find and much prized, and so it was rare to see a flash of colour on the delicate hands of a Russian woman.

My father loved opera; I remember him crying silently at the beautiful voices of Tito Gobbi, Guiseppe Di Stefano, Beniamino Gigli, and the beautiful Spanish soprano Montserrat Caballe, often with a generous whisky in his hand. Because of my father's passions, I arrived in the Soviet Union with some knowledge of the art form, but I was a newcomer to the distinct flavour of Russian opera. My memories of Russian opera will always be bittersweet, as it reminds me of romance, sadness, passion, and melancholia—a mixture of emotions associated with my family and South Africa. It happens that these are also the essential components of the Russian psyche.

Ivan Susanin is a tragedy based on a patriotic hero of the Time of Troubles of the seventeenth century, and tells the story of the eponymous peasant logger who was killed by Polish soldiers. The invaders from the west had been searching the woods near Moscow for the newly elected Tsar Mikhail, the first of the Romanov dynasty. Susanin tricked the Poles and sacrificed himself by leading the hunters deep into the forest, where the whole party got hopelessly lost and ultimately disappeared, ensuring the Tsar's survival. The story was an enduring favourite of Russian nationalists, depicting an ideal of selfless individual heroism in service of Tsar and state. Igor had been desperate for me to experience this particular story as it offered an illuminating window into Russian history and identity.

The opera, rich in folklore and traditional music, is performed with a cast of hundreds, with characters including peasants, militiamen, nobles, ladies, and knights. At points the stage is so packed it can be hard to work out who is doing what, but the show was utterly mesmerising nonetheless. The audience loved it—nobody more so than me.

There were at least two intermissions involving visits to the ladies' cloakroom and an interaction with a toothless *babushka* in a headscarf who demanded a handful of kopeks in return for keeping the area clean. This was a common sight: an army of grandmothers prowled Moscow's public conveniences, museums, galleries, and public transport armed with brooms, dusters, and, usually, buckets of attitude. Many were veterans of the Great Patriotic War and therefore commanded respect, regardless of the circumstances.

These characters were also a frequent sight at the GUM department store near the Red Square, where I once dragged Igor in a futile search for Western goods like moisturiser and shower gel. GUM was the Russian abbreviation of the "State Department Store" found in most Soviet republics and was more renowned for what it didn't have than what it did.

The Moscow GUM's famous façade extends along the eastern side of the Red Square, boasting Art Nouveau, Byzantine, and Russian revival styles. It ceased to be a department store for a while after Joseph Stalin converted it into office space for the committee in charge of his first Five-Year Plan in 1928. After the suicide of his wife, Nadezhda, in 1932, he chose GUM as the site where her body would be displayed. It reopened as a department store in 1953. GUM customarily had the basic consumer goods, but queues were long, often extending into the Red Square. After all that long and varied history, it has now fallen under the ownership of a supermarket company.

Red Square itself was iconic, the site of the stunning sixteenth-century St Basil's Cathedral, or the Cathedral of Vasily the Blessed. Igor said, with a raised eyebrow, that after its completion Ivan the Terrible had blinded the architect Postnik Yakovlev so that he could never build anything so beautiful again. And beautiful it was, with its multi-coloured domes pointing towards the sky, the whole building brilliantly and mysteriously lit at night. Inside are nine vividly decorated chapels, each dedicated to a different saint whose favour was said to have been bestowed upon Ivan the Terrible.

Near the Kremlin Wall is the Tomb Of The Unknown Soldier, containing the remains of a nameless warrior who died in December 1941 defending Moscow against the approaching Nazis. This is an emotional monument for many Russians, considering the enormous losses sustained by the USSR in the Great Patriotic War. It is a place of pilgrimage, where newlywed couples pose for wedding photographs before laying their bouquet on the tomb. The inscription reads, "Your name is unknown, your deeds immortal."

The names of the Soviet "hero cities," the places that withstood the heaviest fighting, are also carved into the stone. And south of the tomb is a row of red urns containing earth from each of these cities: Leningrad, Stalingrad, Kiev, Odessa, Sevastopol, Kerch, Minsk, Novorossiysk, Tula, Brest, Murmansk, and Smolensk. Every hour, on the hour, soldiers from the elite Kremlin Guard goosestep their way to the changing of the guard ceremony. Every time I saw this place and the frozen-in-time theatrics of the guards, shivers went coursing through me. Igor and I would often visit to place flowers on the tomb.

Pride of place in Red Square is Lenin's Mausoleum, where his preserved body, complete with spectacles and luxuriant moustache, has been on display in a glass coffin since his death in 1924, except during periods of war. The Egyptian-style marble construction is discordant with the Red Square architecture, but the experience of seeing Lenin lying in state, surrounded by respectful crowds, piles of flowers, and hushed patriotic music, made up for it. Outside the Mausoleum are the graves of other Soviet leaders. Stalin's is near the Kremlin Wall, but "We don't talk about *him!*" said a tight-lipped Igor when pressed about Comrade Joe.

The Red Square separates the Kremlin, now the official residence of the President of Russia, from a historic quarter known as Kitay-Gorod. It was inside the walls of the Kremlin where I undertook my first driving lessons with Igor and a flat-capped instructor, making good use of the private roads away from prying eyes. The problem, as I sat in the enormous dual-controlled black Volga with my nose just above the steering wheel, was that Igor and the driving instructor had very novel and very different ideas of how to teach me. I spent many hours cruising around the Kremlin with Igor and the driving instructor screaming Russian profanities at each other.

As Moscow's central meeting place, the literal embodiment of the public square, the Red Square was a favourite venue for demonstrators and orators. It moved me to see how ordinary citizens came here to demonstrate for *mir* (peace) and for the President Mikhail Sergeiovich Gorbachev's policies of *glasnost* (openness) and *perestroika* (restructuring). Gorbachev's policies reformed the Soviet Communist Party during the 1980s and heralded a de-escalation in tensions with the West. The end of the Cold War came soon after.

But my most memorable day in the Soviet Union was the October Revolution Parade, which took place in Red Square on a crisp, grey day in 1986. Russians celebrated the holiday on November 7. The leaders of the Politburo and the Central Committee of the Communist Party would gather on the podium of the Mausoleum as guests of honour to watch the military parade at the Red Square. It was a day of great fanfare and celebration and an important date to all Russians.

The night before, my neighbours decorated Gorky Street with red banners bearing the message, "*Slava, Sovetsky Soyuz!*"—"Glory to the Soviet Union!"—and huge posters calling for peace, *glasnost,* and *perestroika,* and lauding the achievements of the workers and the army. Igor and I waited at the apartment window from early the next morning to watch the procession of troops, tanks, and enormous military hardware, including missiles, crawling down Gorky Street to the Red Square, accompanied by a score of patriotic music.

Later that day we braved the crowds to steal a glimpse of Gorbachev, wrapped up against the cold and scowling, watching the Parade from his seat of honour outside the Mausoleum. We had hotly debated whether the famous birthmark on his head would be visible or hidden beneath his winter hat. It was hidden.

As we stood at the foot of the brilliantly lit steps to the Bolshoi that evening, a blushing Igor gave me a red rose, wrapped in cellophane and tied with a curly red ribbon. I knew already about the delicate system of etiquette and symbolism that governed the giving and receiving of flowers in the Soviet Union. Igor had previously explained, in his self-conscious way, that an uneven number of flowers should always be given on occasions (for luck), unless you were going to a funeral, in which case courtesy dictated an even number: four, six, or eight. He said, looking decidedly pink-cheeked, eyes fixed on his boots, that Russians loved flowers, and a symbol of love was a long-stemmed red rose. One could always start with one white rose, and then the type and number of roses can change as love grows.

The Russians consider carnations a practical sort of flower, and it's customary to reserve them for celebrating Russian holidays. Men may receive flowers too, Igor said, shuffling uncomfortably from foot to foot (I wondered if this was a hint?), but only on special occasions and only if they were big and "masculine." This left me pondering the gender of flowers. Noticing my expression, he clarified that flowers for men should only come in dark colours. We agreed that we both liked tulips, and that these would do nicely, whatever one's gender.

I was always the recipient of a bouquet when the Soviet generals, broad chests clattering with medals, came to tea at Gorky Street. In turn, Igor and I presented Nina and Irina with bouquets of mimosa on International Women's Day, and they rewarded us with a smacking kiss on each cheek.

Every September 1st, Russian schoolchildren will arrive to meet their teachers with bouquets, and flower sellers in their stalls and kiosks are a frequent sight on Moscow streets. Flowers are suitable for most occasions, and they are the perfect symbol of the inherent turbulence of the Russian soul: an ephemeral combination of romance, sorrow, and outspokenness I came to know and love. I later discovered that Igor's single rose meant "You are all I have," whilst a bouquet of five red roses would have meant, "I love you." It was all very Russian, but once I had my head around it I found the politics of flower giving to be quite charming.

I discovered too that a complex and distinctly Russian etiquette governed the consumption of alcohol. My hosts always appeared uncomfortable if I could not finish a drink or a toast, and I only learned why when Igor explained it was impolite to refuse, or fail to finish, a glass you had been given. Shots should be downed in one, and the first shot of a drinking session should immediately be followed by the second. I also discovered, to my detriment, an empty glass is always refilled, so it was essential to pace oneself and drink slowly.

A toast and a touching of glasses should accompany every alcoholic drink, except those served at a funeral. This rule drove me to distraction if we had several guests at the apartment, all of whom insisted on giving their own toast. This was Igor's worst nightmare too, since he was the one who had to translate the rambling waffle of the broad-chested military gentlemen who had consumed a few too many in the interest of Soviet and ANC relations. I discovered early on that I too was expected to offer a toast; my favoured subjects were the wellbeing of my hosts and the flourishing of the relationship between the ANC and the Soviet Union. I learned also that the third toast in any set is traditionally, "To love!"—"*Zalyubov!*"

I remember one occasion when whisky was served for the generals. I watched in a kind of trance as the honey-brown liquid trickled into a glass, large cubes of ice floating on the surface. The woody smell of the drink got up my nostrils and into my brain, and it took me all the way back to the day of my political awakening, when I had sat before footage of the Soweto massacre with my father beside me. He had been drinking whisky then, and the smell of peat was something I always associated with the horror of the day Soweto school children fought back, a day that changed the life of so many young South Africans—including me.

I was back there now, looking from the screen to my father's face, washed out in the TV's glow. I noticed for the first time how old he looked. His hair was greying at the temples and thinning; he wore it combed back, but still Brylcreemed to within an inch of its life. The blond curls of his youth had disappeared and no longer fell over his eyes. He was only forty-four.

And just like that I was back in Gorky Street—back at the immaculately laid table with Igor, Nina, Irina, and the clutch of visiting generals. I was crying; the association between the smell of whisky and the murder I had witnessed through the screen was so strong that I couldn't separate the two. I wiped my face on my sleeve before anyone noticed my watery eyes.

***

During my time in the USSR I learned so much about this strange country, a place I had idolised all my life without ever truly understanding.

For one thing, love and sex, I discovered through Igor, were subjects not freely discussed in Soviet society, although Lenin had been very much in favour of free love. During the eighties, most Soviets received their sex education from erotic Western films and literature, as they were never taught the subject at school. By the dawn of the nineties, sex had appeared in anatomy books, but these texts gave little information on emotional intimacy or sex as a means of expressing one's love for another. Most Soviet parents still considered sex too intimate a subject to be taught at school.

Pregnancy was a very private matter too, with fathers often absent from the birth and not allowed to visit their partner or new baby for several days. It was common to pass maternity hospitals and see a father standing outside whilst the mother held the new *malenky*, the child, up to the window for her husband to see. It was a sign of the Soviet Union's diminished economic development that the birth of a baby was only ever celebrated after forty days, when the baby was home and healthy. Thickly swaddled newborns were routinely placed on apartment balconies in below-zero temperatures to "acclimatise." It never seemed to do them any harm, and the Russian babies I saw were all heavy and healthy, untroubled by illness, and not prone to crying fits.

Another quirk of life in Russia had to do with queuing. Russians love to queue and, like most Muscovites, I soon became well-accustomed to it. Igor had a habit of arriving excitedly at the apartment to tell Nina, Irina, and I where he had seen queues on his way through town. In minutes we would be out on the street heading for the nearest one. It didn't matter what we were queuing for—we assumed the prize must be good if people were lining up for it! We would wait patiently, as long as it took, and eventually we would return to the apartment laden with treasures: French soap, Italian toilet paper, breakfast cereals, nail varnish, tights, condoms, or make-up. It didn't matter what it was; if we didn't use it there was always someone we could give it to.

There were so many special days during that time, and so many laughs shared with Igor and my other mentors—when they weren't working me to the bone, that was. On January 7th 1987 I witnessed my first traditional Russian New Year in Leningrad (now St. Petersburg). Russians celebrate the start of the year twice: once on New Year's Day with the rest of the world, and again a week later—a throwback to the old days when the country still ran on the Julian calendar.

After a day exploring the city and the treasures of the Hermitage Museum there followed more dinners and toasts, more generals and sparkling wine. At midnight we ate red and black caviar and tangerines, and we drank more champagne as fireworks burst overhead, their glow throwing into relief the decorated fir tree in the corner of the room. I knew I would soon be finished with my training in the Soviet Union, and a return to Africa was imminent.

A few weeks previously, Ronnie had turned up among the crowd of generals to a dinner party at Gorky Street. Somewhere between the first toast, proclaimed by a fat, florid Soviet general, and the delights of the best caviar fresh from the Crimea, Ronnie leaned towards me and said the words I had been waiting to hear with both dread and excitement.

"Go home," he said, "and when you're ready, find a job that has access to a government department. You will be in Pretoria, after all."

That was that. No further comments or instructions. I watched as he shovelled a dollop of orange caviar, barely balanced on a piece of rye bread, into his open mouth. He raised a furry eyebrow at me and chewed noisily before beaming at the general sat next to him. Our conversation was over.

That New Year's Eve, as I looked out the window at the falling snow—a deep and silent carpet covering the ancient streets of the city—and the frozen blackness of the River Neva, I longed for the dream and the beauty to never end, and for the pain and fury of South Africa to be extinguished forever beneath the thick midnight snowfall.

RETURN TO SOUTH AFRICA, 1987

IT WAS A COLD SPRING MORNING in Moscow when I said goodbye to Igor. We hugged and cried, and as I held him close through his bulky winter coat and breathed in his smell of hair oil, 4711 cologne, and garlic sausage, I knew I would never see my friend again. He squeezed me in his enormous arms and whispered, "Good luck, Susan, I will not forget you." It surprised me he had remembered and used my real name.

The oversized Volga had taken us right to the runway where my plane was waiting. It was a commercial flight at a commercial airport, and it must have looked odd that a government car had driven all the way to the steps for a foreigner in civilian clothes—and a woman, no less. As I turned to climb the steps to the plane, Igor pressed a cassette tape into my hand. He watched me board, waved goodbye one last time, and turned on his heel. Soon the Volga was driving away into the frosty morning. I stared after it through the window for several minutes, willing the car to stop and turn back. I slotted Igor's cassette into my Walkman and pressed play. It was "Susanna" by The Art Company.

Grief and loss welled inside me. I had left a sliver of my heart with a great big Russian bear who I would never forget.

I had come to care for all my instructors, but my feelings for Igor were on a different level. Now I now understood the true meaning and ethos behind the word "comrade." We were comrades all right: we shared the same beliefs, worked side by side, and looked out for each other no matter what.

***

After Moscow, I spent a few weeks travelling—as I was supposed to have been doing all along on my pretend gap year—and acclimatising to the West again. Part of this trip involved the secretive visit to a physician in the UK, who checked my fitness to be redeployed and gave me a tentative all-clear for my neurological problems. Then I went on to a few cookie-cutter European destinations, the kinds of historic cities a young professional was supposed to find interesting. But what struck me, after my relatively austere spell in Moscow, was the sheer opulence and excess of the West. Everywhere I looked I saw greed. The people here were so detached and consumed by materialism. Advertisements were everywhere. It was overwhelming.

It was imperative that nothing from the Eastern Bloc accompanied me into the West, and during the last days of my stay Igor and I had been through every item of clothing and all my belongings to determine what I would be allowed to take with me. We burned my notebooks in the square beside the apartment, with Igor in charge of stoking the flames. I left behind my clothing: the military uniform, the *shapka,* and the colourful set of nylon bloomers bearing the days of the week in Russian, for which Igor had scoured the great GUM department store all those months before.

The flight back to South Africa brought a turmoil of difficult emotions. The further I travelled from Igor and my Russian comrades, the more I grieved. I had still been able to feel close to them while I was in Europe because we were sharing a continent. But as Africa grew closer, my Soviet friends felt another world away. This separation was made all the worse by Ronnie's order never to speak of them or see them again. I was under instruction to deny their existence and to deny the huge part they had played in my life.

I quickly discovered, to my dismay, that life in South Africa had not changed in my absence. If anything, apartheid seemed more vicious and insidious, although that perception may have been influenced by my heightened awareness of injustice after spending almost a year in the USSR. After a gap year spent marching around in a Soviet military uniform, calling everyone "comrade," and espousing the virtues of communism, I now had to push all that to the back of my mind and live once more the legend of the disinterested, apolitical, middle-class White South African woman. Talk about a culture shock.

THE BOMB: HARARE, ZIMBABWE, 1987

I FOUGHT WITH THE LENGTH OF CALICO, stuffing a seam under the foot of Grandma's ancient Singer sewing machine. The room was hot and stuffy, despite the wide-open windows, and I could feel strands of damp hair sticking to the nape of my neck. Domestic life didn't agree with me.

The jacaranda trees were in full bloom, their blossoms an endless umbrella of soft purple that shaded the streets of Pretoria. I loved to stand beneath them, glimpsing the bright blue sky through the branches, waiting for one of the little bell-shaped flowers to fall onto my upturned face. Mousebirds sang and played in the branches, while the gurgling call of the vleiloerie, a species of cuckoo, told me rain was on its way. I longed to be outside, in that world of innocent colours and sensations: barefoot on the grass, the sun on my skin … all of it took me right back until, once again, I became that child who had spent so much time in a Pretoria garden many years before.

It wasn't until I heard the newspaper delivery man arriving on his scooter that I looked up from my sewing. In that moment, I couldn't have been further from the firing ranges of the Soviet Union. It was time for a break, and I would sneak a look at the headlines while I made a cup of coffee, I thought. The needle and thread were still in my hand as I picked up the *Pretoria News.*

The banner headline, smeared in heavy print across the front page, screamed of a car bomb in Harare. The victims were critically injured. Their names were Joan and Jeremy Brickhill. The same Joan and Jeremy—my sister-in-law and her husband—who had introduced me to the ANC.

The bomb had gone off as Joan and Jeremy left an Italian bakery in Avondale, a few streets away from their home. They drove there early each day for break-fast, and in that regard that spring morning was no different. Office workers hurried to their desks, nannies hustled between shops with children strapped to their backs, and buses crawled through the traffic. The surrounding shops were just beginning their morning's trade as the heat rose and the birds called out from the trees.

The initial explosion, as Jeremy opened the car door, blew him off his feet and sent burning lumps of debris hurtling like meteors across the road. The blast catapulted chunks of superheated metal into the surrounding trees, which immediately caught fire. The sound was deafening, and the aftershock—a blunt hammer blow of heat and dust—knocked passersby off their feet. The smell of oil, fire, and singed flesh lingered in the air. In the seconds following the explosion, there was perfect silence. Even the birds stopped singing.

Joan, who was a few steps behind Jeremy, watched it all as though in slow motion. The spot where their car had been was now a smoking crater, and the street that had been so busy with life was now strewn with bodies. Seventeen people were injured.

Joan must have screamed, but she couldn't hear herself or Jeremy because the blast had shredded her eardrums. Everything was heat and dust and acrid black smoke that got into her eyes and left her stumbling, blinded, towards her husband. She couldn't breathe. Burning air cut into her mouth and nose every time she tried. She could taste nothing but dust and grit and the metallic tang of blood. The sky was on fire.

Survivors sobbed and screamed as flames licked through the wreckages of surrounding cars, devouring them one by one. The sky blackened as fire ripped through the trees, which by now resembled oversized torches. Day turned into a smouldering, ash-filled night.

Joan knew Jeremy was badly injured. His midriff had been cut open, and he was bleeding into the dust of the street. Despite her own injuries, Joan ran, choking and screaming, to a nearby chemist, hoping that a pad of cotton wool would keep Jeremy's intestines from falling out.

A few streets away, and just a few seconds earlier, Linda and Jason Brickhill had been playing in the back garden of their home as Janet, their nanny, pegged out the washing. The early morning sun threw dappled patterns against the laundry as it fluttered in the breeze, and the children watched as their shadows played on the concrete by the back steps. They had wanted to join their parents for breakfast at the bakery that day, but they had had to make do with their own games, entertaining themselves.

Then came the explosion. It was close; the orange ball of fire lit their garden like a second sun. Further blasts, like aftershocks, and a plume of black, oily smoke followed the initial thunderclap. Black dust, ash, and grit floated down from the greying sky, dirtying the washing. It was like a volcano had erupted.

Janet grabbed the children and ran inside. As they huddled together on Linda's bed, they heard more explosions as the petrol in nearby cars ignited. The windows rattled and the house shook. The wide-eyed children clung tight to Janet, fearing they were under attack.

Either by the grace of God or someone else, Jeremy survived. Not only had the blast blown him open, but it had shattered his left hip and his arm, and burning shrapnel had lodged deep into his body, all down his back and legs, leaving him scarred and disfigured. It took him eight months to learn to walk again, forever with a limp. But he was alive, and he was angry.

Jeremy (or J, as I knew him), was fortunate to be well-connected as the former second in command in ZIPRA (Zimbabwe People's Revolutionary Army), ZAPU's military intelligence wing. His connections ensured he was flown to the UK for specialist treatment, rather than having to endure the lottery of African healthcare.

Jeremy's injuries left him scarred and crippled, but the look of wildfire in his eyes—always something that endeared him to me—was untamed. He was determined to find those who had tried to kill him; he held them personally accountable for ripping the heart out of his family, for replacing his children's innocence with a fear and anger that no child should know, and for forcing his family to flee Zimbabwe and all that they knew and loved. He would have his moment, and he would have it soon.

Although loath to admit it, Jeremy's psychological scars were far deeper than his physical ones, and my enduring memory of him is his unquenchable anger. The horror of "the bomb" spread outward like ripples in a pond, touching all who knew the family. A shell-shocked and deafened Joan, racked with night-mares and flashbacks, joined him in the UK with their silent children. Between specialist hospital appointments, Jeremy studied at Oxford, trying to put the ever-present pain, anger, and the need for justice out of his mind for a short while. Joan and the children clung to each other.

In years to come, despite the healing effect of passing time and the softness of their English surroundings, Jason and Linda would find they could still not bear the bangs of fireworks on Guy Fawkes Night. Every year, the Brickhills would politely excuse themselves from whatever Bonfire Night celebrations they had been invited to. This was just one way everything changed irrevocably in that instant, a moment that would define the rest of their lives.

A rag-tag group of South African agents was behind the attempted murder. The leader, Christopher "Kit" Bawden, was linked to South African Special Forces and had operated in Zimbabwe since the country won independence in 1980. He was joined by his brother, Guy, and his cousin, Barry. Kevin Woods, a former officer in the Special Branch of the British South Africa Police, and Philip Conjwayo, a former British South Africa Police officer, carried out the surveillance on Joan and Jeremy prior to the attack.

Joan and Jeremy had known, before that awful day, that they were being watched. The whole operation had been clumsy and obvious, and Joan and Jeremy were more than clued-up enough to spot the cars parked down the road from their house, the figures who followed them home and then disappeared at the first indication they had been rumbled. Perhaps the shoddy surveillance had been deliberate, an attempt to unnerve the couple? Or perhaps the agent responsible had just been bad at his job? Either way, the outcome was the same.

The attackers, who were later found to have been culpable for several other atrocities in Zimbabwe, were eventually imprisoned in Chikurubi Maximum Security Prison in Harare. Post-apartheid ANC Presidents Nelson Mandela and Thabo Mbeki were among those who called for clemency for Joan and Jeremy's attackers, although when their release came, it was ultimately (officially, at least) on medical grounds.

Some years later, in the early 1990s, Jeremy met Guy Bawden and asked him why he did what he did. Bawden apologized, but sheepishly; the interaction did little to quell Jeremy's rage.

But back then, standing in the dusty driveway, clutching my newspaper and reading about what had happened to Joan and Jeremy, I wondered if my cover had also been blown. What if the Security Police or National Intelligence joined the dots and realised who I really was? What if the press found out? My work for the ANC could be over before it even began.

My chief concern, however, was for the family members who were, at that moment, in a hospital elsewhere, undergoing urgent treatment. Birds kept singing under the hot African sky, and rain clouds built into huge columns in the distance. Everything seemed so normal, and yet two of the people I loved the most could have been on the verge of death—or already dead—for all I knew. I knew that even if they survived, their lives would never be the same. And there was nothing I could do about it.

I could hear intermittent raindrops, although it wasn't yet raining. My eyes refocused on the newspaper and only then did I notice the bright red spots that had fallen onto the banner headline. Without realizing, I had driven my threaded needle deep into the palm of my hand.

I thought back to the first time I had met tousled, blonde, absent-minded Joan and acerbic Jeremy, who didn't suffer fools gladly but was the life and soul of any party. Their eldest child, Jason, was a toddler and Joan was recently pregnant with her daughter, Linda. Pregnancy and motherhood added to Joan's brain fog, but I liked her immediately, and we got on well. I was more wary of Jeremy and his biting sarcasm, but any doubts I might have had were washed away when the couple fixed it for me to meet Aziz Pahad, the man who sent me back to South Africa disappointed but armed with the plan to make a legend for myself.

There followed another visit to Zimbabwe, and I grew to know Joan and Jeremy better. Their lives became even more chaotic and disorganised after the arrival of Linda, who teethed and howled during our visit. Janet, the nanny, ran the household with military precision; Joan continued to work as a journalist and Jeremy, a dedicated ZAPU comrade, investigated inequalities and atrocities in Mugabe's Zimbabwe.

In later years, after the war against apartheid had been fought and—to an extent—won, I saw less of Joan and Jeremy, only coming together occasionally for fraught family holidays in a post-apartheid South Africa. We were all tired and everyone seemed that much older, shoring up our hurt, our disappointments, our anger, our memories, and our betrayals, all caused by the events we were party to.

Our children were close, despite an age difference. Each of them was scarred by the shared horrors experienced by their parents, and this brought them together. We parents never discussed that horror among us, but it grew uglier and festered over the years until divorce ended both my marriage and Joan and Jeremy's. The scars remain, including for our children. Lives blown apart, and the first explosion, which triggered the subsequent chain reaction, had taken place in Harare, outside the bakery where Joan and Jeremy had turned up in search of some fresh bread and a cup of coffee.

Despite the physical, emotional, and psychological carnage that bomb caused to people I cared about, the whole episode did at least teach me a valuable lesson: never underestimate your enemy or assume they are incompetent. Most of all: don't think a fool isn't dangerous.

PRETORIA BLUES, 1987

AFTER THE COMRADESHIP of the Soviet Union, where I had experienced so much debate around the dining table at Gorky Street and where ordinary people loved nothing more than discussing class and politics, the awkward, tight-lipped reticence of my South African friends and family came as another shock. I felt I had landed on a different planet, a dry and barren place where controversial or unorthodox thought had to be stuffed under the nearest rock for fear of causing offence or getting yourself arrested. My friends and family were always talking, but they discussed nothing at all, and certainly not the ongoing policy of apartheid that was so central to the lives of everyone in South Africa at that time.

The treatment of Black South Africans was so shameful that I think, deep down, my White friends and family must have known they were on the wrong side of history. This would go some way to explaining why no White person ever talked about apartheid, the African elephant in the room. The complicity of their silence disgusted me, but I had to play along with the charade, keeping my true thoughts and feelings buried deep for the sake of my cover.

All around me were lives lacking in purpose and direction—young South Africans looking to escape through the bottom of a beer bottle at their inevitable weekend barbeques. I was drowning in a quintessentially White South African mixture of arrogance, boredom, and entitlement. I felt a greater shame at my heritage, at the colour of my skin, and the name on my passport, than ever before.

Naturally, I will never truly understand what it meant to be a Black South African back then. I have never known how it feels to have your identity and self-worth depend on the colour of your skin. But I wished then that I knew more Black people, if only so I could join a community where I was more likely to fit in. The White people around me didn't understand, and I scarcely knew any Black South Africans. The apartheid government had spent the past forty years making it difficult to forge friendships across racial lines.

In time, I grew accustomed once more to living the legend: I presented myself as an ordinary, bordering-on-conservative young woman who talked about nothing more substantial than marriage and children with friends who seemed to be popping out babies at an alarming rate. I was definitely the odd one out in my failure, back then, to produce grandchildren, to my mother's despair.

But working undercover isn't all gadgets and explosives. It's watching and waiting and tolerating people you would rather not be around. Success in the field is all about becoming unattached and disciplined enough to walk away. In many ways, I had always been the ANC's ideal candidate. I had already endured a childhood that primed me for the lonely life of a spy.

Still, I felt "*Stoksielalleen op n' Saterdag aand*"—"alone on a Saturday night"— the Afrikaans equivalent of Johnny No Mates. I told myself my isolation didn't matter, that I was used to it. And I was, but one thing my experience in the Soviet Union had taught me was that there were other people who were like me, and I had enjoyed the strange and alien feeling of belonging among them. It was only natural that I would miss that.

I kept myself busy, aware that just because I had left the Soviet Union that didn't mean my training was over. I practiced surveillance by myself, creating complex routes through Pretoria and finding sites for dead letter drops in case I needed to pass on documents, photographs, or other information without revealing myself—or knowing the identity of the other party. Ronnie, I knew, was in Botswana at the time, and I considered setting up a dead drop as a means of communicating with him. Getting messages to my handler had always been difficult, but the task seemed to be getting harder all the time.

I found a job at *Pretoria News*—the city's only English-language daily—as I settled back into life in the capital. I was not looking forward to starting in the office, where the staff consisted mostly of English South Africans. These were ostensibly my people, but I saw no kinship with them, carrying as they did the remnants of a past colonial arrogance that suggested (it was never said explicitly; that would be far too crass) that they were more enlightened, educated, and entitled than their Afrikaner contemporaries. The English speakers had a smug otherworldliness about them because of their links to Europe. Evocation of the "Old Country" not-so-subtly implied they were the chosen ones floating to the top of the hodgepodge of colours and creeds that made up the Rainbow Nation.

The Afrikaners I knew and worked with, meanwhile, had a sorrowful, beleaguered, and apologetic psyche. Many of them secretly felt hugely inferior to their

English-speaking counterparts. However, beneath this inferiority complex—and perhaps because of it—burned a nationalistic rage and a fierce protectiveness of their language and collective history, a story of hardship and suffering. Many embraced apartheid, having been blinded by their own nationalistic fervor.

What bothered me most was the unspoken hypocrisy that went with it. These people had endured a fraught and violent history, from which the collective Afrikaner memory still bore scars. Yet for all their talk about the emancipation of their own people, how many of them would ever give up their lives of relative privilege and entitlement to create a better South Africa for their dark-skinned countrymen?

This time round, the legend proved so much more difficult to live. I was growing impatient. I wanted to find a job that would allow me to infiltrate the machinery of the state, so I could get beneath the skin of the apartheid behemoth and finally do the work I had been trained for. It seemed *Pretoria News* was a sensible place to start, but the job was hard to enjoy and the people were harder to get on with. It didn't help that the chief sub-editor and I took an immediate dislike to each other.

Moira du Plessis exemplified the hard-drinking cronyism at the heart of every newsroom. Most of the staff had been there for years, and the place had an incestuous feel to it. They drank after the first edition had gone down to the works and they drank at the end of the working day and into the night, and the next morning they sat red-eyed and bilious at their desks. I was a revise sub-editor, and the copy that came up on my screen was usually riddled with mistakes. The other revise sub, Marianne, was a miserable, moany woman prone to violent migraines and bitter outbursts, and between us we sorted through poor copy written by bad drunks who hid their supplies of booze and empties in their desk drawers.

Friday night shifts were the worst. The top table, where the chief sub and deputy chief sub-editors sat, was always crowned with a six pack of beers for a centerpiece. As the night wore on, the alcohol supply was constantly replenished, and the atmosphere would get progressively more nasty. Monica's face, which was mean to begin with, would become crueler, and her mouth more closely resembled a sphincter as deadlines approached. I often found myself very near breaking point on those Friday night shifts as I cleaned up atrocious copy that, if published, could have landed the newspaper in hot water. Unrest in the townships had been a regular feature of the previous few years, and the intensity and violence of the demonstrations hadn't calmed. The government was taking increasingly draconian measures to ensure order, and a series of successive states of emergency had been declared. As part of these emergency provisions, and to prevent the incitement of further unrest, the press was severely restricted in what it could say about the uprisings. As revise subeditors, it was up to Marianne and me to spot any violations of the latest press restrictions before the copy went to print.

It seemed censorship was part of the South African condition; it surrounded all of us like a noxious mist. The muzzling of the press meant journalists couldn't be honest about what was going on in our own country, and so the population never really realised just how bad the situation was becoming. This artificial state of blissful ignorance had an insidious way of creeping into our consciousness. Living under such a regime teaches you to self-censor, and in this way many White South Africans shut themselves off from the unpleasantness of apartheid. Censorship meant we didn't have to question our responsibility in playing a tacit part in a crime against humanity, which is exactly what apartheid was.

Working as an instrument of the toothless press placed a huge strain on my conscience. It became increasingly difficult to put up with the stress of the job, and I became more impatient and angry. During my training in the USSR I had met people who were genuinely empathic and principled, and I cared about them and missed them; working within this microcosm of South African society made me feel I was drowning in selfish ignorance.

I knew this feeling was one of the danger signs that should prompt a handler to meet and debrief their agent. At my request, Ronnie was able to see me briefly in Botswana, although our conversation lasted for less than thirty minutes, and he appeared disinterested in what I had to say. One drawback of working in deep cover for extended periods is that the agent can become careless or burnt out, and this is when mistakes happen.

I sometimes used coded messages to arrange meetings with Ronnie, which I wrote on postcards sent to a safe address in London. I believe Eleanor, Ronnie's wife, would collect such post. Phone calls for Ronnie, which went through Eleanor's work, were for dire emergencies only as the Kasrils were both under constant surveillance. The couple's work and home phones were tapped, so any conversations would have to be powdered with code words and euphemisms. If we spotted surveillance, we aborted our meetings. There was always a Plan B, which involved a different time, place, and venue.

Despite the challenges of setting them up, semi-regular debriefs are essential to monitor an agent's state of mind and their safety. I had nothing of the sort. I had one such meeting with Ronnie in two-and-a-half years. And later on, when crucial decisions had to be taken, he would be nowhere to be seen. Through his detachment, Ronnie put my life in danger.

I am not the only betrayer in this story.

SECURITY CLEARANCE, 1987

To MY RELIEF, I hadn't been at *Pretoria News* for long before I spotted a vacancy for a less soul-destroying job. The government's Bureau for Information was advertising a post for a writer and translator to work on a new political magazine. I applied and went for the interview a few days later. A large, sad-eyed woman shuffled a pile of papers around her desk before thrusting various propaganda publications my way, most of which showed pictures of White government ministers shaking the hands of various junior Black officials. She asked me questions about my life and my ambitions, and I stuck to the script. I did not meet the editor that day, but my ears pricked up when she mentioned he was the son of a well-known government minister. It seemed this job presented an ideal chance to get closer to the apartheid regime.

However, landing the job shouldn't have been easy. The post required enhanced security clearance, which could only be obtained via a visit to the Security Police headquarters. Basic security clearance involved checking a person's credentials, study and work history, and financial status. This enhanced level called for a face-to-face interview and was needed for anyone whose history included contact with suspicious (shorthand for liberal) institutions. They reserved the highest level of clearance for those who handled sensitive information, usually policymakers and the inner echelons of government.

Back when I worked at SABC, my association with Wits University had made my Afrikaner colleagues suspicious. My alma mater drew attention to me, which was the last thing I wanted. It was the same at the Bureau, and I was sure it was Wits that had set the alarm bells ringing once more.

I regarded the security clearance as a necessary chore, and while I didn't relish the thought of my interview, I looked on it as a test of my nerve and my acting skills. On the day of the interview I arrived early, and an assistant showed me to a cramped office. I was very aware of the mounted cameras that followed my progress all the way down the dingy corridor.

A large, unshaven Afrikaner in shirt sleeves sat behind the desk, picking his teeth. This senior Security Policeman stopped briefly and looked me up and down, consulting a file on his desk. He sniffed like a bloodhound and shifted the toothpick to the side of his mouth. A cigarette burned in an ashtray on the desk, and I noticed a holster tight against his bulging torso. There were wet crescents of sweat showing beneath his armpits. The room smelled of sweat and onions and stale tobacco.

It was approaching thirty-four degrees outside, and the building was stifling. A yellowed fan laboured on the untidy desk, but all it seemed to do was push the hot and stale air from one side of the room to the other. I was sweating too, but more from heat than from my nerves. The test was about to begin.

I greeted the policeman in Afrikaans, as was becoming the social norm. He lifted his bulldog head and considered me. He leant forward and loosened his tie, liberating a few rolls of neck fat. In heavily accented English, he asked me some basic questions about my background and then drew himself up in his chair to look me straight in the eye.

"Ja. So what do you fink about Wits, hey?"

"I wasn't very happy there," I said.

"Why zat?"

"I didn't like the politics."

"Ja. They're all blerry communists."

"Yes, and I was there to study," I said. I could feel myself getting into the swing of things. I added, "I wasn't there to take part in demonstrations and all that nonsense."

"Hm. And what do you fink of living next door to Blecks?"

I stared at him, hoping my poker face would conceal my shock. This hadn't been in the playbook … what the hell was I supposed to answer to that?

"Well," I said, keeping my attention fixed on the policeman's face in case he gave anything away. "I suppose it would be alright if they didn't arrive with their extended families and a bunch of chickens and goats and mess up the neighbourhood."

I wanted to get up and run from the room; I was sure I was going to fail on the spot. But the fat bulldog a policeman just nodded, the sweat on his top lip and forehead glinting.

"Ag, ja, man. I know what you mean, lady." There was a pause and then, content that I was no threat, he said, "Ja, you're okay. You can go now."

We exchanged pleasantries, and I left. My hands shook as I opened the building's front door, and I tasted relief in the fresh air. It took every ounce of composure not to run down the road as fast as I could, to put as much space as possible between me and that revolting sweat-soaked racist and his bizarre questions. But at least I had earned my rubber stamp, and with it the approval to start a new job at the Bureau for Information. I was no threat to national security—and that was official.

"VEE HAH," WYNIE AND THE TEAM, 1988

HE REGARDED ME OVER THE RIM OF HIS GLASSES, his eyes framed from above by a straight, brown fringe that covered his eyebrows. It looked as though someone had placed a pudding bowl on his head and cut around it, and the overriding impression was that I was talking to a slimmer and more dramatic version of Moe from *The Three Stooges*. His long, gangly legs were crossed on the untidy surface of his desk, and there was something camp in his full lips, the way he wafted his hand in my direction as he spoke.

"Welcome," he said in Afrikaans. "Oh heavens, now I have someone who can speak the Queen's English! I'm so happy." He turned to Wynie, his assistant. "Aren't I happy, Wynie?"

"Yes, you're very happy, Vee Hah," said Wynie as he reached out with an ashtray to collect his boss's spillage. The room was cloudy with cigarette smoke that clung to my clothes and hair and scratched the back of my throat.

I couldn't take this "Vee Hah" character seriously. He was far too volatile and excitable, and his demeanor made me imagine a child playing the role of an editor. Tears were never far away, and he was looking at me even now with a dewy expression and a quivering lower lip.

But then Vee Hah seemed to switch back to an affected and over-the-top enthusiasm, swirling his hand around in the style of a royal wave as he launched into an emotional speech about how wonderful the team was and how lucky I was to be joining them. Was I supposed to curtsey, I wondered, or break into grateful tears, or kiss his hand in a gesture of gratitude for being handpicked for this role? I was now the English translator, sub-editor, and writer for the new glossy political journal *RSA Policy Review*, published by the Bureau for Information's propaganda department.

Wherever you encountered Vee Hah (an abbreviation of his real name: Van Heerden Heunis), you could bet you wouldn't be far from the ever-dutiful

Wynie, who simpered and chain-smoked and clung to every word his boss said. They had both come up to Pretoria after working on an Afrikaans newspaper in Cape Town, *Die Burger*, where they had been news and parliamentary reporters. Their journalistic experience was limited, but Vee Hah was well-connected, being the son of a government minister. And in a society like ours, connections opened doors. Both Vee Hah and Wynie disliked Pretoria and longed for their old life in Cape Town, where they had rubbed shoulders with younger and more liberal officials and junior ministers of the ruling Nationalist party.

Vee Hah was explosive, and Wynie was the unlucky lackey who had the job of talking him down whenever he wound himself up so much he couldn't think straight, a regular occurrence as each deadline approached. Vee Hah combined a dangerous lack of sleep with an obsessiveness bordering on OCD, and he would check and recheck every line of copy before our wooden, deadly-dull interviews with deadbeat government ministers went to the printers.

The rest of my team consisted of Estee, Ilsa, and Wilhelmien. All spoke Afrikaans, but they also had a proficient command of English and often spoke it in my presence as a mark of respect—a kindness that didn't go unnoticed. Meanwhile, I always made a point of speaking Afrikaans if it was proper to do so.

Much of the ever-present tension between Afrikaans- and English-speaking South Africans revolved around who conquered who, and when, and why. Collective memories of the Afrikaners' subjugation by the British and the concentration camps of the Boer War were never very far away, and the English language struck many Afrikaners as a reminder of their ancestors' oppression. Language is such a sensitive part of any cultural identity, but it was felt by nobody as keenly as the Afrikaners—so much so that the government had been prepared to risk widespread civil disorder in Soweto and elsewhere by making theirs the country's official language. Although my spoken Afrikaans was not grammatically perfect, my colleagues appreciated my attempts to speak it. If I struggled, my interlocutor would usually, and graciously, switch to English, and we largely got along fine.

"The team" was polite and easygoing, and through these traits my colleagues enabled Vee Hah's indulgent and often ridiculous behaviour. Vee Hah was the youngest son of Chris Heunis, the Minister of Internal Affairs. Our team and his entire extended family knew Chris Heunis as "Pappie," and Vee Hah often

treated us to lengthy speeches praising Pappie's eternal wisdom. These mono-
logues were usually laden with anecdotes from the latest family get-together,
and Vee Hah's obsession with his father struck me as completely over-the-top.
As a senior figure in the apartheid government, Pappie struck me as a nasty,
sour-faced, racist bastard, and I often watched in horror as Vee Hah kissed his
father's photograph in moments of histrionic and tearful gratitude for his fine
parentage. Under Vee Hah, office life was an endless stream of team-building
exercises and tedious dinners, but what I was holding out for was an invitation
to Pappie's Pretoria mansion, where Vee Hah also lived with his long-suffering
wife, Chrissie, and his two sons (exact miniature replicas of himself).

On the work front, we settled into a routine of sorts, with many of our tip-
offs coming from Pappie's leaky government department. Through Pappie,
Vee Hah was kept abreast of the latest discussions taking place in government
circles. By now, the government was badly bruised by international sanctions
and the withdrawal of investments in South Africa. The thinking at the top
table was that it was probably time to talk to those few elements in the ANC
who didn't want to string up the whole lot for crimes against humanity. To
boost the government's flagging popularity, Vee Hah had lined up a dull succession of junior government ministers to be interviewed for puff pieces. My job
was often to translate what they said and try to make it sound interesting. It
was deadly.

At one point, it was decided that I should interview various parties involved
in the ongoing independence process in Namibia, including the Minister
of Foreign Affairs, Roelof "Pik" Botha. Vee Hah thought we needed to add
substance to the flimsy content of our magazine, which was turning out to be a
total flop. The truth was that hardly anyone read us, so nobody knew or cared
who we interviewed. Hence Pik.

Pik was a controversial and short-tempered man, rumoured to love wine,
woman, and song. He gained his nickname from the Afrikaans word *pikkewyn*,
meaning penguin, a reference to the dinner suits he wore as he flitted from one
highbrow function to another.

Prior to the interview, Pik sent in a list of questions he thought I should ask,
which prompted a seismic tantrum from Vee Hah, who felt nobody should tell
him what to do. For a while there were various rumblings about journalistic
integrity that had Vee Hah threatening to resign, Wynie in a panic, and the rest
of the team in tears. After they had cried themselves out, my colleagues reached

a compromise, and I went off to interview Pik Botha clutching a reworked but still pre-approved set of questions that made a mockery of journalism. But we were playing Pik's game by Pik's rules, and if he didn't like the questions then he didn't like you, and then there was no interview.

I duly arrived, questions in hand, at Pik's ministry, and his people showed me into his darkened office. To my surprise, there was no security either inside or outside. Given that he was a senior figure during a fraught time, I was surprised nobody had tried to pick him off.

My eyes adjusted to the gloominess of Pik's office while I was still contemplating the lax security. Someone was watching me. In front of me was Pik's back and, beyond him, his reflection in the mirror, looking right at me. I stared back. He didn't blink as he ran a comb through his hair, which was thick with oil. His eyes were just as black and there was no hint of a smile. Then he turned and looked at me directly, his eyes travelling up my body until they rested on my cleavage, where they remained for our entire conversation.

I didn't know it at the time, but my interview with the lecherous Pik would start a chain of events that would bring me to the moment I had trained for, when I would shrug off my cover and finally, finally, finally—after all that watching and waiting and pretending—strike a blow against the apartheid government. I was always on the lookout for opportunities to put my training to use, but so far nothing seismic had presented itself. So I did what I had been told to do: I stuck to my deep cover, and I lived the legend.

After all, if I was going to give the game away and expose myself, it would have to be for something good. Little did I know that that something was waiting for me in Namibia, and it was my interview with Pik that started it all.

NAMIBIA, 1989

BACK THEN, Namibia was a flashpoint in the continent-wide struggle for dignity, freedom, and independence. Formerly known as (German) South West Africa, the country was among the many victims of the European colonial powers' "Scramble for Africa" in the late 19th century. By 1914, almost ninety percent of Africa was under European control, as Britain, France, Germany, Italy, Belgium, and Portugal fought for raw materials—such as rubber, cotton, timber, tea, tin, and cocoa, amongst others—in demand in Europe. Africa's wealth in diamonds, gold, and precious stones made the deal even sweeter. The European colonialists felt entitled to this bounty, and they didn't care how much blood had to be spilled to get their hands on it.

The result was that Africa was not only stripped of her natural material wealth but also her indigenous cultures, religions, languages, family structures, legal systems, and ancestral lands. Her people were subjugated by slavery and subjected to the mores of their colonial occupiers, who believed they were enlightening the benighted savages of a dark and barbaric continent. Of course, it was the Europeans who behaved like savages, but that didn't seem to matter at the time.

A long-standing effect of the "Scramble for Africa" was the arbitrary carving up of the continent by remote and detached European administrators. Colonialists—usually people with little knowledge of the lands they now presided over—partitioned Africa into areas of influence by drawing straight lines on a map, with no consideration of the culture, language, and religious and ancestral influences of the people they were arbitrarily grouping into nations. This resulted in conflicts that have endured for generations and continue to hamper Africa's economic development today.

Namibia's story is, sadly, a typical one. The arrival of the Germans in 1884 sparked repeated clashes between the European occupiers and the indigenous population. The Germans had the technological advantage, and they were able to subjugate the native Namibians on account of their superior weaponry and equipment. Hundreds of thousands of indigenous Herero, Damara, and Nama people were killed or interned in concentration camps. History records that out of a population of 80,000 Hereros, just 20,000 survived the colonial extermination campaign.

In 1886, Germany opened negotiations with Portugal, the colonial power responsible for Angola, which borders Namibia to the north. Through these talks, Germany ultimately gained control of the Caprivi Strip, a parcel of land stretching eastwards from Namibia towards the heart of southern Africa. Control of this land was crucial for strategic reasons since it provided access to the Zambezi River and other African territories. If you look at a map of modern-day Africa, you can see the Caprivi Strip jutting from Namibia in a way that seems awkward and nonsensical. But this is the legacy of the carving up of a continent based on arbitrary divisions. It should be no surprise that Africa is home to so many troubled—and, in some cases, failed—states, given that men in dusty European drawing rooms got to decide where Africa's nations should start and end, with no input from the people who had to live with the decisions.

Colonialism's roots are buried deep beneath this beautiful and troubled continent, and a German influence remained in Namibia long after the occupiers left. I knew this already, but it still surprised me when I arrived in Windhoek, the capital, and encountered German newspapers, street names, and architecture. Many languages are spoken in modern-day Namibia and, of course, German is among them.

In 1915, beleaguered by the First World War, Germany surrendered Namibia to the Union troops of South Africa. Administration of the country was handed over to the then South African Prime Minister, Louis Botha. In effect, one colonial oppressor was exchanged for another, and when the National Party rose to power in South Africa in 1948, Namibia's fortunes worsened. The ruling Afrikaners saw the country as an extension of South Africa, a fifth province to be presided over from afar. Apartheid, with all its evil trappings, was extended to Namibia, forcing millions more into the system of racial division that tore families apart, systematically deprived the rural poor of education, jobs, and healthcare, and created an attitude of mistrust and suspicion between races.

Now, in 1989, having endured foreign governance for over 100 years, Namibia was on the verge of gaining independence from South Africa. The

UN oversaw the independence process, which was watched closely around the world. But the Nationalist South African government didn't want to give Namibia up; the ruling Afrikaners were prepared to empty their sleeves of dirty tricks if it meant they could cling to their fifth province. The prevailing attitude at the Bureau for Information, and throughout government circles, was that Namibia was ours, and we would not simply hand it over. The plan was to spite the UN—regarded as a bunch of interfering foreigners—by making the independence process as awkward and as drawn-out as possible. Every spanner we had was earmarked to be thrown in the works, in the hope that the world would just decide Namibian independence was more trouble than it was worth and leave us all alone.

But the more the South African government tried to disrupt the independence process, the more determined I became to expose the dirty tricks they employed. This, I decided, was to be my battleground. This was what I had trained for.

***

Work at the Bureau continued, and I made sure to keep my head down and play the part of the diligent employee. Life was a parade of interviews with boring junior ministers—men with bad haircuts and expensive suits who were struggling to reassure an increasingly angry nation that democratic change was well under way if only everyone would stay calm and sit tight. South Africa felt like a tinderbox, and throughout the White suburbs many sleepless nights were spent fretting about a large-scale Black uprising. Meanwhile, the pressure of sanctions and boycotts continued from outside South Africa, and the government was forced to adopt an unhealthy siege mentality to make it through this war of attrition. Apartheid's days were clearly numbered.

I was stuck with these dull and desperate ministers on one side and the ever-hysterical Vee Hah on the other. I continued to build my relationship with my boss, always keeping my eyes open for opportunities. One came when I was invited to a "team building" barbeque at Pappie's official residence in Pretoria.

The barbeque—or *braai*, as we South Africans call it—is a fundamental part of life. The *braai* at Pappie's place was a big deal, and Vee Hah's friends, family, and colleagues from the Bureau peopled the lawns. Among the crowd was Vee Hah's wife, Chrissie. A few weeks before, Vee Hah had blown his latest *Policy*

Review pay cheque on a slick new motorbike and an even slicker oil painting of Table Mountain. There was a quiet anger in Chrissie's big brown eyes that no amount of food, drink, or merriment could conceal.

Chrissie disappeared inside while Vee Hah frolicked in the swimming pool with his children. The rest of us mingled and ate, conversation lingering on the parliamentary sessions we had reported on in Cape Town. On our last work trip to the legislative capital I had posed with the team on the steps of parliament, enjoying the irony of my position.

Later in the afternoon, I excused myself from the forced festivities and wandered into the residence. It was furnished beautifully, with expensive paintings on the walls and huge velvet curtains draped beside every window. I peeked around an open door and found myself in Pappie's study. The desk was enormous, and after closing the door behind me I set about opening the drawers, which were stuffed with documents. I started reading the neatly stacked papers, but I was deterred from more drastic action by the thought there might be CCTV on the property. I ran my hand across the smooth surface of the desk and wondered where I could attach a mine.

There had been very few opportunities for using my initiative within the narrow confines of my job at *Policy Review*. Admittedly, it was appealing to imagine Pappie—an enabler of apartheid—getting the biggest (and last) shock of his life when he next sat down to sign some papers, but this was always just a fantasy. Instead, I focused on the idea that Namibia was the way to go; my interview with Pik Botha had planted a seed that was growing all the time.

Soon after the party, I came to Vee Hah with a pitch: we should divert more of *Policy Review*'s attention to Namibia, and he should send me out there as a special correspondent. Such an assignment would allow me to gather first-hand intelligence on the independence process, and I hoped some of this information would prove useful to the ANC. It would also get me out of the office and its overwrought atmosphere. Of course, this wasn't how I justified my pitch to Vee Hah. Instead, I spoke of the chance to elevate *Policy Review* into the international spotlight, to drag the magazine into a world of newsworthy events, and boost our flatlining circulation figures.

Vee Hah proved difficult to convince, as he believed the magazine should focus on the more esoteric aspects of policy, not news. He was insistent, at first, that we should leave the reporting to the newspapers, but I badgered him into accepting my ideas by planning a series of interviews with those involved with the independence process. We had already made a strong start by interviewing Pik, I said.

I resorted to flattery, telling Vee Hah that we were the only publication capable of producing meaningful and detailed interviews with the main characters in the Namibian story. I lined up a meeting with the then-Administrator General of Namibia, Louis Pienaar. I also scheduled an interview with the United Nations representative responsible for overseeing the independence process, Martti Ahtisaari. This was something of a coup, given the contempt with which the UN and the South African government regarded each other, and my initiative won me some leeway with Vee Hah.

In addition, I got myself a place on a press tour going up to Windhoek, and then on to the northern towns of Oshakati and Ondangwa, where South African troops had their bases on the border with Angola. The UN had called for the withdrawal of all South African troops from the area, and I thought the withdrawal process in itself would make a newsworthy piece as a backdrop for the interviews.

Although I was triumphant at landing these interviews and pleased with my ability to persuade Vee Hah of their necessity, I was forever fearful of being exposed. This was a fear I had to bury, pushing the anxiety deep inside myself, where it stayed hidden. My legend was watertight; I was one of them.

Namibian independence had been a hot subject for decades, but it calcified from a possibility into a certainty in 1978 with the adoption of UN Resolution 435. The resolution formally stated that South Africa's occupation of Namibia was illegal, and it presented proposals for a ceasefire and the country's first round of UN-supervised elections. At the time, the country was still known as South African-controlled South West Africa, but as part of the resolution the name Namibia was adopted. When something has a name, it's harder to ignore. And from then, independence became a matter of when, not if.

The resolution established the United Nations Transition Assistance Group (UNTAG) to oversee South African withdrawal from the territory. A peace-keeping force was installed from April 1989 to March 1990 to monitor the process and assist the administration of the country's first free and fair elections. UNTAG oversaw the deployment of these peacekeepers, as well as military observers and police. The idea was that South Africa would be allowed to administer the elections, but only under UN supervision and control.

Pik Botha, the man who had inspired my involvement in Namibia, was a key player in this process. He was a signatory of the Tripartite Accord, signed in 1988 at the UN headquarters in New York, which concluded an agreement on independence. As part of the agreement, Cuban troops would also withdraw from neighbouring Angola and Soviet Military aid to the Namibian independence movement, known as SWAPO, would cease. Such were the tangled webs of geopolitics and proxy involvement that played out behind the scenes of every African story. Other signatories were the Angolan Foreign Minister, Afonso Van-Dunem, and the Cuban Foreign Affairs Minister, Isidoro Malmierca Peoli.

It amused me to see a quote from the then-United States Assistant Secretary of State for African Affairs in the Reagan administration, Chester Crocker, who said watching South Africa and Cuba at the negotiating table was like "watching two scorpions in a bottle." Having found myself on the wrong end of Pik Botha's death stare, I knew this was an apt analogy.

I visited Namibia on several trips during 1989. My first interview there was with Louis Pienaar, the Administrator General. He proved to be a soft-spoken, nervous man who seemed out of his depth dealing with the well-established and endlessly complicated machinery of the UN. Pienaar did not get on with the UN Special Representative, Martti Ahtisaari, who had arrived in Windhoek in April to head UNTAG and Namibia's transition to independence.

As a child, I had pored over that map of Africa on my wall and developed distinct fixations with each country I studied. But Namibia had always been a place of particular interest, partly because of the German influence—unusual in a continent historically dominated by the British and the French—and partly because it happened to be on South Africa's doorstep. I had stared for hours at pictures of the abandoned mines and ghost towns reclaimed by the desert, at stamps depicting strange rock formations and cave paintings from another era. And now I was lucky enough to go there for work, all while devising a plan to counteract the South African government's efforts to frustrate the independence process. If it all sounds complex, that's because it was. If betrayal was easy, everyone would be doing it.

Namibia was certainly a troubled country, but I found the place fascinating, unlike anywhere I had ever seen before. Its colonial past echoed still in the refined coffee houses of Windhoek, where the well-heeled liked to pass the sultry summer days. The country appeared more cosmopolitan than South Africa, despite the majority of its landmass being consumed by a desert.

Windhoek certainly seemed like a capsule of European culture, dropped from a dizzy height onto the African continent. The hot and dusty winds that licked through the town reminded me that I was still in Africa, but the place lacked a certain African-ness. There was no hubbub of traders, none of the usual frantic African energy or vibrancy or colour. Instead, the city had been washed out by an austere Teutonic influence that took some getting used to. It was as if the indigenous Namibians had never been here at all, like the Germans had found an empty country and built their own version of Namibia from scratch.

There was something unsettling about a place steeped in indigenous history and yet stripped of all signs of it. There were few overt nods to the violence of Namibia's recent past, one of which was the *Südwester Reiter,* the Rider of the South West, a statue of an armed horseman that commemorates the soldiers and civilians who died on the German side of the Herero and Namaqua War of 1904-1907. There was no mention of the casualties on the other side, even though the native factions suffered losses fifty times greater than the Germans. After independence, this monument would be moved. But for now its rider's brass rifle was still glinting in the unrelenting sun.

Opposite the statue stood the gingerbread-like *Christuskirche,* Christ Church. It had been built in 1907, following a series of wars against the indigenous Khoikhoi, Herero, and Ovambo people. Known colloquially as the "Church of Peace," to my eyes it was anything but. The longer I spent in Namibia, the more I noticed these subtle reminders of the country's bloody history.

Haunted as it was, I was desperate to stay in Namibia for as long as Vee Hah would let me. Thankfully, the Pienaar interview went a long way towards placating him, and after my sit-down with Martti Ahtisaari, the Special Representative, I got the impression that Vee Hah was firmly on-board with my Namibian project.

Ahtisaari was a melancholic and ponderous character, dripping with mistrust and cynicism. His caution would later prove well-placed: later that year he avoided a brush with a trained South African assassin because he changed his mind about attending a function—where the would-be attacker was waiting for him—at the last minute. The perpetrator, the notorious assassin Ferdi Barnard, later told the Truth and Reconciliation Commission that he had been ordered by his bosses in the security forces to rough up Ahtisaari but not kill him.

The botched attack would have sent a clear message: Ahtisaari and the rest of his UN entourage were not welcome in southern Africa, and this message served in no uncertain terms as an introduction to the campaign being waged to upend the independence process. The South African government was just getting started; if the rest of the world wanted Namibia to be free, it would have to come and get it.

THE HONEY TRAP, 1989

WHILE MY *TÊTE-À-TÊTES* with the great and the good of the independence process had been interesting, I was more excited about my press trip to the north of the country. A whingeing photographer from the Bureau accompanied me as we flew up on a military plane from Waterkloof Air base in Pretoria. Over the months I made several journeys up to northern Namibia on the huge Lockheed C-130 Hercules troop carriers, affectionately known within the Air Force as "Flossies." In time I grew to enjoy the experience, but on that first trip it was more apt to evoke the plane's other nickname: the "vomit comet."

We were joined by a Canadian film crew, and the pilot took one look at his pampered, middle-class human cargo and decided he would have some fun with us. We were strapped to bench seating, each of us supplied with a sick bag, and warned to expect a bumpy ride. It was all going so well until we approached the Namibian border, when we started shedding altitude at an alarming rate. It turned out the pilot wanted to treat us to a stomach-churning display of treetop flying, the canopy so close to the belly of the plane that the landing gear would have brushed the leaves had it been down. When we were almost there, the pilot went a step further, opting for the kind of corkscrew landing that was usually only attempted under heavy fire from anti-aircraft guns and missiles.

The Canadians, who had enjoyed a hearty meal before take-off, choked and spluttered throughout the descent. The photographer beside me started screaming; she was sweating bullets and already I had taken a dislike to her. It was like sitting in a galvanised sick bucket, thousands of feet in the air, in forty degrees, with the five most irritating people on the planet.

The plane eventually straightened out, and we thumped down onto the dusty landing strip at Ondangwa Airport. Our giant tin can was prised open, and I caught a wicked smile on the pilot's face as his retching, squealing passengers staggered out into the heat.

It hit me like a wave, sapping my mood and my energy. There was a permanent glare in the whole Oshana region of northern Namibia that left you with watering eyes and a thumping headache. The midday sun was unbearable and there wasn't a shady tree around.

Out of the heat haze strolled a wiry, sun-tanned White man in shirt sleeves with an enormous nose and curly black hair. He was laughing as he approached the plane, enjoying the sight of foreigners in severe discomfort—among them two hot, flustered women.

This was Colonel Heston de Bruin of the South West African Police Force (SWAPOL), our guide and escort for the next few days. De Bruin introduced himself and said he would keep us company as we explored the northern region and informed the "folks back home" about how the local police was playing its part in the independence process.

I was busy scanning my surroundings for shade as I performed a desperate mental rain dance. But soon I realised why the name Heston de Bruin was familiar. De Bruin was one of the Security Police spies who had infiltrated the student council at Wits. In doing so, he had betrayed scores of radical students to the state, condemning those young idealists to torture and abuse. That set him firmly in my sights. My mission, I decided, was to befriend Heston de Bruin, any way I could.

De Bruin was in his early forties and had a roguish charm about him. His half-smile was crooked, and whenever we spoke his steady brown eyes focused in on me like heat-seeking missiles, never leaving my face. There was also something irreverent in his attitude that I enjoyed, particularly after spending so long surrounded by my obsequious, fawning colleagues at the Bureau. This man was the sum of my whole Namibian experience; it was as if he had arrived in a cloud of dust in front of me, just as the tornado whisks Dorothy away in *The Wizard of Oz*.

De Bruin looked like he too could take off at any moment down the Yellow Brick Road in search of the Emerald City. He appeared lost and out of place: liked yet not liked, respected yet despised. This combination of factors created the potential for an unpredictable and explosive situation, and I never let myself forget that he was a trained spy who might still be dangerous, even if he had left the espionage game behind.

I soon discovered that de Bruin's company was surprisingly enjoyable, and to an extent I was happy to let myself get swept up by a man whose gaze and audacity swallowed me whole. He was a curious mixture of humour and malice. He was pensive and yet he contained an odd, uneasy energy that unsettled me whenever it showed itself. He was a man who demanded my full attention, and he got it—and living on that edge enticed me. I didn't analyse my feelings; I just went along from one moment to the next, mindful that a friendship with de Bruin might present the best chance I would ever get to sidle up close to the beleaguered apartheid regime.

De Bruin and I clicked, right from the off. It helped that he was familiar, albeit in a way I couldn't quite place. Sometimes he reminded me of myself: the spy in me, the sense of un-belonging. He and I differed in that he possessed a deep vein of cruelty and ruthlessness, traits that made me watchful around him.

We were two spies working for opposing sides, thrown together in a strange and unsettling time and place. I knew he was more than he ever let on, but did he know the same was also true of me? Or did he fall for the impression of the pretty and benign White rose that I had spent so many years cultivating? Did he know I was secretly a moonflower, toxic to the touch? Throughout our relationship I would sometimes catch him smiling at me, and when I asked what he was smiling about he always claimed he didn't know.

As promised, de Bruin served as my guide to the Oshana region, a stronghold for the pro-independence South West African People's Organisation (SWAPO). SWAPO subscribed to a Marxist-Leninist political outlook, and the struggle for Namibian independence struck me as a cause that any true socialist should hold dear. Although if de Bruin ever heard me talk like that, he would have run a mile.

It was no coincidence that it was here where the majority of South Africa's military might was concentrated, and the presence of so many soldiers created an uneasy atmosphere. The region felt like a pressure cooker, in more ways than one. It was so hot that the handful of tar roads were melting, black sludge weeping towards the scorched residences on either side. Away from the urban centres, rows of flat, ugly, magnolia-painted houses with tin roofs squatted on either side of dirt tracks. My feet burned through the soles of my shoes, and everything, everywhere, smelled of motor oil.

Oshakati is the largest town in northern Namibia. Barefoot, snot-encrusted children, powdered with fine sand, played in the roads with chickens and stray dogs. Sandstorms were common, and when the winds picked up the white dust would stick to your hair and get up your nose. Tumbleweeds bounced from one side of town to the other.

Even the gardens were sparse and dusty, and they all seemed to be studded with five-pronged plants called *duiweltjie*, the "devil's thorn." If you stepped on one without shoes, the spines would shoot deep into your foot, where they would stay until they were prised out with a penknife. If you were lucky, you would be left with a few deep and painful holes where the thorns had been. If you were unlucky, you would be left with a few deep and painful holes where the thorns had been, *and* you would get sepsis.

Ondangwa is the only other major town in Namibia's far north. It is surrounded by inland water channels, white sand, and palm trees. The road through town was fringed with open-air stalls selling everything from flyspecked raw meat to shoelaces to dried mopane worms (a popular snack). Everywhere I saw squat, gaudy "Cuca shops" or *shebeens*, unlicensed drinking houses, stocked usually with Cuca, a Portuguese beer brewed in Angola. There was a rumour that the South African-backed Democratic Turnhalle Alliance (DTA) was giving out free Cuca to encourage people to vote for them. According to my palate, that was not much of an incentive.

Dilapidated minibuses and taxis buzzed down the roads, and the blaring of horns was a constant accompaniment to our trips through the town. The local pedestrians were fearless, thronging in the streets without a care for the shabby vehicles that weaved and dodged through the crowds. In those days, there was little formal contact with nearby Angola, but small traders still drove their wares back and forth across the border. I noted this detail in case I ever needed a quick getaway and an ANC-friendly country to cross into in a hurry.

Ondangwa Airport was connected to Oshakati by one of the area's few tarred roads, which was almost comically busy with farmers and their cattle. Our party was due to stay at a nearby barracks, recently abandoned by a withdrawing SADF battalion, for this leg of the trip. The barracks turned out to be a total dump, and I suspected the soldiers who had been living there would have had no qualms about leaving the place behind them. There was no running water, the toilets were all blocked, and the beds were filthy. The mess was deserted, and the pantry had been stripped bare.

The conditions were enough to send my photographer spiralling into a full-on tantrum, and I was quietly relieved when she booked herself a seat on the next Flossie back to Pretoria. The Canadians, meanwhile, headed to the nearest guesthouse for a cold beer and a clean bed for the night. This left me and Colonel de Bruin, who offered to put me up at his place in Oshakati. I was all too happy to accept. If he noticed my eyes lighting up at his typically auda-cious invitation then I hoped his ego would override his capacity for logic and he would assume I was simply excited to spend the night with a rugged local police hotshot.

And so began an uneasy relationship between two spies. Our contact continued for several months as Resolution 435 spluttered along. During this time I was all over the place, moving back and forth between Pretoria, Windhoek, and Oshakati, juggling my job at the Bureau, which was becoming increasingly irrelevant, with my growing interest in the powder-keg that was Namibia.

I have several lasting memories of my time with Heston de Bruin, the most emotional of which was when I made a trip to see him at a police camp in Rundu, on the Angolan border. I found him sitting alone on the edge of the Kavango River, waiting for me. We sat together in silence, sharing the sunset, our arms entwined and our bare feet dangling in the refreshing water. The sound of laughter and singing skipped across the river from the UNITA camp on the opposite bank. We watched the sky change colour until it was soaked through with glorious pink and orange. Fireflies danced around our heads. As the stars shone the moon rose, and hyenas laughed in the darkness.

De Bruin grew to trust me, and in time he spoke openly in my presence about the involvement of SWAPOL, the South African police force (not to be confused with SWAPO, the Namibian pro-independence party), in the Oshakati and Ondangwa areas. De Bruin either didn't care what I thought or, more likely, assumed I was nothing more than his ditzy little bit on the side. I cultivated this impression, not caring about the morality of catching a man like de Bruin in a honeytrap. Sometimes the ends justify the means in intelligence work, and some opportunities are just too important to pass up. This was one of them.

I saw no ethical problem inherent in my relationship with the Colonel. Sleeping with him didn't strike me as crossing a line in the sand; sex was a way to extract information, and an effective one at that. I always had to consider the context of these situations. Did I feel guilty or uncomfortable with my role in the honeytrap? Not at all. I recognised it for what it was, and I was careful not to become too involved. I was a married woman, but this wasn't about love. It was about control.

De Bruin, too, wasn't exactly unattached. He was between marriages although, by the time I got involved with him, he and his fiancée were serious enough that they had set a date for their wedding. After the wedding he told me he wanted to spend some time with his new wife—a weekend or so—before she returned to her job in Windhoek. Then I would be free to see him again. And all this was said without scruples or hesitation—despite the pledges of faithfulness he had made at the wedding. It's fair to say fidelity wasn't a strong suit for either of us.

After my trips to Namibia I always returned home to Pretoria feeling drained and empty. Officially, the rule on sharing information was simple: don't. The only person who should have known what I was up to was my handler, and even then there were good reasons to divulge updates on a strictly need-to-know basis. I had been told enough times already that being a spy—and staying a spy—meant staying alert and defensive, always. There was only one person on the planet I could completely trust, and she was me.

There was always going to be potential value in cosying up with a man like de Bruin, a known spy who was now in a position of seniority amid the politically fraught battleground of the Namibian independence process. Still, I tried to soften the pain as much as I could, and I recognised that it was important for me to keep my boundaries and, wherever possible, my silence. In this way I was able to partition my feelings and, with practice, the lie became easier to live.

De Bruin was magnetic, certainly, but as our fling continued I learned how difficult he could be. The role I played with him demanded a lot of me; ironically enough, it took a great deal of brainpower to convey the impression I was nothing more than an unthinking piece of skirt. And for all his unguarded shop-talk, pinning down de Bruin was like trying to catch mercury. He was there, but not there. Gleaning information from him involved a delicate balancing act; I had to work out when to be available to him, and when to back off. It was exhausting, yes, but it was also exhilarating.

This attraction to danger had always been part of me. Until now, it had lain dormant, curled like a snake on the verge of striking. The fear, unpredictability, and adrenalin of work on the edge, the balance on a knife blade, made me feel alive.

It took a few months, but eventually de Bruin started to show a greater interest in my life. I soothed his suspicions before they had a chance to arise with stories of my White, middle-class background. I told him about my work in journalism, my suburban upbringing, the garden of my childhood. I left out all the bits about making contact with the ANC, military training in the Soviet Union, and redeployment to South Africa. At any time he could have had one of his lackeys run a security check on me, and in all likelihood such a check would have uncovered my connection to Joan and Jeremy Brickhill and, through them, the ANC. It was pure luck—and pure sloppiness on de Bruin's part—that he never dug deeper into the life of the woman he was cheating with.

One spring day he even paid a visit at the Bureau in Pretoria. We held hands in my office and looked out over the jacaranda trees whose blossom shaded the streets. The thunderstorms of the night before had disturbed many of the delicate little flowers, and the blossoms lay like a purple carpet on pavements, shimmering in a haze of spring sunshine. It was a very different view to the blistering sun and white sand, the panorama of desert nothingness we had grown used to in Oshakati, where we spent most of our time together.

De Bruin complimented me on my dress and said he preferred the smart, high-heeled, made-up, and perfumed version of me to the more laid-back, jeans-and-T-shirt girl I became in Namibia. When he asked me to wear more dresses in the future, I laughed. He didn't. I made a mental note to dress up next time I went north; his sexism was repulsive, but if it made him more likely to lower his guard around me, I would do whatever he asked.

I wanted him to see our connection as a no-strings-attached fling, and I discouraged him from having any expectations of me. I tried to be light and fun around him, knowing that if I aroused suspicions he could have me checked out at any time.

Thankfully, de Bruin's work kept him busy. He was about to enter the media spotlight as a spokesperson for SWAPOL, dealing with the return of exiled People's Liberation Army of Namibia (PLAN) insurgents—a condition of Resolution 435. I was worried that my increasingly close connection to de Bruin would invite scrutiny, but as far as I knew I was viewed by everyone who knew him as his harmless, fluffy little bit on the side. De Bruin's colleagues knew I was a journalist, but SWAPOL was so desperate for positive publicity that the officers I met—burly sunburned Afrikaners, all of them—treated me with respect. Everyone knew de Bruin—or "Hoof," as they called him, meaning "Chief"—was involved with me. The fact he was engaged to someone else didn't seem to bother anyone.

It was hard work, but I was eager to cultivate good relationships with de Bruin's colleagues. I knew it could mean trouble if anyone in his circle decided I was worth investigating, so I did my smiley best whenever I visited him in Namibia. Still, I was aware of his colleagues' heavy energy, the malice they concealed behind handshakes and pleasantries. There was a threat, too, in the physical surroundings of Oshakati. I smelled danger lying dormant in the squat houses and saw malignant forces lurking in their dustbowl gardens. There were threatening whispers in the boreholes that creaked and sighed in the wind that whipped through the town like the devil's breath.

I didn't have time for ethics, and there was no room for fear. There was a risk in what I was doing, but there was a reward too. This may not have been the way I planned to operate, but this line of work demanded a careful and constant balancing of the stakes and the prizes. When you decided on a course of action, you flew with it, and you flew with confidence. There was no other way to operate. My instructors in Moscow would have agreed. But without exception, I know those kindly veterans would acknowledge the danger of what I was doing. As a woman, I had my own vulnerabilities, and a man like de Bruin would not take kindly to my deception.

In the honeytrap, discipline is everything. One cannot, and must not, allow the luxury of emotional involvement. If you develop feelings for the subject, you have no alternative but to pull back. It is opportunistic; the skill is knowing when to withdraw.

I was fond of de Bruin, in a way, but I knew his death would have repaid the debt of many a murdered ANC cadre. Countless men and women had been killed at the hands of his Security Police colleagues. The most dangerous of this group would have been trained at the special operations (read "dirty tricks") section of Vlakplaas, a farm outside Pretoria which served as the headquarters of the South African Police counter insurgency unit C10—later known as C1.

C10 was a paramilitary hit squad tasked with either killing or "turning" key figures in the Anti-Apartheid Movement. Griffiths Mxenge, a civil rights lawyer and ANC member, and his wife, Victoria, were among C10's most high-profile victims. Police officers stabbed Griffiths over forty times and beat him with a hammer before they cut his throat. A few years later, they came back for Victoria. She was shot and hacked to death in front of her children. Without question, a debt was outstanding.

It would have been possible to eliminate de Bruin and disappear with the correct support. It would certainly have sent an appropriate message to de Bruin's cronies at Vlakplaas and to his old university buddy Craig Williamson, the self-styled apartheid super-spy who had been involved in the assassinations of ANC activists at home and abroad. I was in position, and I was close enough to de Bruin to get away with it. All I needed was approval from the ANC, and de Bruin, one of the upholders of apartheid, would have been dead.

I contacted Ronnie to update him: my work had put me in contact with Colonel Heston de Bruin, and I had lured him into a honeytrap. Ronnie and I rendezvoused in Gaborone, Botswana, where, to my surprise, my handler was unimpressed with what I had to tell him. Ronnie clearly didn't see what I saw: de Bruin was a high-profile target, for more reason than one. It happened that he was related to Olivia Forsyth, the government spy, who was arousing interest in ANC circles at the time. She had recently surfaced in Zimbabwe, where she had made contact with the ANC and asked if she could work for them as a double agent.

De Bruin himself was guilty of more than just his past. He was also, in the present, an active participant in the illegal disruption of the Namibian independence process. He was heavily involved in interfering with the area's rural Ovambo population and was open with me about the violence and intimidation meted out by his colleagues in SWAPOL and Koevoet (the police counter insurgency unit) to jeopardise the local elections.

From the materials I found in de Bruin's home, including press cuttings relating to Vlakplaas and the assassinations of prominent ANC activists, including Griffiths Mxenge, it was clear he was aware of the activities being carried out in his name. I found fake passports in his desk and a folder of other documents, which seemed to support various "legends" under different aliases. This made me wonder just how much he knew: probably even more than he let on.

And all this was not to mention de Bruin's past as a spy. He had caused considerable upheaval some fifteen years earlier when he infiltrated the student council at Wits, a betrayal resulting in the arrest and torture of student activists and ANC supporters. The way I saw it, de Bruin was a thorn in our movement's side, and he wasn't about to just go away. But Ronnie's noncommittal response left me confused, adrift in deep cover with no clear instructions and no obvious course of action.

Was Ronnie just half-soaked and indecisive about de Bruin? Did he fear him and de Bruin's associates at Vlakplaas? Did all this have something to do with Olivia Forsyth and discussions that were taking place way over my head? Was Ronnie out of his depth and unsure how to use me? If he was trying to protect me, he had a funny way of showing it. He never briefed me on contingency or getaway plans. He was uncertain about what I should do and said it would be better to drop the whole thing and let de Bruin go. But it was too late to just go back on all my work, to pretend my time in Namibia had never happened. By then, I had established contacts in SWAPOL and Koevoet, and the relationship with de Bruin had ripened to the point where I had a decision to make.

I wasn't used to feeling so confused. In truth, I wasn't used to feeling anything at all. Throughout my life, I had looked on my emotions as an indulgence best kept in a box under the bed. My personal concerns rarely saw the light of day.

I was a spy, a spook, an undercover agent. I was many things, but I was not an assassin, and I was never supposed to be deployed as one. In spite of this, I found myself thinking back to those freezing afternoons on the range with Igor and Pytor, the weapons training that had preceded those wonderful trips to the ice cream palace.

Could I pull the trigger on someone I knew? Someone I may have cared about, even if I didn't want to admit it? I am not without sentiment, but I knew I had it in me. It wouldn't have been easy, and the aftermath would haunt me for the rest of my life. But I could have done it.

And yet when I tried, I found it hard to imagine de Bruin, a man made of restless energy, lying lifeless across a blood-soaked bed in the hot, airless bedroom in Oshakati. I couldn't quite bring myself to smell the blood heavy in midday heat. Not yet.

De Bruin had shown me Namibia and given me a feel for the place I otherwise would not have had. Our excursions had included trips to the Koevoet base, various police camps, towns, villages, and the Ruacana Falls and dam. He had introduced me to several Ovambo chiefs, who were on the SWAPOL payroll and briefed to inform on SWAPO activity in the territory. Every day with de Bruin was rich in opportunities to gather intelligence, and I took as many as I could, relying on my memory to retain everything I was told, everything I uncovered when de Bruin thought no harm could come from leaving me alone in his house. I filled my head with names, dates, and contacts. I prowled his property and picked his brains. I drank him in, and then I considered killing him. Did de Bruin suspect me? I believe he was probably too self-absorbed to consider me a danger. At worst, he most likely regarded me as harmless or stupid.

In another life, could he have grown to love me? And could I have "turned" him? I think so.

The theme of "turning" enemy agents came up frequently during my training. Even now, I can still hear the words of Valery Pavlovich, my intelligence instructor. "Quite frankly, Deana, the matter is that everyone has a price, and anyone can be bought." Valery taught me that before you try to turn anyone, you have to first identify their vulnerabilities. Then it's a question of working out how best to encourage them to jump ship. Blackmail is one option; if you study any target closely enough, and for long enough, you can usually find something to hold over their head. Are they having an affair? Are they in debt? Do they visit sex workers? Do they have a gambling problem? Find the vulnerability and hone in on it. Stick a finger in the wound.

Money can be an incentive too. As Valery believed, everyone has a price. And the better the information, the higher the price. Alternatively, one can attempt to appeal to the greater self: what are your target's beliefs, ethics, and values? Does patriotism, idealism, or even nationalism inspire them? Coercion is another approach, although a little risky. But there is often a way.

All this was good to know, but in the moment it did nothing to help me. I had tangled my life in de Bruin's, and now I needed to know what to do with him. Should I push him away or push him off this mortal coil? It led me to consider who de Bruin was working for. Was he a double agent acting for the ANC? This would explain Ronnie's reluctance to act against him. But who was Ronnie protecting? Me or de Bruin?

I thought, as I watched Nelson Mandela walk free from prison on a sunny February day a few months later, that I recognised a dark, curly-haired, bespectacled figure behind him who looked familiar, but I wasn't sure…

A HUNTING HE WILL GO, 1989

THE BLACK AND WHITE FISCAL SHRIKE, better known as the "butcher bird," tore into the lizard's soft underbelly. The butcher bird was so called because of its tendency to catch prey, impale it on a thorn tree, and come back later to eat it alive. This particular butcher was ready for its feast, and now it took its hooked beak to the lizard, scything through reptilian flesh like it was liquid. The bird's bright eyes met mine from its perch among the thorns, many of the spines bearing ragged evidence of small creatures the butcher had already finished with. There was a snapping sound, the beak pulling at the lizard's belly, as the stricken reptile writhed on the thorn. The bird watched me as it ate, afraid that I would chase it away. I was still, taking in the scene. A savage hunter in a brutal, murderous place.

Shadows grew long as light bled from the day, a welcome relief from the white-hot heat of Oshakati in mid-February. The desert sky changed into its evening dress, a kaleidoscope of orange and yellow streaks. Mosquitos emerged from dark corners: large, black, long-legged pests that settled on my arms and ankles, a sharp pinprick on my skin as one drank its fill. These Namibian mosquitos were tenacious creatures, and even the heaviest nets were useless against them. I would lie at night, breathing in the suffocating smell of dust as they buzzed around my head and tangled themselves in my hair. The creaking ceiling fan was the only thing that worked to keep them away, the turbulent air all that stood between me and the swarms that gathered like clouds outside. Malaria was rife in the north of Namibia, and this was the season for it.

The town's white dust covered my bare feet. My skin was red and still carrying the sun's heat from earlier in the day. Lizards and skinks—those who had so far avoided encounters with the Cape's winged butcher birds—scuttled over the concrete steps, savouring the last rays before the coolness of a desert night set in. A column of red ants marched across the dry, cracked soil of the yard to a nest built from white sand.

The windmills from the boreholes nearby creaked as the breeze picked up, adding to my growing unease. Its tendrils spread from my gut to my chest, squeezing the breath from me. I had to focus. Tonight was the night.

The sound of humming and running water came from the bathroom as de Bruin drew his evening bath. By now I knew the ritual: a hunting he will go. He had received the call that afternoon and had run to the bedroom to pick up the receiver by the side of the bed.

"Yes, General ... I'll be there," in Afrikaans. That was all I heard.

Through my proximity to de Bruin, I knew more about South Africa's involvement in Namibia than almost anyone in the country. De Bruin's unguarded pillow talk was often awash with intelligence ... when he wasn't blathering on about his great unrequited love: the hostess on an intercity coach who had cheated on him and broken his heart many years ago. He still wasn't over it.

Oshakati, with its wide dusty streets and gardens of tangled chicken wire, was the home of the notorious paramilitary police counter-insurgency unit known as Koevoet, the Afrikaans word for "crowbar." Among the information I had gathered from de Bruin was the knowledge that Koevoet was still very much operational, even though it should have been well on the way to being wound down by now, as per the conditions of the Namibian independence resolution.

The idea was that Koevoet soldiers were the only ones capable of prising SWAPO cadres out of the bush. De Bruin worked with Koevoet as a press liaison officer, but he also used to go along on operations "for the ride." The counter-insurgency force was chiefly occupied with "neutralising" insurgents belonging to the People's Liberation Army of Namibia (PLAN), the armed wing of SWAPO. These fighters usually entered Namibia from Angola, where they were trained by the Angolans and their Soviet and Cuban allies. Colonialism was supposed to be finished, but Africa was still looked on by the great powers as a proxy battleground, a frontier for broader geopolitical conflicts that seemed to become more complex and yet more detached from the lives of the African people as the years went on.

Koevoet officers went out under the cover of night, I learned, flushing out PLAN insurgents from among the local population. Officers tortured and killed SWAPO sympathisers too. I suspected tonight's outing with the General would be one such grisly hunting trip. By his own account, de Bruin had a lot of fun conducting "interviews" with terrified local villagers. More evidence, as if I needed it, that de Bruin, behind his charming smile, was a monster.

Not only that, but from the newspaper cuttings I had seen hidden in the filing cabinets and wardrobe of the spare room, de Bruin was doubtless aware of the atrocities happening at Vlakplaas, the South African Police "farm" near Pretoria where captured ANC members were incarcerated, interrogated, and tortured. I had heard horrific stories about that place: executions conducted by strapping explosives to the victim's body, leaving little in the way of obvious human remains and nothing to be identified.

Whatever his involvement, de Bruin was certainly keeping tabs on Vlakplaas, which was only just emerging—via the press—into the public consciousness. I often snooped around the house while he was out, looking for morsels of information wherever I could find them, but now I resolved to go one step further. I would go through every document in search of clues pointing to de Bruin's personal involvement with Vlakplaas and the atrocities committed there. I would copy what I could and smuggle the paperwork out to Ronnie, who could circulate it among the big guns of the ANC. I also wondered whether de Bruin might keep information on his cronies in the Security Police. His study was a potential goldmine; I just needed some time to go through it all.

He was still clattering about in the bathroom. I knew that by now he would have dimmed the bulb and lit a neat row of tea lights by the side of the bath. I could still hear him whistling and humming under his breath. He liked to balance his ashtray and his burning cigarette next to the regimented bottles of shampoo and bath salts.

Then, "Mrs. Kid! Get in here."

Through the steam and the bubbles I saw his sinewy body in the tub, his shorts discarded on the tiles. I made my way in and perched obediently on the edge of the bath, letting him look at me in the candlelight. One of his tanned arms was perfectly dry, the cigarette burning between his long fingers.

"You should join me," he said. Then he half-closed his black eyes in the dim light and leaned back. He looked peaceful, soft. Coils of dark hair fell damp against his skin.

I watched him as I ran a swift mental calculation. Did I have the strength to push him under? Probably. Could I hold him there for long enough? That was a different question. Official verdict: death by drowning, perhaps after too much to drink.

His voice interrupted my reverie. "Penny for your thoughts, Mrs. Kid? What's going on in that pretty little head?" He opened his eyes a crack, sucked on the cigarette and blew a ring of smoke into the candlelit room. I shrugged and moved over to the edge of the bath where I knelt beside him, curling a tendril of his dark hair around my index finger and looking wide-eyed into his face.

"Where are you going?" I asked, dialling up the petulance. "Do you have to?"

"Work, Mrs. Kid. I have to work tonight." He smiled. "We have a few visits to make," he added, with a laugh.

I placed my left hand on the warm, soft skin of his chest. Hair, bone, and rippling muscles beneath my outstretched fingers, pruning already in the hot water. I rested my hand on his solar plexus, summoned all my strength, and pushed hard. His head slipped back, parting the bubbles and leaving clear water between me and his wide-open eyes. I knew then, in that moment, that I was no match for him. If it came to it, he would fight me with all his strength, and he would win. I took my hand away, and he resurfaced, taking a large mouthful of air. I laughed, as if my attempt to drown him was nothing more than a game between lovers. He paused, his eyes locked on mine. Then he laughed too, loud and deep. Water glistened on his tanned face in the candlelight.

"I'll make it up to you, Mrs. Kid, I promise."

I got up and moved to the door. "You'd better," I said, looking back over my shoulder at the Colonel, the spy who could have loved me.

We had lain, side by side, that hot afternoon, on the daybed in the enclosed front porch. It was the coolest spot in the house, and the porch windows had been flung wide open beneath the shade of the enormous "monkey puzzle tree" that dominated the dry, scorched front garden.

De Bruin and I had been drinking Diet Coke with ice and lemon. While he wasn't looking, I fished out a few slices of lemon and wrapped them in a tissue. There were documents to read and copy, and I had to take my chances. SWAPO and Ronnie needed proof of what was going on in Namibia.

I planned to make use of de Bruin's absence that night to mix some invisible ink from lemon juice, a trick I had been taught years ago by Valery Pavlovich, my Soviet Intelligence instructor. I had a spare notebook, and I planned to fill it. It was risky, but this was the only way to operate. I did not bring a camera to document my trips to the north; de Bruin had warned me from the off that his men were "camera shy."

Now I lay on the bed and watched him dress. He picked up his always-loaded revolver from the bedside table, and I watched as he checked it and slotted it into his holster. Even though I feared him, I relished my hidden power: he did not know who he invited into his bed each night. He did not know that, if I wanted to, I could ensure he would go to sleep and never wake up. I turned away so he couldn't see my smile.

No doubt the loaded and polished weapon was there to encourage the "interviewees" he planned on seeing that night. When I asked him about it he laughed, a dry, hollow sound, not unlike the call of the butcher bird. In my imagination I saw the bird of that morning, the front of its plumage wet and matted with blood. He kissed my forehead and left.

I stood alone in the dark house listening to him drive away. The tin roof creaked as it cooled from the heat of the day. Crickets called from the dry grass outside, their chirruping mixing with the whirring of the ceiling fan. My heart pounded in my chest. I did not know how long he would be, and I needed to work fast. What I wanted was in his study, where there were no curtains or blinds. If anyone walked around the back of the house they would see me rifling through the filing cabinets. The best option was to gather the documents and work in the long hallway that ran the length of the house, where I was invisible from outside.

My bare feet were cold against the parquet floor as I crept around the house, checking the doors. I made sure they were all locked, and I left the spare key in the front door so it wouldn't open from the outside. One by one, I flicked every switch, leaving most of the house in perfect darkness. In the kitchen I produced the hidden lemons, squeezed them, and mixed the juice with water. I took a handful of cotton buds from the bathroom and headed for the filing cabinet. I read cross-legged on the floor of the passage with de Bruin's papers fanned out around me.

I wrote with great speed, taking down all I could copy. The only sounds were my breathing and the lemon juice squeaking across the page. My invisible writing filled the blank pages of the spare reporters' notebook that I had brought. I would send the post to Ronnie at a safe address as part of a bundle of art supplies for "my dear nephew's birthday." The plan was to package it with coloured pencils, felt-tip pens, a sketchbook, and a signed birthday card. Nobody would suspect a thing, apart from Ronnie—who would know the blank pages contained information in invisible ink. He would be able to decipher my message simply enough; when heat was applied, the hidden text would become visible. It was a quaint but effective way of passing on information, and I was sure my scheme was so brazen it would not arouse suspicion. This was pure, vintage espionage, working in plain sight.

I never knew what exactly I was looking for among de Bruin's files. I had no explicit instruction or briefing from Ronnie, so I was left to act on my initiative. If something looked relevant, I would either copy it or memorise it. Stealing paperwork wouldn't be an option; I had to move through airport security when I travelled to and from Oshakati, and if I was searched it would be game over.

Valery Pavlovich had taught me well. As I worked, the smell of lemon juice took me back to the dining room table at Gorky Street. It was a chilly November day, and Irina and Nina had been put to work ferrying bowls of various substances around the house for Valery to use in his demonstrations. He dipped a fingertip into each substance, sniffed it, sometimes tasted it, and then wiped his finger on a neatly folded cotton handkerchief that peeped out of the top pocket of his best grey suit.

"Quite frankly, the matter is that one must use what one has at one's disposal," he said, his gold teeth glinting in the light. "That is my pieces of advices to you."

It had taken me some time to grow used to my mentor's endearing assassination of the English language. Valery's favourite dog breed was a "puddle," and he had been lain up for a while with "pnoomonrea." I loved him just the same.

He had always insisted I use the same "hands-on" technique to acquaint myself with the household substances we transformed into invisible ink. We experimented with various homemade inks, including lemon juice, baking soda, and vinegar mixed with water (really, any acidic substance would do). To make the invisible ink appear, all one had to do was hold it over a heat source and the words would reveal themselves: quick and easy. We had made various concoctions at the dining room table, and I'm sure Nina and Irina were none too happy about the mess we made. However, a few ink stains were nothing compared to the scandal once caused by Sergei Sergeiovich, the flamboyant explosives instructor. Sergei taught me how to make bombs out of agricultural fertiliser, much to the housekeepers' disgust and to Igor's horror when he realised we had enough mixed to turn the windows of the apartment into glass confetti. Gorky Street was only just spared an explosion to knock the dentures out of the *babushkas'* mouths.

But that was then, in the cold of the Soviet Union. Here I was, now, in the searing heat of northern Namibia. My friends were thousands of miles away as I sat isolated in that dark, deserted house with death so close around me. But I had a job to do.

More memories came flooding over me as I worked. I saw that summer day in Golders Green, North London, when I met Ronnie for the first time. He had taken my ambition, drive, and raw talent and handed it to those in the Soviet Military who trained me, teaching me the tradecraft of secrets: how to keep your own and how to unearth everyone else's. My legend cushioned me in a fitted cocoon; I was like the silkworms that had fed on the mulberry leaves in the sun dappled garden in Pretoria all those years ago.

Moonlight streamed through the windows, and the crickets' calls reached a crescendo outside. A black-backed Jackal barked in the distance, calling for its mate. These were the sounds of the Namibian night.

I replaced each file I borrowed, careful not to disturb anything. The top drawer of de Bruin's cabinet was locked, but picking the lock was for another night. The notebook was full and the invisible ink had run out. It was ready to send my gift to "my dear nephew" in the post. I placed it at the bottom of my bag and walked towards the bathroom, keen to wash off the sweat and fear of the day. Something made me stop.

Footsteps crunched in the gravel at the back of the house. I was dead still, my back tight against the wall. I clicked off the light in the passage, falling to my knees.

The hair on my neck prickled. I willed myself not to move, prayed my heart would not beat for those few seconds. I turned my head towards the sound and listened. My eyes were wide open, searching for a pinprick of light in the velvet dark. My first response was to find the source and stifle it.

I crawled along the passage on my hands and knees and waited, not daring to breathe, as the steps continued around the yard. A dog barked next door. A nightjar, disturbed by the noise, whistled and flapped its pointed wings in the darkness. I inched through the hall until I reached the study door and pushed myself up to get a better view.

Standing in the ominous dark, in that house filled with secrets and newspaper cuttings telling of violent and gruesome deaths, nothing else mattered except the stillness. There was no separation between intellect and instinct—they were the same. The cause I believed in sweated from every pore.

A shadowy figure was looking in through the window, hands cupped against the glass to see inside. I knew it wasn't de Bruin; the footsteps weren't his and now the shape of this man's body was different. My heartbeat reverberated in my ears, my hands shook, and my legs were unsteady. I watched through the crack in the door ... who was he? Had he seen me at the filing cabinet or mixing the lemon juice? I saw a holster strapped to his body, the metal of the gun blinking in the moonlight, but I couldn't see his face. It occurred to me I should get out. If de Bruin's cronies suspected me, they could kill me and dispose of me easily enough. No one would be the wiser. But I was in control. This was my game, and I would say when it was over.

I turned and snapped on the light, moving for the front door just as the figure rounded the corner to the front of the house. I opened the door and stepped into the moonlight—I would confront this specter directly. A pale, round face floated through the blackness towards me.

"Good evening, Miss," he said, in Afrikaans. "The chief wanted me to check everything is in order."

That flat disc of a face disappeared back into the gloom. I swallowed hard and watched as the lights of his car flashed into life and faded, two bright beads, down the dusty road and into the distance. Should I believe him? Was de Bruin checking up on me? Did he suspect me? Had he sent Moon Face to intimidate me? I would have to be more watchful.

STRONG HANS AND THE CROWBAR, 1989

HESTON DE BRUIN and I had so much in common, although he didn't know the half of it. We were soldiers in the same war, and this in itself induced me to feel a dangerous proximity to him. Of course, we were fighting on different sides, but our experiences tallied so closely that it was hard not to form a deeper connection. It was even harder to keep the truth concealed.

I liked living dangerously, and de Bruin was the ultimate hazard. He was also profoundly enigmatic, and this only made me more attracted to him. When he wanted, he could be sunny and personable and welcoming, a real charismatic character. To have found him in the middle of the desert, a magnetic and generous presence amid the dust of northern Namibia, seemed an almost impossible stroke of luck. He seemed, at times, to be a kind of human oasis. And yet, at the same time, he was a total psychopath. I never could have loved him but, as much as he repulsed me, I was fond of him nonetheless.

As our relationship progressed, he and I started to have more meaningful conversations about politics, people, the country. I think he spoke to me more than he spoke to any other woman—including his poor wife back in Windhoek. Despite his infidelity, it was clear that he cared for her, and at times he let me see how guilty he felt about our fling. At other times, however, his attitude towards her was downright strange. On one occasion, he lovingly patted a stack of her red, lacy underwear in his wardrobe. He turned to me and said, "You must never wear these." It was all a bit odd.

And while de Bruin was protective of his wife, he was paternalistic towards me. He used to hold me close and say things like, "Let's make babies," but at the same time we never made any serious long-term plans. Instead, de Bruin suggested I should look for work in Namibia, so he and I could be closer. He wanted me to get a job in the police, and in time this desire would calcify into a firm offer. But for now, I was still his bit on the side, and I was getting exhausted at juggling de Bruin, domestic life in Pretoria, and the demands of my job.

My cumbersome, slow-witted bosses at the Bureau were now trying to convince the world, through a series of dull interviews with the senior players, that South Africa was playing fair in the Namibian independence process. The truth was the apartheid government was up to its eyeballs in dirty tricks, disrupting the elections primarily through a vicious campaign of voter intimidation.

Koevoet soldiers made for remorseless hunters. They tortured and shot locals who hid PLAN insurgents, and despite the official line that Koevoet was being disbanded as part of Resolution 435, the organization had never been busier. Koevoet bullies would also go from town to town roughing up SWAPO sympathisers. They warned everyone else to expect the same treatment unless they cast their vote for the DTA, the party backed and funded by—you guessed it—South Africa.

Koevoet trackers, drawn from local Ovambo communities and placed on the South African police payroll, used their skills to find the tracks of insurgents entering from Angola. These master bushmen were usually able to tell at a glance exactly how many insurgents had passed through, when they had arrived, if any of their number were wounded, and whether they had been moving in a hurry. Trackers followed the trail on foot, supported by Casspir armed vehicles, deadly traveling arsenals bristling with sophisticated South African weaponry. With the technological advantage firmly on South Africa's side, in every instance it was only a matter of time before Koevoet flushed out their quarry. Depending on the mood of the day, captured insurgents were tortured, shot, or both, usually in front of an assembled crowd of their comrades. Known SWAPO sympathisers were often dragged to the sites of these impromptu executions to watch.

Koevoet soldiers operated on a bounty system and received rewards and bonuses for their kills. Casspirs often returned to base with dead bodies draped over the spare wheel as trophies. The message this sent to local communities was clear: step out of line, and you'll be next.

I asked de Bruin if he could set up an interview for me with the leader of Koevoet, Lieutenant General "Sterkhans" ("Strong Hans") Johannes Dreyer, a character respected and feared by everyone who knew him. I told de Bruin my bosses at the Bureau would be delighted with such a high-profile subject, and he fixed it for me to sit down with the feared and despised Strong Hans.

"Dress it up, Mrs. Kid," de Bruin said on the morning of the interview. "You look good, he'll like you."

To this day, I still do not know who exactly Mrs. Kid is supposed to be. The pet name functioned to de Bruin as a reminder of my status; I was a woman when he wanted me to be—a pseudo-wife, even—and yet he still thought of me as a child. I didn't question it, and besides I was too busy picking out an outfit for Strong Hans. I supposed kitten heels and a low-cut blouse might appeal under the circumstances.

At first, I was apprehensive about the meeting; it was well known that Strong Hans was not partial to the press in any shape or form. However, it must have been clear even to him that some good PR could be useful, given the intense scrutiny he—and his organization—was under.

I soon found myself standing opposite the man answerable for Koevoet, and I could have sworn that on that day there was a chill in the air—something I never expected to say about red-hot Namibia. Still, I held my ground and looked the surprisingly small, wiry man in the eye. His was a wizened face, burned into premature age by the sun, and dominated by a large mustache and glasses. He smiled when I greeted him in Afrikaans. I shook his hand, thanking him for setting aside the time to meet me and explain developments in the area.

Strong Hans soon switched to an easy English. He listened intently to my questions, and his demeanour reminded me of a small spotted genet: coiled to spring at its prey, always on the brink of unleashing that fearsome temper. He made no eye contact as he spoke. The atmosphere was subtly menacing, but he warmed up after I buttered him with lies about my politics, claiming I was on the side of the South Africans against the pesky Namibian independence movement and the UN meddlers who were so hell-bent on making it happen. Shortly after, coffee and biscuits appeared on the table between us. Here was a man whose hands were soaked with blood, offering me a custard cream and a cup of *Koffiehuis*. The general smiled and purred into his coffee cup, loving the attention I was giving him.

Strong Hans Dreyer had formed Koevoet after an illustrious career as a policeman. In founding Koevoet, he drew on his knowledge and experience from his time in the Selous Scouts, a reconnaissance force that had fought as a counter-insurgency unit in the Rhodesian Bush War.

He certainly struck me as a man who understood the art of war. He recognised that propaganda was a weapon as effective as any other, and he was committed to winning the "hearts and minds" of the Namibian people—even as his men were intimidating, rounding up, and killing local SWAPO supporters.

He knew well the value of informers and deployed those on his payroll into local SWAPO-supporting communities as spies. His success rate was phenomenal, and he had rooted out countless insurgents through this holistic approach to conflict. Now his organization was supposed to be winding down, and the public line was that Koevoet was already well into the process of being disbanded and absorbed into de Bruin's police force. However, we in that room knew his men were out intimidating the locals and hunting down Namibian insurgents even as we spoke.

Strong Hans and I parted on the best of terms. The Lieutenant General even promised me a go in a Casspir, as though he were offering me a donkey ride and an ice cream on the beach.

In fact, we got on so well that both Strong Hans and de Bruin said I would be a good fit as the new police liaison officer for the area. I told them I would consider their generous offer.

That was how a Lieutenant General and a Colonel tried to recruit an ANC spy.

THE COLONEL AND MRS KID, 1989

I LOOKED UP AT THE COLONEL and stroked his cheek with my forefinger. A bead of sweat glistened on his top lip. Two white bodies tangled among the thin sheets, among each other. And I was a coiled snake—a Cape cobra. He just didn't know it yet.

I traced his eyebrows with my finger and moved to a spot above his nose, right between his eyes. I drew a small circle with my fingertip. For the bullet, I thought. A nice, neat hole. No mess. The exit wound would be different, of course, and blood could get so sticky in this damn heat.

He shifted towards his bedside table, where he had left his lighter and his cigarettes. And his gun, which he always kept loaded.

"Penny for your thoughts, Mrs. Kid?"

There he was, Heston de Bruin, naked and foetal, his body slim, tanned, and exposed. That hair curled dark against the pillow, the long fingers with the gold signet ring which caught the setting Namibian sun.

That night, I endured his pillow talk until he fell asleep, and then I found myself with the revolver in my hands, de Bruin snoring on the bed before me. The sensation of the gun as an extension of my body, and the smells and tastes of the Moscow firing range: snow falling against my fur hat and gunpowder in the air. Each crack of the rifle spoke to the promise of ice cream, yet to be enjoyed, with Pytor and Igor.

Heston de Bruin was a monster—that much was certain. What fell within the grey area was the question, still a source of anguish, of whether I should kill him. On the one hand, I knew of de Bruin's past as a government spy, and I knew of the horror which had been inflicted upon the Wits radicals he had exposed. And he was involved with Koevoet—a key player in the apartheid regime's campaign against the Namibian people. I had reason to believe from the newspaper cuttings and scrapbooks he kept (trophies, perhaps?) that he had more than a passing interest in the deaths of prominent ANC activists both in South Africa and abroad, although I had little proof of his personal involvement. I suspected he was connected with Vlakplaas, home to the death squads which were terrorising the local countryside and desperately trying to prevent the birth of Namibia as a free and independent nation. On the one hand, the world would be a better place without him sullying it. It was a case of spy versus spy.

So what stopped me from pulling the trigger right there and then? Why did I hesitate? For one, I hadn't been told to kill him. If Ronnie had ordered me to scrub de Bruin from the face of the Earth, he would have been dead already. But it was clear the ANC didn't want him dead—or, if they did, they didn't want it that badly. Killing him would mean blowing my cover, burying the legend I had lived for so long. Would there be other, bigger opportunities to come my way, if only I held on a while longer? Would my path cross with a more high-profile target or would I be presented with a more opportune moment to strike a greater blow against apartheid? If, like a bee, I would have one chance to sting before I died, would this be a big enough hit to be worthwhile? I wasn't sure, and that in itself spoke volumes.

I still had no answers to my increasingly urgent messages to Ronnie. None. I was alone in the field, with only the dangerous and unbalanced de Bruin for company. I could remove him from the equation, but was he worth it? How do you put a value on a human life?

It was not a trivial decision. But I was not a trained assassin, and he wasn't the prize.

Colonel Heston de Bruin smiled in his sleep, that slow, narrow, sidelong smile whose meaning I often questioned. He looked utterly defenceless. And as I looked tenderly at the Colonel, I put his gun back on the bedside table without making a sound. Today was not the day.

DIRTY TRICKS, 1989

AFTER I HAD BEEN MOVING BACK AND FORTH between Windhoek, Oshakati, and Pretoria for a few months, I came to hear of a special task force from the Bureau that would be regularly going up to Namibia to provide "support" during the run-up to the elections. I thought this sounded interesting and ominous, given South Africa's interest in disrupting the independence process. It occurred to me that it might not hurt to apply for a post on this task force and see what they were getting up to. Such a job would give me even more freedom of movement in Namibia as the elections approached, and the task force seemed like a potential pipeline of intelligence about South Africa's meddling in Namibia. The UN and the international community would be in uproar if someone could produce evidence of how South Africa was contravening the terms of Resolution 435. The apartheid government would be named and shamed in such a disclosure. The bad publicity might even finish the Nationalists off.

The "communications" (or rather "dirty tricks") contingent was a seven-strong team comprising of journalists and representatives from the military and intelligence communities. The aim of the task force—never stated publicly, but always obvious from within—was to reduce SWAPO's vote share in the upcoming Namibian elections. One way to achieve this was to sow division within SWAPO and another was to back opposition parties, chiefly the Democratic Turnhalle Alliance. My colleagues in the dirty tricks contingent were also instructed to obtain personal information about UN officials that could later be used to discredit them.

The South African government financed the whole show to the tune of R3.5m (worth around £5m in today's money). The aim was to make friends and influence people, and to this end the entertainment budget alone was over R100,000. Grants were given out, under instructions from none other than Pik Botha, to promote the DTA in the press and ensure negative media coverage for SWAPO. This directly contravened the terms of Resolution 435.

Botha played an ambiguous role in the whole Namibian story, arguing vehemently against Resolution 435 and delaying its implementation for several years. On the day implementation began, April 1st 1989, he persuaded the UN's Martti Ahtisaari to allow South African armed forces to engage PLAN insurgents who mistakenly thought they could safely enter Namibia to be disarmed. Almost 300 people were killed in the ensuing bloodshed—273 on the PLAN side and 23 South Africans.

My colleagues at the Bureau openly discussed how we could persuade people to shift their votes to the DTA. Although it was unlikely SWAPO would lose the elections, my bosses believed we could at least reduce their winning majority, which is exactly what happened. SWAPO ultimately won the election, but not as decisively as had been expected.

The dirty tricks group was led by Karel Breedt, previously from the Bureau of State Security (BOSS). He employed me along with another journalist, Marlene Kromberg. I would deal with English press releases and interviews, and Marlene would handle the Afrikaans. We would have access to National Intelligence and Military Intelligence reports, which we would feed through to sympathetic journalists in South Africa and abroad—many of whom were on our payroll—in an attempt to influence the narrative.

The attitude at the Bureau was that our electioneering was a "dry run" for what would happen in South Africa in the future. If we successfully encouraged anti-SWAPO feeling now, then we would be better prepared to encourage anti-ANC feeling in the future, when the ANC finally got to the polls (as seemed inevitable, by now). The thinking was that it would be good to get the practice in before we had to fight on our own turf, where the stakes would be much higher.

The man at the head of the Bureau, Dave Steward, knew of and approved the activities of the contingent, and the Administrator General of South West Africa, Louis Pienaar, was fully aware of our presence. We received accreditation through his office.

I was eager to get started on the dirty tricks team, not least because it provided the perfect excuse to see more of Namibia and cozy up even closer to de Bruin, who I was still very much seeing. But on the day the team flew to Windhoek, chaos awaited us. No accommodation had been organised, and they sent the team to two different houses, both dilapidated and with no supplies. There were beds but no linen and an empty kitchen with no food, drink, crockery, or cutlery—not even a teacup. Marlene and I headed for the local shops and did the best we could to equip the place using some of our generous entertainment allowance, but the ill omens of our arrival were a sign of things to come. We quickly discovered there was no hot water or light bulbs, so icy showers and candlelight had to make do. The telephones were not connected either, so we found ourselves sitting in the dark—cold, hungry, and incommunicado. Not a brilliant start. To add to the discomfort, Karel Breedt, the supposedly straight and sober leader of the delegation, fell off the wagon spectacularly and spent much of his time in a drunken daze before being sent back to Pretoria in disgrace.

After a shaky start, we got to work. Marlene and I pumped out copy, and it was subsequently confirmed that our involvement was fuelling a significant increase in anti-SWAPO and anti-UNTAG coverage in the Namibian media. As verified by Nahum Gorelick, the then-director of Namibia Peace Plan 435, a group monitoring the transition towards independence, some of these stories were ridiculous fabrications aimed at making SWAPO appear bungling, inefficient, and corrupt. We played on the suggestion of rifts in the organization and bought-and-paid-for journalists lapped up our half-cooked stories. We provided the ammunition, and media lackeys pulled the trigger.

I was asked to use my contacts in SWAPOL (chiefly de Bruin) to show the world how Koevoet was being integrated into normal policing duties, in line with Resolution 435. Of course, no such thing was happening. Koevoet was still actively patrolling the border to the north and picking off PLAN insurgents if they tried to enter Namibia. De Bruin had a network of informers and co-operative Ovambo chiefs who kept him up to date on SWAPO activities. Armed with this information, Koevoet would sweep in when necessary and eliminate the cadres.

My bosses also wanted to promote South Africa's image as a peacemaker. Even as we worked to present this false version of ourselves, we were told to emphasise allegations of divisions within the SWAPO leadership. We trumpeted the suggestion that there was a power struggle within the organization, all in the name of destabilising Namibia. Some peacekeepers we were.

And then there was the Anton Lubowski story. Lubowski was a celebrated White Namibian anti-apartheid activist who was outspoken in his support for SWAPO. Naturally, he was despised for his views by fellow White Namibians and by the South African authorities, and he was frequently ridiculed in the apartheid government's pet press. Lubowski was involved with the Namibian trade union movement and made a name for himself defending political prisoners. He had just been elevated to the SWAPO Central Committee when a South African hit squad murdered him at his home in Windhoek.

The timing of his death was shocking. The hit was carried out a week before SWAPO's leader, Sam Nujoma, was due to return to Namibia after 30 years in exile. The aim of the assassins was clearly not only to kill Lubowski, but to derail the independence process. Black Namibia was still reeling from the shock, even as the dirty tricks contingent prepared to step in and exploit the situation. My colleagues pushed the lie that Lubowski had been killed by a militant faction within SWAPO that sought to oust Sam Nujoma and install their own man at the head of the party. In reality, Lubowski was killed by the South African state, the latest in a long line of its victims. But it wouldn't do South Africa's reputation any good if the world were to know that, so we worked hard to cover it up.

Martti Ahtisaari was another target. We pushed stories saying he—and, by extension, the UN—was satisfied with South Africa's involvement in the independence process. This too was a lie; Ahtisaari was already suspicious of South Africa, and he had every right to be. But, again, our job was to convince the world that the South Africans weren't the bad guys in a conflict in which we very clearly were.

My colleagues and I struggled on in our dilapidated accommodation. We got the phone working, and I called de Bruin to explain why I had not been able to make it up to Oshakati for a while. I said I was busy with the Bureau but told him if he hung on a few more days, I would be able to see him.

Then, later that day, an unexpected call came.

I can't remember whose voice it was on the other side, but it would have been someone senior in the Bureau or elsewhere in the South African government. I was told that I had been headhunted for a job. The position was for an English translator and media officer in South African President F. W. de Klerk's office. I jumped at the chance, thinking that this was exactly the kind of opportunity I should be chasing—all the way into the belly of the beast.

The only catch was that I would need enhanced security clearance, but I couldn't let on that this was a concern. I pushed my worries to the back of my mind and reminded myself how easy it had been to pass my last security check. I supposed that so long as it consisted of nothing more than a face-to-face chat with a small-minded racist, I would be able to charm my way through it.

I was ecstatic, delirious with possibility. I was told that F. W.'s people would contact me in due course, and then an interview would be arranged. I had barely started at the dirty tricks contingent and already an even riper opportunity had presented itself. I was sure now, for the first time, that I was on the cusp of something truly great.

TIME TO GO, 1989

MY OPTIMISM WAS CRUSHED with another unexpected phone call, not long after the last one.

"Stay in the house," the anonymous man on the other end of the phone said. He had a curt, clipped Afrikaner accent. "Wait there, and someone will be over to collect you. There are some questions we need to ask." The caller told me I was going to be put on a private flight back to Pretoria. What came next I didn't know exactly, but surely it would be nothing good.

For the first few seconds of that call, the fear and horror of being discovered didn't register. When it sank in, it was my body—not my mind—that reacted first. My chest tightened and my heart started to beat so fast I had visions of my ribs snapping like wishbones. My hands shook as I replaced the receiver, the spare room already growing dark as light filtered out from the day.

I was in Windhoek, in the house I shared with my colleagues from the dirty tricks contingent. There was no furniture in the spare room—just the black government-issue telephone. This was the same phone through which I was issued instructions from my bosses in Pretoria, and it dominated the corner of the room like a malevolent demon.

I had squatted on the floor to take the call, and now I found myself staring into the carpet, noticing for the first time the white flecks amid its beige. I crawled into the corner and sat there, trying to steady my thumping heart as I worked out what to do next.

This was the dreaded day I had imagined for so long. It had come at last, and I knew exactly what had prompted it. It was because of my interest in the job with F. W. de Klerk's office. This time the background check must have been done properly and thoroughly. I assumed (correctly, I later discovered) that the police had uncovered my link to noted ANC members—and assassination attempt survivors—Joan and Jeremy Brickhill. It was game over.

Not only was I a White South African ANC member, but I was one of the very few trained as a military intelligence officer, a spy, in the hated Soviet Union. I was White, and I was a Red. That placed a price on my head.

Also, I had had the audacity to slip into unusually sensitive positions. I had interviewed government figures, planted myself in the Bureau of Information, and worked and socialised with a government minister's son. I had lied, and I had deceived, and in the process I had betrayed not only my country but my race. Already I was the one they were desperate to catch. And, finally, the *coup de grâce* was that I was the sister-in-law of the much-despised Joan and Jeremy Brickhill. The price on my head just doubled.

I got up, unsteady at first, and looked out over the twinkling lights of Windhoek. I would never see them again. As I moved through the house, I noticed a distinct change of atmosphere, a coolness from my colleagues. The contingent was a multi-disciplinary team, and among our ranks was a representative from Foreign Affairs who I had always guessed to be a spy. He was watching me, I knew. He would have been instructed to keep an eye on me until reinforcements arrived to get me on that flight to Pretoria.

My thought processes were foggy and sluggish as I tried to ground myself and think, *What would Valery Pavlovich do?* Should I stay put and see what came of it—and hope I'd be able to talk my way out of whatever mess I had landed in—or should I run?

I waited until dark descended in earnest, biding my time until most of the others were asleep. If I was going to go, now would have to be the time. I crept out of the house under the cover of night and unlocked the government car to which I had been given a set of keys. I reversed slowly down the drive, too scared to turn on the lights in case my spook housemate realised he had let me out of his sight for a second too long.

I should have been under surveillance already. But somehow I was able to slip away—perhaps because my enemies had underestimated me. It was also to my advantage that we were in Windhoek, where the professional police force was shabby and unserious. There was no Security Police presence nearby, and a lack of resources, or perhaps just a simple communications breakdown, may have explained why nobody was watching as I made my getaway. Either that, or I had been allowed to slip away and was being tailed even as I drove to UNTAG headquarters, the nearest safe place I could think of.

At the UN's office I explained my situation and came clean—for the first time—about who I really was. I explained I needed to claim asylum, and the clerk at the front desk looked at me blankly. Some hours later I was taken to the Soviet observer mission in Windhoek, where I would receive a reception far colder than I had expected. The warmth of my instructors back in Moscow was not shared by the staff at the mission in Namibia. The Administrator General was throwing a party that night, and the Russians had been invited. I turned up at the worst possible time.

My friends in the Soviet Union had been tigers. But the men I encountered at the Russian observer mission were pussycats. I was met in the lobby by two irritated Russians dressed in their Sunday best, obviously looking forward to cocktails and sad little sausage rolls with the great and the good of the Namibian independence process.

These two resembled a comedy duo in their ill-fitting brown suits, scuffed shoes, and striped ties, an ensemble that evoked the GUM department store on Red Square. Grudgingly, glancing frequently at their watches, they listened to my story. They telexed Moscow to confirm my identity and received proof I was indeed an ANC agent in need of help. But, for whatever reason, they refused to aid me. Before anything had been resolved, my saviors excused themselves to leave for the party. I learned later that they were disciplined for their negligence. They should never have left me.

I was exhausted and desperate, and it was the middle of the night. I feared for my life, and I knew there was a good chance I had been followed all the way here. But now my exhaustion turned to fury.

I had to think fast and without emotion. This was a game of cat and mouse, and I had little time. I was light-headed from the surge of adrenalin. I would not go down without a fight, I resolved, as I hopped in a taxi for the airport. My first plan was to get on a flight to Europe—anywhere in Europe—and then travel on to London, where I could claim asylum.

At the airport I discovered there were no European flights due out of Windhoek for several days. I didn't have anything like that kind of time; I had a head start of hours, at the most.

My next plan was to head for Botswana, the nearest ANC-friendly country. There I thought I could try the Soviets again and hopefully have more luck at the embassy there. I had my credit card with me, but no cash. I didn't even have a road map; all I had was a pocket diary that contained a tiny map of southern Africa. I tore out this little map and made for the car-hire booth at the airport.

It was possible to drive directly from Namibia to Botswana, but the route passed right through the desert, where there were few proper roads. I needed a four-wheel drive, and it turned out there were precisely zero four-wheel drive cars available to hire that day. So there went that plan.

Instead, I mapped out an alternate route—one that didn't involve off-roading in the desert. I would have to double back into South Africa and pass right through the danger zone—where I was a wanted woman—before crossing the border to Botswana. It was a journey that would take around three days, although this way I had the advantage of following a route that would have surprised my pursuers. I knew it wouldn't be long before they realised I was missing at the house, and from there a woman-hunt would be set in motion. They would come looking for me at the airport first, I suspected. Driving back into South Africa would never occur to them.

So I did the only thing I could do. I hired a car, crossed my fingers that I hadn't been followed, and set off in a direction nobody would expect.

THE KALAHARI DESERT, 1989

I LAY CURLED ON THE RED POLISHED FLOOR, my forehead pressed against its coldness. The smell of Sunbeam polish was harsh in my nostrils. A column of black ants marched back and forth from a hole in the wooden skirting.

The dusty curtains moved in a slight breeze from the open window. The curtains hid me from the world outside, and from where I lay I had an unrestricted view of the door. I stared at it, waiting for the handle to move. I strained to listen for any noise from the compound. There were no footsteps.

I had arrived at the Kalahari Gemsbok Rest Camp a few minutes before it closed for the evening. The gates shuddered shut behind me (would they keep me in or my pursuers out?) and I drove towards a cluster of tin-roofed outbuildings, surrounded by a red polished *stoep*. My heart lurched.

Police.

Two unoccupied police vans were nose-to-nose outside the accommodation block. I kept my face expressionless as I parked the rental car and got out. I had no idea who—if anyone—was watching me, but I knew I had to act the part. The reception desk was inside the main building, past the vans. Radios crackled from inside, scratchy calls in obscure code offered to the airwaves and left unanswered. I checked in under an assumed name.

My room was down the red *stoep*, and I hurried along without giving in to the urge to look over my shoulder. As soon as I was in I locked the door behind me and pulled the curtains closed. A fat black fly circled, avoiding the ribbon of sticky flypaper hanging from the ceiling.

From the window I had an unobstructed view of the compound and the police vans, whose occupants were now noisily washing the vehicles, throwing buckets of soapy water over the dusty paintwork. I watched rivulets run down the sides of the vans and pool on the sandy red earth. Each streak suspended in time.

Hadedas squawked and squabbled on the roof, jostling each other out of the way and standing on each other's long toes. A pair of hornbills called from the thorn trees outside the compound, and the evening sky became streaked with pink. I watched the day fade and drank in the unreality of my situation. The sounds and sights beyond my window were, in many ways, so normal and so natural. But my life was in turmoil, and already I knew it would never be the same again.

My room was spartan, its furnishings few and functional: bed, table, toilet, sink. As soon as the lock had clicked behind me I started looking for escape routes, but there were none. I was well and truly cornered. My only hope was to shelter throughout the night and flee at first light. There was no chance of me driving through the desert at night; that was a recipe for getting lost and, besides, the gates to the compound had already closed. If I left now, it would look suspicious. I had counted four policemen washing the vans, all of them armed. My best option was to stay put and rest. I would have to blag my way out of it if I was caught.

I shuffled uncomfortably beneath my curtain. The fine red dust of the Kalahari covered my hair and clothes, and I could feel its grittiness in my mouth. My head ached and my eyes burned after driving all day, and it was only now I realised how dehydrated I was.

The stink of *braaied* meat wafted into the room, and voices picked up in the compound outside. I could hear the crackle of the police radio and the clink of beer bottles as the policemen settled down to tend their fire and relax. I wasn't sure if they had seen me, but the radio worried me the most—it was likely that a description of me had already been blared over the airwaves. I wouldn't be able to hide for long.

I had picked up surveillance earlier that day when I stopped to fill the car with petrol and to get something to eat and drink in a nondescript and dusty little town. Such towns often comprise nothing more than a main street and an OK Bazaars Shop, which is where I went. The store had wide aisles and was well-lit ... the perfect setting to flush out a pursuer. I strolled up and down the aisles, studying the shelves, giving any watchers the opportunity to see me and assume I was distracted by my hunger. I made out like I was absorbed in reading labels. Then I rapidly spun around so I could see down the brightly lit canyon of the aisle. I caught a man and a woman scurrying away, dipping around the corner, obviously desperate to find cover. Gotcha. I supposed I was dealing with a team of three: one would be back in the vehicle (I had already noticed a car tailing me) and these two were operating on foot.

I quickly gathered enough supplies to keep me going, and all the while my pursuers kept as close as they dared, watching in case I dropped anything off or picked something up from a designated hiding place in the store. The next step was to draw them out and see if anyone would follow me to the Kalahari Gemsbok Park. No doubt the surveillance vehicle would be different, but the team would be the same. Following me would be difficult, however; we were in the desert, and the vegetation was sparse. There was nowhere for anyone to hide.

I arrived unaccompanied at the camp. But my pursuers must have known roughly where I was, and perhaps they even knew exactly. If that was the case, I feared they would close in quickly, before I had a chance to disappear. Or maybe they were content to wait for me outside the camp, knowing I wasn't going anywhere that night. The net was closing in.

I later learned why my pursuers were content to wait the night, rather than striking while they had the chance. A lot had to do with my father, of all people.

When the Security Police realised I was missing from the house in Windhoek, they contacted my parents to see if they knew where I had gone. The police explained to them that I was an ANC spy and a race traitor and a communist to boot. My parents were horrified.

The Security Police devised a plan to bring me in without making a major spectacle of my arrest. They wanted my father to accompany them to Namibia, and they hoped he would be able to talk me into surrendering without a fight. To save face—and cover the fact that an ANC agent had infiltrated the apartheid regime—the official line was that I was a deluded government employee who was having a major mental breakdown, and the optics of my father coming all that way to collect me would have certainly reinforced this narrative of the lost girl playing out her espionage fantasy. But my father didn't have a passport, and as the South Africans waited for him to get his travel documents in order, they were content for local cops to tail me and keep tabs on where I was. Of course, I would never have gone quietly—and certainly not just because my father was there. But the South Africans were desperate to avoid a scene. The last thing they needed was a media scandal, what with the Namibia situation balanced on a knife-edge and the ANC growing bolder with each passing day.

I was also told, much later, that, despite the lukewarm reception at their mission, the Russians had been keeping tabs on my situation all along. I have no way of knowing if this is true, but it might also explain why I was allowed to slip the noose that day in the desert, since there was nothing the South Africans feared more than a diplomatic incident with the USSR. Whenever there was a superpower in the game, the South African motto became "the quieter, the better." Hence: bringing my father along in the misguided hope that he could talk me down and convince me to come quietly.

There was one more factor that was stacked in my favour, beside the involvement of the Russians, my father's passport delays, and the South Africans' desperate need to save face at any cost—and that was the bureaucratic inefficiency that characterises all aspects of life in Africa.

If I was on the run in Europe, powerful and well-organised governments would have been able to immediately mobilise an integrated response from the police, the armed forces, and civil society. Pictures of me would have popped up on the next day's front pages, and the interconnected might of Interpol would be wielded against me. In Africa—certainly back then and, to an extent, still—things move slowly as a rule. We joked often about jobs getting done on "Africa Time"; if you called a government department after lunch on a Friday, you knew you would be waiting until Monday at the very earliest for a response. It was endlessly frustrating to deal with the state, and inefficiency permeated every system—including the police. When you were operating on Africa Time, things got done when they got done. I suspect this general administrative sluggishness helped me get ahead of the police and stay on the run for as long as I did. Who knows how long my file sat on the desk of some provincial Namibian police chief before he signed off on joining the hunt for me? For once, I found myself thankful for Africa Time rather than frustrated by it.

So I had these factors on my side. But still, I felt particularly exposed as I waited in my room at the desert camp. I felt particularly alone, too. There was no help, no safe house, no disguise, no travel documents or fake identity, and very little money. I was practically unarmed. My only weapon was a can of mace attached to my keyring and a fork I had stolen from a Wimpy when I stopped for coffee. If need be, I could stab someone in the face or hand with it, giving me a few moments to slip away.

No doubt about it, I had been thrown to the wolves. The Russians at the Soviet mission had been useless, and there was no sign of Ronnie or anyone else from the ANC riding in to save me. I had betrayed my country and my family, and now the people I thought I could count on had betrayed me.

Dusk turned to darkness in the airless little room. Moths circled the paraffin lamps outside on the *stoep*, casting confetti shadows onto the floor. The conversation outside, in Afrikaans, grew louder, and I flinched as the radio crackled once more in the background. Crickets sang in the clumps of dry grass outside the compound.

A gecko emerged from a crack in the whitewashed wall, its toes splayed as it eyed a fly that had come to rest nearby. Creatures of the desert stirred outside the walls, and night proper descended like a cloak, filling the spaces between the buildings.

"Hey, lady!" came the shout, waking me from an uneasy half-slumber. "Hey, lady? You in there? Open the door!"

Bile rose in my throat. The door handle rattled in the dark. I could make out boots in the thin strip of light that seeped under the door. The gecko—just visible in the murk, startled by the vibrations—swallowed hard, blinked, and ran back through the crack in the wall.

I crawled out from under the curtain. They wouldn't take me lying on the floor. They could take me standing, and I would look them in the eye as they did. With shaking hands I unlocked the door, the floor cold beneath my bare feet. I flung it open and blinked at the man standing there.

"Hello," I managed, trying for my best smile and looking straight at the clean-shaven, tanned face of a young police sergeant. Thoughts of Moscow crowded into my head. Unarmed, I had no chance against a man so much bigger and stronger than myself.

"Hey, lady. Howzit? We was thinking would you like to join us for a *braai*? We got a nice *braai* out there. Would you like a beer?"

Time was still. I looked at the boyish man before me. The crickets screamed in the bush, and a bullfrog croaked nearby.

"Oh," I said, relief sticking in my throat. "Thank you." I brightened my smile even further and made an excuse of my tiredness in my best Afrikaans. He met my eyes and a slow smile followed.

Always find the familiar ground, hold eye contact, and turn on the charm. Here, I was speaking his language, and that dispels suspicion like nothing else. He had seen me but wasn't sure who I was and assumed at first that I was a tourist before his curiosity had got the better of him. Now he apologised for disturbing me and shook my hand vigorously.

"If you need anything, or if you change your mind, we'll be out there."

I had opened the door fearing for my life, and now this young policeman couldn't do enough for me. After what felt like an eternity, I bade him good-night and closed and bolted the door behind him. As soon as I was sure I was locked safely in my room, my cell, I fell to my knees. At that moment in the darkness, in a night full of dangers and secrets, I allowed myself to cry, tears mixing on my cheeks with the sweat and dust of the day.

The night was long, and my rest was the shallow rest of a woman on the run. At even the slightest sounds from outside—boots on the *stoep*, the screaming of birds, a clinking of beer bottles—I would be jolted back awake and into my thoughts of the life I had left behind forever.

CAT AND MOUSE, 1989

I CIRCLED THE WIMPY CAR PARK, staying in second gear. It was already hot and the morning sunlight was streaming through the open windows of the dusty little car, its light making dancing patterns on the passenger seat beside me. My arms were burned brown and a fine film of dust covered my body. I was in the desert, alright.

It was my second day on the run. I had left the police camp in the national park, driving out at 6:00 a.m. just as the gates were clanking open for the day. Above me the sky throbbed with streaks of pink and orange. Thorn trees gleamed in a sheen of dew, and hadedas picked their way through the dust, their hooked beaks searching for life amid the dead sand. I drove past a watering hole and stopped for a moment, appreciating what I feared would be my last view of wild Africa.

Several zebras stood in the shadow of a thorn bush. On the back of one zebra was perched a couple of oxpeckers, also known as tick birds, looking for parasites concealed in the fur. Impala grazed nearby and a herd of springbok stood stock still, the beautiful beasts watching me, intent on holding my gaze as their cinnamon fur, resplendent with streaks of white, glowed warmly in the sun. An African hornbill inspected the car from its perch on top of the thatched hide, where visitors gathered to watch animals at the watering hole. Hoofmarks abounded in the baked mud and the paw prints of a black-maned Kalahari lion bore testimony to other guests who had visited during the night. There is nowhere as beautiful as Africa, an assertion I held even as I was being chased across the Cape. Once again, the natural splendour of the place belied an ugly spirit, in the tradition of that strange and dangerous continent. But that was Africa. My Africa.

The line between reality and unreality blurred as I left the watering hole, driving through dust that rose across the road in dirty mushroom clouds. I felt I was in a horrible dream sequence that must end soon—one way or the other.

The Soviet Embassy in Gaborone, Botswana, was my only hope of slipping out of the country. From there I planned to spill the secrets of what had really been happening in Namibia and start a new existence as an exile. Otherwise my life—figuratively, and perhaps literally—would be over.

The horror of Oshakati's evening hunts and the duplicity of my bosses in Windhoek had seeped into every pore and become impossible to wash off. I was the journalist who window-dressed and whitewashed untruths, smiled at the faces of murderers, and the spy who meticulously recorded and remembered all they said and cared nothing for their fate. A two-faced Janus looking at the past and the future of both my country and Namibia, standing on the threshold of each, helping to end the old and usher in the new order of things.

I was comfortable with moral ambiguity. No conscience snapped at my heels or forced me to beg for forgiveness. I was used to lies and deceit and sat side-by-side with deception. Although it was never spelled out in the job description, it is what spies do best.

The revulsion and anger festering in me reached new heights as I realised what everybody's "normal" was in this world of actors and spies. A normal that twisted the truth, glorified the corrupt, and denied the rights of the many. A normal that tortured, shot, and blew up its opponents.

The car spluttered as I slowed down and turned at the edge of the car park, taking in the surrounding scene. Street traders, all Black women, were setting up their pitches in the morning shade of the sparse acacia trees that lined the roadside. These locals were busy setting down colourful blankets and unfolding battered trestle tables to display their wares: everything from saucepans to fruit and shoelaces to *mealies*, what we call corn on the cob. Women laughed and gossiped, their legs outstretched as they breast-fed their plump babies. Others had small children strapped to their backs, drowsing in the heat. Above them, in branches of the acacias, the mynah birds squabbled, their masked faces peering through the leaves as they eagerly eyed the fruit laid out beneath them.

Dew glistened on the clumps of grass by the roadside, and the air felt clear even though the sun had risen in the sky, casting blunt shadows across the car park. Pied wagtails scuttled over the pavement and between parked cars. It was a perfect summer morning in this small, dusty, Northern Cape town—a town oblivious to the events developing around me each minute and the niggling mixture of fear and anger that grew, like a tumour, in the pit of my stomach every time I glanced at the rear-view mirror.

I knew that by now the contingent, the Bureau, and the Security Police would be searching for me. Right about now, the penny would be dropping that an ANC spy had been allowed to operate in their midst, the consequences of which didn't bear thinking about. The South Africans would have surely expected me to take a flight out of Namibia, and I hoped I had bought myself some time by taking to the roads. And now here I was in the car park of a Wimpy, circling once more in an attempt to get an unobstructed view of the white South African government-issue Toyota that had appeared from a side street on the edge of town and followed me ever since. I was good enough at flushing out pursuers, but to do this properly I would have to stop, which was a risk. It was possible that police officers were waiting to capture me, but the safest option was to stop in a busy place where any attempts to grab me would be frustrated by the presence of witnesses.

A parking spot opened in front of me, and I nudged the car into the gap and sat for a minute, watching the Toyota crawl past. A glimpse in the compact mirror as I tidied my hair revealed a fat, florid, and meaty White man in his mid to late forties, with sweat gleaming on his forehead and plump hands strangling the steering wheel. He tried not to look in my direction as he scoped out a place to park. But his attempt to keep his eye on the prize, drive a car, and look nonchalant wasn't working and I noted, with some amusement, the colour rising in his jowls. Gotcha already. Follower identified, and we haven't even started the game...

I felt more irritated than anything and decided this brief episode would be for Valery, who had always enjoyed our cat-and-mouse surveillance games. I could hear him talking even now, that broken English that always took a moment to process but endeared him to me all the more.

"Frankly, the matter is that one must take the advantage as soon as possibles, and maintain that control throughout. My pieces of advices to you is to think on your feets at all times."

Yes, I would think on my feet, and I would try to enjoy the game. If this fat fool was the apartheid regime's attempt at surveillance, it was a pretty poor show. I'd gone from playing a dangerous game of spy versus spy with de Bruin and dodging clued-up and suspicious colleagues in Windhoek to taking on a small-town cop doing a poor job of tailing me around a car park.

I locked the car door and took a moment. Ostensibly, I was surveying the market, in the manner of an overwhelmed tourist. Really, my focus never strayed from my pursuer, who was still looking for parking. The small square was becoming busier with shoppers heading for the street-traders and the smattering of stores: a dry cleaner, a butcher's shop, a bank. The Wimpy bar was filling up with those, like me, who were longing for their morning coffee. I made for a *tuisnywerheid*, or "home industry," shop that had an unobstructed view of the parking area and my pursuer and positioned myself behind a shelf of sweets and dried flowers. I was hidden behind a golden array of *koeksisters*, a traditional Afrikaner confectionary made of fried dough infused with syrup or honey, and *melktert*, a dessert consisting of a sweet pastry crust containing a custard filling made from milk, flour, eggs, and sugar. From behind my delicious screen, I watched. And so I became the pursuer.

The policeman, who had finally found a spot to park, rolled out of the Toyota like a Weeble and mopped his brow with a handkerchief. He was a short, fat man with several chins hanging from his disagreeable face. He looked around anxiously, craning the fat rolls of his neck while scratching his crotch. He wore a powder blue safari suit, the kind with a tunic-style top with large pockets, and shorts with matching light blue socks. The tunic strained over his enormous belly. That told me Weeble was a lover of beer and red meat and that I could outrun him if the situation called for it. His short sandy hair was Brylcreemed and parted on the side. I also noticed he had a holster in his belt, underneath the tunic of the safari suit. Everything about him screamed Security Police, but this was the cheap and cheerful small-town version. The officers I had known in Pretoria were the National Intelligence or Special Branch sort: slick and urbane, rather reptilian, with smug expressions to match. Nothing like this country boy, in well over his head chasing around a trained ANC operative when all he had wanted was a spot of easy weekend overtime to put more beer money in his pocket.

I moved to another window for a better view, watching Weeble through the eclectic display of gooey confectionary, homemade jams, locally distilled moonshine, crocheted blankets with matching bed socks, and biblical quotes etched on slabs of wood. He stopped to light a cigarette to calm his nerves. His fat, nicotine-stained fingers were shaking.

Weeble appeared to be on his own, and the last thing I wanted was for him to get flustered and call for backup. My plan was to play with him for a bit; I would let him think he had me in his sights then slip away unnoticed.

I strolled out of the shop, clutching a loaf of freshly baked bread, a newspaper, and some biscuits for the journey. I marched towards the Wimpy, which looked to me like a faux-red-leather, chrome-and-plastic, Stars-and-Stripes tribute to the tastelessness of capitalism. I chose a window seat facing the entrance, ensuring I had a clear view of the toilets and the other diners as well as a wide vantage of the square and street outside. I even caught Weeble ducking behind a parked car—a comical moment, until he moved to nervously adjust his holster. Even from a distance I could see the crescents of sweat blooming beneath the armpits of his safari suit.

The chrome table was sticky to touch and the floor was grubby, but I pretended to be absorbed in the garish menu with its plastic-looking food. The toilets were through an open door near the kitchen, up a flight of stairs. That could be my getaway route, if only I could lure him out.

I made a few quick glances over the top of the menu as Weeble wobbled his way towards the Wimpy. My revulsion gave way to nostalgia. I missed Valery and our surveillance exercises: slick, well-planned, and well-executed outings. My sparring partners then had been masters of disguise, liable to don caps, wigs, or glasses on the move, changing coats and often discarding items of clothing in telephone kiosks or bins around the city. Together we worked the Metro stations, the streetcars, and the buses, and left chalk marks on trees in the Gorky Central Park. Now I was looking at apartheid South Africa's version of the same thing: a fat little rat of a man. Here I sat, watching him watch me over a laminated Wimpy menu. James Bond this was not.

Weeble puffed and plodded his way inside the diner and thumped himself down at a table some distance away. He stared at me as if I was Public Enemy Number One. I studied my newspaper and tried to ignore his stare. I felt every ounce of his hatred: for being English-speaking, for being a race traitor and a betrayer of my country, and most of all because I was a "*kaffirboetie*" member of the ANC.

To my surprise, he summoned a waitress to demand a mince omelette and a mug of black coffee. I thought he was there to arrest me, but he clearly wasn't in a hurry. Was he waiting for someone? Had he called for reinforcements? Were there even any reinforcements in this Godforsaken dust hole in the middle of nowhere? Then again, it was the weekend. And nobody worked on the weekend—certainly not on Africa Time. Perhaps the logic was that a dolly bird on her own didn't pose much of a security risk. Not for the first time, I found myself grateful for being underestimated.

Weeble sat over his mince omelette, shovelling it down between mouthfuls of black coffee. Fat glistened on his lips and a drop dripped down his chin, edging its way over his stubble until it fell onto his blue safari suit, leaving a greasy stain that bloomed into the fabric. He belched and wiped his short, fat fingers on the paper napkin. I noticed he wore a signet ring on his right hand and a wedding band on his left. It made me think of Valery Pavlovich's hands, so different with those long fingers and manicured and buffed nails. Everything about Valery was meticulous. He would certainly know how to play this fool.

Weeble sat back and stared at me, a toothpick protruding from between his nicotine-stained bottom teeth. His eyes were half shut, and he looked as though he might doze off, a soporific consequence of the fatty omelette. He hated me, and I hated him back. He was a caricature of everything I loathed about South Africa: its narrow-minded racist provincialism, its paternalism, its misogyny, and its discrimination that was so much a part of everyday life that nobody even gave it a second thought.

I decided I had had enough and made for the bathroom. He sat upright and watched me walk towards the door. As I turned to go up the stairs, I heard a chair scrape back against the tiled floor.

"*Vokken kommunistiese kont.*"

So he was coming for me. Although he was everything I despised, I could not afford to underestimate him. Stupid is dangerous too. My heart reverberated in my chest, and I felt unsteady. I only had a few minutes if this was going to work.

I dashed up the next flight of stairs, past the ladies' cloakroom and into the gents' on the next floor, where I paused until I heard his heavy footfall coming up the stairs. I heard him kick open the door of the ladies' and order me to step out, otherwise he would shoot me "right between the eyes." He sounded guttural, like a pig with his head buried in a trough.

I ran down the stairs again as I heard him open each cubicle of the ladies' toilets, his huge, flat foot thumping against the doors. There was a scream as one of the doors swung open, and in my head I saw a terrified woman sitting there with her knickers around her ankles. She screamed even louder when she saw the gun pointing at her face.

Within seconds, I was in the car and reversing out of the bay and into traffic, hoping to cause enough of a commotion to get away and ahead before he even had a chance to call for backup. As I stopped at the first set of lights I heard a loud crunch of metal behind me, followed by the smashing of glass and a car alarm. For a moment, even the mynah birds fell silent.

Then a wave of sound rushed in to fill the void: screams, babies crying, and the crash of twisting metal. The smell of melting rubber mixed with the rising heat of the day and I found myself intensely grateful that I hadn't eaten at the diner. A glance in my rear-view mirror confirmed my hopes: a South African government-issue white Toyota had sped into the road, paying no attention to the haphazard queue of vehicles idling nose-to-tail across the junction. The lights had changed just as the Toyota shot forward, and my pursuer had sent himself face-first into a truck laden with pipes. The collision sent the truck's cargo rolling into the road like so many oversized Pick Up Stix, blocking off both lanes and sending cars swerving to avoid them. Everywhere behind me, chaos reigned. The mess would take hours to clear.

In the rearview mirror I saw broken glass shimmering like diamonds in the morning sunlight, and a fat little Weeble, red-faced and sweating in his safari suit, kicking a metal pipe. Shouts of, "*Fok! Fok! Fok jou!*" floated past me like dust in the wind, disappearing beneath my laughter as I put my foot on the accelerator and sped down the road towards Gaborone.

EPIPHANY 1: GABORONE, 1989

FLUSHED FROM SLEEP, I sat at the window of the flat in the compound of the Soviet Embassy in Gaborone, the capital of Botswana, and looked out onto a perfect African spring day. Above me, high white clouds vaulted amid acres of blue sky.

I heard birdsong outside and opened the window to breathe the crisp air. Excited children were playing in the swimming pool below, and my new Russian friend was splashing his young children in the clear water. The sounds of laughter, cut through with the slap of splashes, rose to my window. It was the very picture of family happiness, a million miles from anything I had ever known. I looked out an endless sea of tin roofs, baking in the midday heat.

I left open the window for the gentle breeze and lay on my back on the soft, white sheets of the double bed. The sheets smelled of Russian soap, and I closed my eyes to see a thousand swirling images of Moscow unfold before me, filled with light and sound and colour. I turned and buried my face in the pillows, breathing in the clean fresh laundry of Gorky Street once again before falling into a restless sleep.

I woke up with my joints aching and my head throbbing. I had been taking regular steroid tablets to control my spinal disease and beat back my other rheumatological problems. My exodus had forced me into an unplanned withdrawal, and now I was suffering without my medication. I had nothing with me except two changes of clothing and a rudimentary hand-drawn map of my escape route. I had grabbed a handful of my medication when I left, not knowing in the rush that steroid treatment must be reduced slowly and not stopped abruptly, otherwise you ended up with the kind of unpleasant side effects I had woken up to. My head was spinning, and I longed for a deep sleep to shut out the pains of the moment and the terrors of the preceding days.

I had arrived in Gaborone in the dark, having picked up South African surveillance tailing me on the route I took through town. I did not know where the Soviet Embassy was, or even if someone was on-duty in the evenings, but I knew I needed a *Yellow Pages* to find the embassy phone number and its address, and I had to do it fast.

The car that followed me came from the outskirts of a town nearby, where I had been stopped at a roadblock. Armed soldiers were checking the cars ahead and to my dismay I too was waved aside by a grunt with a gun. I thought this was it, and the South Africans were going to intercept me at the finish line, on the road to Gaborone with the Soviet Embassy so close.

I watched on with disbelief rising like bile in my throat. A soldier tapped on the driver's side window of the car ahead of me, and the driver duly rolled the window down. The soldiers were asking questions, and I supposed they might be looking for something, or someone. I saw how they looked into each vehicle, scanning the passenger seat and the back. Surely to God I hadn't come this far for everything to end this way?

There was nowhere for me to go; I couldn't drive past the car in front, and by now there were cars parked up close behind me so I couldn't reverse or turn around. I was in trouble.

A huge soldier strolled up to my dusty, weather-beaten little car, rubbing a finger through the caked Kalahari dust, examining the tyres, the number plate, and the windscreen. He stared at me, long and hard in the fading light. He held what looked like a riding crop in his hand, which he tapped like a drumstick against his thigh-high boot. I smiled and battled to control my breathing and my thundering heartbeat. He tapped the car boot with the crop, which served as an instruction to pop it. This was standard procedure, a check for weapons smuggled across the border. I opened the boot from inside the car and heard him rummaging. I watched him in the rear-view mirror, and he watched me watching him. He met my gaze without blinking.

He slammed the boot and strode round to the driver's window, which he tapped in turn. I wound it down and smiled at him, holding his stare. Breathe, I told myself. Focus and breathe.

"Name?" he barked.

I told him, trying to ignore the rising panic in my chest. By now it was too late to lie; if he asked for documents after I gave him a false name then it would all be over. I didn't know it at the time, but the delay with my father's passport—and the South Africans' insistence that he should be the one to escort me home—was the only thing keeping me from being arrested there and then.

"Where are you going?"

"Gaborone. To visit a friend."

"Your headlight is broken, Miss Susan," he said. "Get it fixed."

I assured him I would. He stared again at me and, after a tense couple of seconds that felt like much longer, waved me on.

Relief flowed through me, and my muscles finally relaxed. I realised only now how hard I had been clenching the steering wheel throughout our fraught conversation. I looked down at my hands and saw blood where my nails had dug in. Small red lines with beads of blood bright against my pale skin. I hadn't even noticed the pressure, nor the pain.

I sat back. I was drained, exhausted, but so grateful that I had avoided arrest. I had made the right decision by thinking outside the box and taking this route, and it had bought me valuable time. But none of that meant I could relax. I had to keep moving to avoid detection. It was all about speed. And I might just pull it off if time stayed on my side.

I put my foot down, hoping to get to Gaborone before dark. The shadows grew longer, and the road was silent, the tall pine trees silhouetted on either side. Despite being one of Botswana's major arteries, the road was nothing more than a narrow strip of potholed tar. A few enormous trucks—my main company at this time of night—blew their horns when my little red car sped past them.

Then I saw the white car behind me. It sped up to move in closer behind. I recognised it straight away—it had been parked in a bay near the border crossing, before I had run in to show my passport. They had been waiting all along ...

I felt the familiar snake of fear twisting through me, tensing and tightening my muscles, crushing my insides, and twisting my belly. My knuckles turned white against the wheel as a prickle of cold sweat made itself felt in the nape of my neck.

Here we go again.

I overtook the large lorry in front of me. The dark shapes of trees and the shadows of an unfamiliar, terrifying landscape smeared past the windows as I stuck my foot on the accelerator. I could not see the face of my pursuer in the darkness, and neither could he see mine: two faceless shapes in the night, anonymous players in a road game of speed and terror.

As predicted, the white car made the overtake too, and then settled on my tail right through to Gaborone. It followed me all through the streets until I reached the Holiday Inn. There wasn't much time, and I didn't have the option of hiding out somewhere during the night. I drove into the parking area, grabbed my bag, and ran in, booking one of the few remaining rooms. As I swept through the lobby, I was aware of someone standing just inside the entrance, lurking in the shadows.

I caught the lift to my room. It was on the second floor, overlooking the car park. I stood in the dark and observed, under the streetlights, that my pursuer's car was parked outside, not far from my little red steed. I went into the adjoining bathroom and opened the bath and basin taps all the way. The sound of running water would drown out my voice and make my words unintelligible.

I checked the room and the phone for bugs, dashing my hands over the walls, into the inner workings of the lamps. I even unscrewed the telephone receiver. Nothing.

I rummaged through the bedside table, casting aside the Gideon's bible, a notebook, a pen, and the restaurant menu to reach for the *Yellow Pages*. I dialled the bedside phone. After a few seconds, it rang—the number was right.

"Good evening," came the greeting on the other end. It was spoken in Russian, a man's voice.

"Good evening, comrade," I replied. Then I launched into a hurried monologue. I spoke fast, explaining who and where I was, that I was being followed. I said I needed help, and I had nowhere else to turn.

I finished talking and tried to catch my breath. There was an awful silence over the line.

"Yes, I understand," he eventually said. "Meet me outside the back entrance of the hotel in thirty minutes. Be careful and do not be followed."

I turned off the lights, bolted the door, and placed a chair against it. At least that way I would hear the commotion if someone broke in. I peeled off my dusty clothes. With half an hour to kill—and little chance of my pursuer breaking into my room without backup, I took a quick shower, grateful for the free toiletries in a basket in the bathroom. I dried myself and changed, pulling my long, wet hair up into a bun. I hid it beneath a cap.

The corridor was clear; I gathered that much by pressing my ear to the door. I opened the door a crack and peered out, just to make sure, before I darted for the fire escape at the end of the hall. I made my way down through the eerie darkness, punctured only by the glow of a single streetlight above the loading bay. I stepped back into the shadows, allowing myself to be absorbed in the night. There was no surveillance as far as I could see.

I didn't have to wait long before a blue car screeched into the loading bay, driven by a young, dark-haired man wearing a blue sun hat. Suddenly I came over all tranquil. Detached, even. If a single shot were to come now and end it all, at least I would know I had died trying. I had always tried my best; I hoped Ronnie realised that. But the game wasn't over yet.

I took one last glance at the African sky, enjoying the brightness of the stars and the shape of the clouds that drifted through the moonlight. Then there was nothing left but to take a deep breath and step forward, anticipating a bullet even as the stranger leaned over and opened the passenger door for me.

"Get in, get down, and wear this hat," he said.

I did as I was told as he sped through the evening traffic. Curled in the footwell, I could see streetlights and the tops of trees as we sped along. After what seemed like an age, we reached a set of automatic gates that opened onto the Soviet embassy compound. My companion drove around the rear of the premises to another building, then he stopped the car and ran round to the passenger side to let me out.

He held my hand and helped me to my feet. For a moment I was still. I looked up at the sky, breathing in the cold freshness of freedom. Tears of relief came from nowhere. Another man took my hand, and I turned away so he wouldn't see me crying. A tear fell to the rocky ground, where it glistened like glass in the moonlight.

This new man lightly took my arm, guiding me up a flight of steps and into an apartment. He bolted the door, and I noticed the film of sweat on his forehead. He was tall and slim and barely thirty years old, with sad brown eyes and a worried expression.

"I am Anatoly Alexandrovich," he said. "I am a Soviet representative here. I trained in the military and worked at the same centre as yourself in Moscow. I have verified your details, Comrade Deana, and I have notified the centre that you are now safe. They send their best wishes and congratulations, and I assure you we will do our best to get you to Europe safely. You can stay here until Tuesday, when we will get you onto a direct flight to London at the last minute. We will supply travel documents and tickets. This is a secure apartment in the embassy grounds under diplomatic immunity, and we are now protecting you.

The Boers cannot enter here. It is very fortunate that you arrived when you did; the Boers are looking for you throughout Gaborone."

It was like coming home. The soft lilt of his accented but perfect English was accompanied by the smells of Moscow that permeated the apartment. These scents, rich with significance, emanated from the carbolic soap in the kitchen and the rye bread on the dining table, set with a samovar and a plate loaded with slices of cheese and Russian sausage. The flat was clean but spartan, and what little furniture there was wouldn't have looked out of place at Gorky Street.

Anatoly showed me around and, anxious at my obvious exhaustion, called a nurse to examine me. I was told that it was essential for me to rest, to be well enough to leave in a few days' time.

Anatoly asked if I was ready to talk; we sat together well into the night. We agreed this conversation would serve as a formal debriefing in the absence of an ANC one, and that my information was as of much value to the Russians as it would be to the ANC. In fact, there was a far better chance of it being used properly and acted upon in the hands of the Russians.

My debriefing took several days, in all. I told Anatoly everything, from my first meeting with Ronnie and my happy days in Moscow to the desert of Namibia, de Bruin, and all. I recounted how I had slipped out of the Windhoek house in the middle of the night and dodged the police while I had been on the run—a journey that had now taken me here, to kindly Anatoly and his evocative little apartment. I had no regrets then, and I have no regrets now. Telling the Russians everything was, without doubt, the best thing for me to do in fulfilment of my training and my function as a spy.

Over the course of those days, I realised it was all about the Russians ... it always had been. They were the ones who had trained and protected me, and now they had saved me. My organization, the ANC, and my handler, Ronnie Kasrils, deserved neither my loyalty nor the fruits of my labour. When I had needed his help, Ronnie was nowhere to be seen. I was not the only player in this game with more than one face.

Ronnie, the chameleon, made it his habit to play upon the naïveté and idealism of youth, harnessing the energy and willpower of young people impatient for change. He would see to it that these young idealists were trained, and then he would send them back into deep cover with no more input. He was a handler who would discard his agents in the field with no support structures for extended periods, leaving them to fend for themselves to an extent not feasible even for a spy. In my case, he had either suffered a lapse of memory or he had exhibited a cynical disregard for his agent. Both were unforgivable.

My fury would grow, later, when I came to understand this was the period in which Ronnie had been dealing with the antics of Olivia Forsyth, the high-profile double agent. How could he abandon a recruit who was so well (and expensively) trained in the USSR—and who reached the belly of the beast on more than one occasion—for the small fry Forsyth proved to be?

Did the ANC have a clue what to do with their spies or the information they provided? Did Ronnie forget about me? Was he was busy? Perhaps he thought I was a double; the ANC was riddled with them, for all I knew. I still do not know why he abandoned me, and now it does not matter.

But at the time, Ronnie's betrayal filled me with revulsion. My outrage, my sense of injustice—which had always been strong—spread through me like a poison. Pure betrayal flowed through my veins as Anatoly and I talked long into the night. Many times he would look at me and shake his head as I told him of the decisions I had made and the choices I had faced, and how, through it all, I had held on to what the Soviets had taught me, knowing nobody else had ever had my back like my mentors in Moscow.

Moths danced around the lamps of the apartment that sticky African night. Crickets sang in the damp grass outside, and in the heavens the moon rose bright, a ball of molten silver surrounded by the burning flecks of silver stars. We talked until I fell asleep. It was over.

SPECIAL DELIVERY, 1990

IT WAS BULKY AND SMELLED OILY, but there were no greasy fingerprints or wires coming out of the package. No obvious signs of a parcel bomb, but something wasn't right. It didn't feel right.

I was in London, living as an exile. The Russians had seen me safely to Europe, and now I was in the process of building a new life for myself. Heavily pregnant with my first baby, I had just returned from several weeks' bed rest at the local hospital. I avoided going into labour at twenty-four weeks and again at twenty-eight. My obstetrician didn't understand why my blood pressure was so high and innocently asked if I had been under any stress of late. How about fleeing my home and constantly fearing for my life, I thought? Could that be it?

I had arrived in the UK seven months earlier. My departure from South Africa had been accompanied by a chorus of death threats from right-wing apartheid supporters who couldn't cope with the collapse of their beloved racist regime. South Africa was crawling with bitter White vigilantes, sore losers who were hell-bent on revenge. I was a traitor, and I had been in the news. That made me a target.

My father and I weren't talking—he insisted he couldn't forgive me for what I had done—but I had endured many tearful phone calls from my mother, who wanted me to know that her home was being watched and she was being followed whenever she left the house. What better way to get back at me than through my parents, who were already frightened and vulnerable after being harassed by the press, the Security Police, and National Intelligence?

I was forced to tell the obstetrician an edited version of why I wasn't an example of blooming and contented motherhood-to-be, and I was admitted to an antenatal ward for extended bed rest and observation. From a security perspective, this was a nightmare. The ward was near a flight of steps leading to an unguarded entrance: easy access for any would-be assassin.

To make matters worse, during the morning ward round the consultant cheerily disclosed my circumstances to anyone who would listen, resulting in junior doctors, fellow mummies-to-be, and the tea lady staring at me open-mouthed for the rest of my stay. The consultant, a large, fleshy man in a dickie bow, couldn't have done a better job if I'd handed him a megaphone and a soapbox and directed him to Hyde Park Corner.

I eventually escaped the jowly consultant and his gaggle of prodding midwives. I was sent home, where I promised I would relax for the rest of the pregnancy—as much as I could relax while weighing up the likelihood of being assassinated by a South African hit squad. At the same time, I was dealing with PTSD, family meltdown, press interviews, and the logistical gymnastics required to claim political asylum as a refugee.

My mother struggled with the instruction not to post baby clothes for her first grandchild to my house. I explained over and over that I was a target, which was why all post had to go via the ANC's office in Penton Street. There it could be checked for explosives or any other nasties.

During this period there had been several high-profile attacks on prominent ANC activists from Europe. The Royal Protection Squad was assigned to keep me safe, as was the case with many other well-known ANC members. The officers were always discreet, and they were polite with me if ever there was a security issue. Many of their interventions were prompted by suspicious or unexpected post arriving from South Africa; on one later occasion I would barricade myself and two toddlers inside the house whilst a bomb disposal engineer and his dog circled a package at the bottom of the garden, much to the interest of my curtain-twitching neighbours. It turned out that this particular parcel was completely innocuous and had been sent to me by accident.

Many anti-apartheid activists did not survive the struggle. Dulcie September, the ANC's Chief Representative in France, Switzerland, and Luxembourg, was assassinated outside the ANC's Paris office on March 28, 1988. She was shot five times in the head.

Ruth First, an academic, South African Communist Party (SACP) member, and wife of SACP leader Joe Slovo, was killed by a parcel bomb back in 1982. She was murdered on the orders of Heston de Bruin's university buddy, Security Police Major Craig Williamson.

Albie Sachs, an ANC activist and lawyer, had his arm blown off by a car bomb planted by South African agents in Mozambique in 1988. The explosion also blinded him in his left eye. And it didn't stop there. Throughout the 1970s and 80s, there were several cases of ANC exiles receiving poisoned clothing in the post, which is why I was so suspicious when I received that strangely bulky, oily-smelling package of baby clothes from South Africa.

That day in North West London I put on some gloves and an apron and placed a damp dishcloth over my nose and mouth to protect me from any fumes. I gently placed the package on some newspaper, slowly cut the string, and peeled off the Sellotape.

I could tell when I had been sent something by my mother because she always wrapped each item in tissue paper, which acted as a slight deterrent for anyone wanting to tamper with the individual packages. Inside this particular delivery I found hastily folded baby clothes, bootees, and a matinee jacket, none of which were wrapped in tissue paper. They smelled musty and were tacky to the touch. The letter that usually accompanied such parcels from home was missing. I bagged and double bagged the contents and dialled the number of the Protection Squad. The depravity of these people was staggering: how could any human being try to poison a baby because they disagreed with the politics of its mother?

I suppose I shouldn't have expected anything different. The apartheid police were a versatile bunch ... so versatile they even had their own in-house poisoner, a monster of a man by the name of Chief Deputy Commissioner Lothar Neethling.

The adopted son of Dr. J. C. Neethling, a leading "Black Shirt" in the South African Nazi Party, Lothar Neethling grew up to be a gifted scientist. He held doctorates in forensics and founded the South African Police's Forensic Unit, which he used as cover for his work as a poisoner.

In 1989 Captain Dirk Coetzee, a police death-squad commander, revealed how Neethling used the police forensic laboratories to supply "knock-out drops" for the murder of ANC suspects. The concoction was known as "Lothar's potion."

In 1989 the former general secretary of the South African Council of Churches and anti-apartheid activist Reverend Frank Chikane became a victim of poisoning. His clothing, unbeknownst to him, was saturated with a lethal nerve toxin, and he became dangerously ill after wearing it. The FBI investigated and concluded his clothing had been impregnated with poison.

Sue Dobson

The names of the policemen responsible emerged during the trial of the Apartheid government's biological warfare expert, Wouter Basson, otherwise known as "Doctor Death." Basson, a cardiologist by profession and physician to State President P. W. Botha, served as head of the biological and chemical warfare programme "Project Coast" from 1981 to 1995. The Civil Cooperation Bureau (CCB) tasked him with developing chemical weapons to use against ANC activists. He was also the doctor who researched the sterilisation of Black women, hoping to limit the growth of non-White populations. He was a busy man, and his other projects included developing poison-tipped umbrellas and screwdrivers to be used as weapons by the agents of apartheid. He also experimented with cigarettes containing anthrax and milk and whisky laced with toxic substances. Our very own Dr. Mengele.

No wonder I was so paranoid.

AFTERMATH, 1990–1993

I WAS LATE TO THE CLINIC. I was always late these days.

My life had changed three weeks ago with the birth of my son. My body was still in rebellion after a difficult pregnancy and labour, a forceps delivery, a postpartum haemorrhage, and blood transfusions, replete with subsequent anaphylactic response. My son, my baby boy, was a wispy, large-eyed, pink-cheeked fallen angel. To look at him, you would never guess he had taken me to the brink of a bloody, torture-on-a-rack kind of Medieval death.

My daughter was there too. She was all hair and inquisitiveness—so much so on the first count that she resembled a blonde cloud—and with the advent of her motor skills she had recently become fixated on exploration and discovery. Now she screamed at my side. My baby boy, who until then had been sleeping peacefully, opened one eye, grizzled for a second, and let rip with a mighty roar.

I loitered in the hallway, peeking through a gap in the door at the convivial circle of fluffy new mummies. They had been bouncing their plump, cherubic, gurgling babies on their knees, but when they saw me and my entourage they stopped mid-sentence and stared open-mouthed. I felt I had just arrived from Mars.

The health visitor, alarmed at the disruption, advanced to soothe my daughter. She found me a seat in the gaggle of mothers, and some kind soul thrust a mug of tea in my hand. All eyes swivelled towards me. Panic rose in my chest. Who were these people? What was I supposed to say to them?

As a new arrival in the UK, battered by PTSD, nightmares, and flashbacks of living in apartheid South Africa, I found small talk and the staid predictability of other people's lives frustrating. Crowds left me anxious and exhausted, and after any stretch of time in the company of other people I would find myself longing for silence and solitude. Adapting to a society that had not known prolonged war or deprivation for forty years, where living standards were sky-high and everyone enjoyed such a surplus of personal freedoms, was bewildering.

Mandela was still in prison, for now, and South Africa was still headline news. International campaigns and concerts were the order of the day. We had become a popular cause, and the ANC was suddenly fashionable. I found the images of apartheid—the cruelty, brutality, and suffering—anything but. The media's gratuity also struck me as offensive, as voyeuristic, ignorant, and patronizing. But motherhood soothed my stress and proved to be a healing and grounding distraction. With my sweet and wide-eyed children beside me, it was possible to imagine none of it had ever happened.

As part of my debrief, I had told the Russians everything about South Africa's campaign of election interference in Namibia. I had seen the operations of the "dirty tricks" contingent first hand, and I spilled everything I knew about the group's aims, budget, and personnel. My disclosures about the apartheid regime's interference made it into the papers, and for a while I found myself somewhere I had never wanted to be: in the limelight. I was interviewed, photographed, and gawped at countless times in the ANC London office in Penton Street. My face and name appeared in various international publications, and the inevitable hit pieces duly emerged in the South African press, slandering me and denouncing me every which way.

The ANC had offered no help with interviews after the Namibian story broke, although they did issue a press release about me, confirming my version of events and admitting to the world that, all along, I had been working undercover as a spy.

I was described as a "fragile, emotional child" by an insufferable spokesman for the SADF in Namibia—a man who had met me in passing and had neither the time nor the expertise to offer any serious analysis. Now he was smearing me in the pro-government press. That line spoke volumes; even in my childhood, I hadn't been fragile or emotional. There hadn't been room for it, what with my mother's galloping madness and the detachment of my capricious, racist father.

Even he got involved in the press-feeding frenzy. Never renowned for his loyalty, my own father described me to a journalist as "some sort of James Bond" and publicly speculated I must have had a nervous breakdown—the official line the government had planned to use to get me back to Pretoria without making a scene. I would also soon learn of my father's plans to join the police search for me, sacrificing his own daughter to absolve some of his guilt at having raised a race traitor and a spy. As the old line goes, they fuck you up, your mum and dad.

Finally, however, I had struck my blow against the apartheid state. I had exposed the illegal interference in the Namibian independence process, and in doing so I had undermined the Nationalist government's credibility. UN officials, including Martti Ahtisaari, had long suspected that South Africa wasn't playing by the rules, and I gave them the proof. My reward was that the world was offered a glimpse behind the curtain, yet another peep at the true, ugly face of apartheid. And I was pleased to have played my small part in the Namibian independence process, helping to usher in the birth of South Africa's new, independent neighbour.

Sam Nujoma was sworn in as the country's first president at Namibia's independence celebrations on March 21st, 1990. Mandela was standing by his side—brothers in arms, as they had always been. I watched through tears of happiness, and longing for Africa, as I settled into my new life in London.

My victory—one of a thousand cuts—came at a great personal cost. My experiences had scarred me, and I emerged into a life of exile carrying a severe case of PTSD among my baggage. I was left to my own devices by the ANC, abandoned to wrestle with my demons every night as I sat in the drab home office and relived the events of the past years.

Every time I closed my eyes a rogue's gallery paraded itself in my mind: Sterkhans Dreyer and his Koevoet killers; Foreign Affairs Minister "Pik" Botha, combing his Brylcreemed hair in the mirror, his black salamander eyes watching my every move; Colonel de Bruin, eyes shining with excitement as he prepared for another night of "SWAPO hunting"; and the Russian diplomats in Windhoek in their sad brown suits who refused to help me because they had been invited to a bash at the Administrator General's residence.

I would stand in the shower at the end of each haunted day and try to wash them away, visualising those faces swirling down the plughole. Whenever I left the house I saw men with their features hidden beneath caps, drivers who seemed to be following me at every turn. I took cover if a car exhaust backfired and I checked for surveillance obsessively, making up long and elaborate routes to wherever I was going, determined to smoke my pursuers out. When I snatched at sleep I would see the little red hire car driving deeper and deeper into the desert, now veering off the road, now drifting towards a tree, with me fast asleep at the wheel. In my dreams, I would suddenly wake, hit the brakes, and steer myself back onto the road.

Therapy and counselling were considered bourgeois and indulgent, and I was duly left by the ANC higher-ups to just get on with it. A lack of post-operation support contributed to the deterioration of the mental health of many exiles, many of whom turned to drugs or alcohol to quiet the voices. For those who had been detained, tortured, or placed under house arrest, now exiled away from their homeland and friends and family, life in rainy ol' Blighty was the last straw.

Even after I fled, I lived a life constructed of lies and secrets. I was drawn to the shadows, where I had always felt safest. I had lived a legend back in South Africa, and in many ways I continued to do so after my exile. Being wary and mistrustful had, back then, been a way of staying alive. Now I was back among the civilian world, it wasn't a case of flipping a switch and forgetting everything that had been drilled into me. It was clear from the off—my adjustment to this new life would be a slow and painful process.

Friendships and relationships remained difficult for me, and even after all these years I still find emotional intimacy claustrophobic. Back when I was in the Soviet Union, my instructors had been surprised that I never succumbed to homesickness, never missed my friends and family. But my childhood had conditioned me for a life of solitude, and the way I saw it: the more friends I had, the more people I would have to lie to. The friends I did have had never known the truth about me, not until I appeared in the papers.

In the days shortly after my arrival in the UK, I often found myself dreaming of Moscow. In my mind I relived the conversations I had shared with Valery Pavlovich, a man with a clear understanding of it all.

"Quite frankly, Deana, the matter is that relationships complicate matters. If you take my pieces of advices you will remain on your own and remain safe. Trust no one!"

He had a point. Spying is for the emotionally distant and detached. I was used to my solitude, and it did not bother me. I wore it like a cloak around me. It protected me.

But when you weave such a tangled web of lies, it's easy to get caught up in them. Not everyone appreciates or forgives deception, and it naturally takes time and patience for family and friends to trust an outed spy again. I had no qualms about being dishonest and living the legend, as I knew it was the best way to protect those I cared for. If I had shared my secret life with them, I might have compromised their safety with the burden of knowledge. I would have given them the responsibility of knowing the truth, placing them in danger. Lies were just how I showed my love.

My father remained resolute in his refusal to forgive me. He told me how ashamed he was, how I had betrayed not only South Africa but all White people, everywhere. Five years passed, and we didn't speak. I said nothing of his own betrayal—choosing his country and his race over his daughter. I also held my tongue when he got stuck into the press interviews, tantamount to a character assassination of his only child. My mother, on the other hand, forgave me, although the subject was best avoided in her presence. Her sadness at my betrayal was assuaged when I introduced her to her grandchildren, on whom she doted. I sensed a forgiveness in her love for my children, and an apology, too, for how she had never known how to show her love for me.

My father remained obstinate and unapproachable. When I returned to South Africa—my first trip back—to repair some of the damage of the past, he agreed to meet me, but only so he could "look at" his grandchildren. Stony-faced, he positioned himself some distance from the barriers in the arrivals hall. The children, however, had other ideas. Intrigued by his scowl, my two bundles of energy ran over to examine this strange man they had heard so much about. It was the perfect ice breaker, and I witnessed him thaw as soon as my children threw their arms around him. The moment was accompanied by a tear and much nose blowing. I never said a word.

We reconciled, but neither of us ever spoke of the past. Even at the time of his death, it remained between us like the proverbial elephant, a bitter memory. My relationship with him was complicated, needless to say. I still abhorred his racism; and his lack of loyalty towards me stung for the rest of his life and probably will for the rest of mine too. But he was still my father.

I originally decided to keep my past a secret from my children. My family seemed to have suffered enough because of politics. But secrets rarely last. On a much later visit to a South African bookshop, my then ten-year-old son picked up a book on military intelligence written by the late Peter Stiff.

Across the crowded shop, my son's voice rang out. Several pairs of eyes latched onto me, and the South African habit of staring, open-mouthed, at a subject of interest ensued.

"Hey, Mum, is this you in here?" asked my little foghorn. The words echoed off the racks of books and magazines and bounced back at me.

"Er, yes," I said. "Shall we go?" I made for the door.

"Hey, Mum, this says you were a spy!" said the foghorn, some decibels louder.

And so I was.

EPIPHANY 2: LONDON, 1993

"MUM, MUM, MUMMM ..."

My daughter, my cloud of flyaway blonde hair and blue eyes, tried to get my attention as she swept past, pushing a laden doll's pram through Ward 4B, Great Ormond Street Hospital.

I smoothed the sheet and placed the teddy bear in the corner of the cot where my son would be able to see it. From the grimy window I watched the sun setting over the London skyline. The Christmas lights of Russell Square and Holborn twinkled in the cold December evening, and the sounds of rush-hour traffic drifted up to the fourth floor. The apnoea monitor in the cot next to ours beeped, and a nurse rushed over to check the tiny body inside, a human being lost in a mass of tangled tubes and wires.

My little blonde cloud began another lap of the ward, negotiating the spaces between cots. Word had come up that there were complications after my son's surgery, and that he had had a seizure. They were waiting until he was stable before bringing him back upstairs to the ward, to his cot. The wait felt like an eternity. My heart thumped in my chest.

I longed to hold his little body and feel his baby breath on my cheek.

The heavy Victorian doors swung open, and there he was: a small, broken boy lying on an adult-sized trolley, his brown curls dark against the crisp white sheets. A large, blood-stained dressing covered him from breast to pelvic bone. He was restless and cried despite the sedatives he had been given. The gastrostomy tube that fed him was curled on his belly, taped in place with a fresh band of micropore. We all hated it, that tube, and what it meant.

The nurses tried to soothe him as they transferred him to his cot. A small army of them scurried around him, monitoring his temperature, heart rate, and breathing, checking the oxygen cylinder and mask attached to the wall above his cot, next to the notice and stickers that bore his name.

One woman swept his soft brown hair to the side with a gentle hand, but in the fading light I could see the pain pinched in his face. His eyes opened briefly, and I glimpsed a spark of recognition before they clouded again in pain and confusion. He fell into an uneasy sleep, and I placed my hand on his chest to feel the reassuring beat of his heart.

I scooped up the blonde cloud, who nestled into my neck and sat comfortably on my hip. Her breathing slowed as she fell towards sleep. I knew then that these children must come first. I owed them that. I owed South Africa and the ANC nothing.

Already, too much had been taken from my children. The same was true of so many of South Africa's young, who had been robbed of their childhood, their innocence. It was one of the few fates that befell almost every child, regardless of race. South Africa did that. South Africa had brutalised me, and hardened me, and took away the mother I could have been.

I was free now to return. On paper, I had been granted amnesty from prosecution, my pardon published in the *Government Gazette*, South Africa's official record. I was free to collect my £2,000 resettlement grant and return to the country of my birth. Many exiles, who loved and longed for their homeland, had already gone back. But I was different. My family and I were too high profile, even now. We regularly received death threats in the post, and I was still considered sufficiently at-risk to have members of the Royal Protection Squad watching over me.

South Africa, meanwhile, was a seething cauldron in which a handful of disparate political movements had been stirred with the grievances of past and present. The toxic mixture was seasoned with civil unrest, creating an atmosphere of turmoil that set the country vibrating with violence and anger. For a period there was a reckless settling of old scores. Retribution was the order of the day.

During this time, anti-apartheid activists were frequently hounded, hunted, and attacked by White right-wing extremists. The news soon filtered through to me: I was still very much a target in Security Police circles. They were protective of their own and didn't care for the bad press Koevoet had received from the interviews I gave in London.

My safety did not worry me, but I feared for my family in South Africa and, above all, my children. Many of the people I had crossed had long memories, no doubt, and my activities were not the sort that could have been easily forgotten.

If I were to return to South Africa, what security could I provide for my children? How could I take them into danger, into a viper's nest of traitors and murderers? I would stay away. I owed them that. The deeds of South Africa's assassins were still fresh. The death squads were alive and well, active all over the globe, and I was on their list. The fear I felt for my children is something that has never left me.

It was some weeks after arriving in the UK as a political exile that I discovered I was pregnant. I was homeless, penniless, and ravaged by PTSD. I had no family, and at first I had no friends either.

Determined to banish the gallery of ghouls that haunted me during my every waking moment, I found a therapist who tutted and sympathised and an acupuncturist in Chalk Farm with connections to South Africa who had successfully treated many war-weary exiles.

It worked. The faces receded into the ether. My hour-long treatment sessions in the cosy, scented, candlelit room made me feel safe and sane. However, nobody mentioned that acupuncture can boost one's fertility ... considerably. I suspect this treatment had a lot to do with my falling pregnant at what seemed, then, like the worst possible time. But things were looking up, despite the hardships I still faced.

I hadn't been in the UK long before I met the Rivonia Treason Trialist Dennis Goldberg. Dennis, his loving wife, and his wonderful daughter placed me firmly under their wing. They gave me clothes and baby things from the supplies Dennis had collected for ANC cadres in the camps in Angola and Zambia. Their support was invaluable, their generosity unmatched.

And to my surprise, pregnancy was exactly what I needed. It gave me a focus, beside myself and my troubles. It was as if the universe picked me up, dusted me down, and sat me on a fluffy white cloud of maternity that proved a welcome distraction.

The challenges that followed: a premature baby; a second pregnancy and horrendous delivery not long after the first; chronic illness; a sick child, and all the challenges of adulthood and parenthood were grist for my mill.

All of it was worthwhile. It meant I was alive, and I had survived. I relished it.

EPIPHANY 3: A LONDON GARDEN PARTY, 1995

THE OLD MAN SHUFFLED TOWARD THE PODIUM, minders poised on either side to catch him if he fell. His once broad shoulders were thin and stooped and his eyes were dull. The heaviness in my chest felt like grief, but I couldn't be sure.

I had expected to see him bounding towards us, hands outstretched, his presence filling the tent. A smile would be like an embrace for the little crowd of exiles who had waited for hours to shake his hand at South African High Commission's garden party. We had hoped for energy and zest. Instead, the great man looked frail, ill, and exhausted. His hand, when I shook it, was warm and dry to the touch. It was a hand you wanted to reach out to again, just to hold for comfort a moment longer.

It wasn't the first time I had seen him. Soon after his release, Nelson Mandela had visited London with his wife, Winnie. They came to the ANC office in Penton Street to meet a group of South African exiles who had made London their home. He wanted to thank them for the work they had done behind the scenes for the struggle.

Then hugely pregnant, I arrived early. I had hoped to slip in unseen before the event started, but I was spotted and ushered to a seat in the front row. The room was buzzing with excitement. He had not forgotten us, even though we were stuck here on this wet, draughty, little island.

And suddenly, there he was. The man who had inspired me for so many years. He was tall and powerfully built, his energy was immense, and his aura contained a rare combination of strength and gentleness. Everything about him was dignified and statesmanlike.

The audience jumped to their feet and roared the verses of "*Nkosi Sikelele*," fists raised in salute. He broke into a slow, beautiful smile. And time changed. The moment didn't end. And throughout that brief eternity, I felt humbled, and grateful, and glad to be alive.

Many of the elderly exiles were in tears. Some had not seen him since before the Rivonia Treason Trial in 1963 and his subsequent imprisonment. It was around that time that many in the audience had left the country after being detained, banned, or placed under house arrest for their role in opposing apartheid. But it would be worth it. In their lifetime there would be a democratic South Africa.

Almost unnoticed, Winnie walked in beside him. She was a controversial figure and increasingly disliked, proving wilful and difficult to control. Rumour had it that the ANC was urging Nelson to distance himself from her and her high-handed actions. They would divorce in the end, and he would eventually marry Graça, the widow of Mozambican president Samora Machel.

Winnie glared at the audience. She dressed expensively, with a turban and diamond earrings that twinkled under the lights. A poor choice, some might say, when appearing before an audience of exiles who had lived a life of near poverty in a foreign country for years.

To Winnie's horror and embarrassment, and my amusement, a group of young men broke into a toyi-toyi. The entire room followed suit, heralding a surge of noise, voices calling out as one. The place was abuzz with movement and excitement, the elderly exiles riding a dizzying tide of happiness that had been long in the making. Nelson grinned. Winnie looked like she had just stepped in something nasty.

But that was then, and this was now. Nelson looked as though he was dying right there on the spot. I took myself off to the side, waiting under a tree as I tried to compose myself. I focused on the audience, scanning the faces. Many, like me, were with children or grandchildren. My boy dozed in the shade in his pushchair, while I had blackmailed my blonde cloud into a party dress and pigtails. She was moaning now that her feet hurt. Other children were looking hot and bothered in their Sunday best, and I guessed I had an hour, tops, before my children decided enough was enough.

I grabbed the blonde cloud by her little hand, and we headed off for a stroll through the gardens. We came upon a row of portaloos under the trees. A door flew open and out stepped ANC Deputy President Thabo Mbeki.

We stared at each other for a few seconds. He was sweating in his double-breasted striped suit, and he mopped at his brow with a crumpled handkerchief. I greeted him. He raised an eyebrow but said nothing. So this is the ANC *wunderkind*, I thought.

I introduced myself. He blew his nose. I explained who I was, offered a handful of names he knew, mutual friends. His bloodshot eyes looked at me from above the hanky. I told him I had worked in South Africa as an intelligence agent for MK.

"I have to go now," he said.

And with a flick of the wrist, and before you could whisper "retrovirals," he was gone. He resembled a rubber chicken as he bopped along towards the tables of sandwiches and cakes.

I had lain my life on the line for people like him. Who the hell did he think he was? We risked our lives doing their dirty work, and we didn't get so much as a "thank you" in response.

My heart thumped and my throat closed, and still the stain of rage grew on me. I gathered up the children and left without a word.

It would be my last contact with the ANC.

GOING HOME, 1995-1996

THE DARKENED SOUTH AFRICAN AIRWAYS (SAA) aircraft shuddered to a halt at O. R. Tambo International Airport, Johannesburg. I rested my forehead against the seatback and took a deep breath of stale, recycled air. My head throbbed and my throat hurt. Every joint and muscle ached after an eleven-hour flight in a cramped economy-class cabin.

Coming in to land I had seen the familiar green treetops and the winding roads. I recognised the stadium with its emerald playing field, nestled among the red roofs of houses and the swimming pools glittering like turquoise gems in the spring sunlight. As we came in closer, the canopy of blossoming jacaranda trees cast a purple haze over suburban streets.

Next to me, stretched out over two seats, her soft, fine hair tousled every which way, my blonde cloud slept soundly. She had fallen asleep again after I had washed, brushed, and changed her and her brother into respectability, following an SAA breakfast of stale croissants and orange juice at 4:00 a.m. My small boy sat in the window seat, his eyes wide with excitement at the airport scene outside, beloved Woody and Buzz Lightyear toys clutched to his chest. Their innocence made my heart ache.

The aircraft smelled of feet, and around us lay the detritus of a long-haul flight: discarded shoes, cans, empty wine bottles, socks, and newspapers. Even the crew, beneath their plastered-on smiles, looked jaded. The hostesses looked greasy, their faces appearing to melt, Dali-esque, into the garish SAA scarves knotted ridiculously around their necks. I gathered up the Barbie dolls, comics, and crayons that we had spread out, all the time keeping watch as to who was around us and what they were doing.

I had checked for surveillance at the airport, and again before boarding the plane, but nothing looked out of place and I believed we were safe. Checking for surveillance while herding two small children is an art; the horror of complacency, getting it wrong and exposing them to danger, would be a constant fear throughout their childhood. I knew then, as I know now, that they would be the target: the quickest and easiest way to break and destroy me both as an agent and as a mother. It is a fear that haunts me even though my children are now adults. My choices and my actions have always made them vulnerable, and my first responsibility is to keep them from harm.

I got up as soon as I could and had one last look around me. Nothing appeared out of the ordinary, and nobody seemed to be watching us. Because we were sitting towards the rear of the aircraft, I had been afforded a good vantage point of the rest of the plane, without having to worry about who was behind me. It worked well, until the morning queues for the toilets, which made us the object of bored scrutiny as yawning, dishevelled, and sleep-befuddled fellow passengers waited for the busy cubicles.

I looked like any other mother after a long flight with two young children, which is exactly what they wouldn't expect. Several flights from international destinations landed around the same time, and I knew it would be easy enough for me to hide, as always, in plain sight among a crowd of arrivals. I was too ordinary to attract attention. Just like old times.

Anyone searching for me would look for a woman travelling alone, possibly in first class or business class because it afforded more privacy than the cheap seats. They wouldn't expect a harassed and overwhelmed mother, which was (unintentionally) very much my mid-nineties look. I looked very different to the young spy who had fled southern Africa just a handful of years ago. By now I was in my early thirties, and I had swapped the dresses and my trademark long hair for a shorter style and more casual clothing.

As I was taught during my training many years before: put yourself in your enemy's shoes. What would they expect from a high-profile spy returning from exile? They would not expect me to have arrived with my children, and nor would they expect me to be met by my family at the airport. Instead, they would watch the exits for those who got off the plane first, looking for anyone who seemed to be in a hurry. Taking the least expected course of action had worked for me back then, and it would work again for me now.

South Africa is a chauvinistic place: women travelling alone attract attention, and many seldom do because of security concerns. My mother would often comment when she saw a woman out by herself, "Ag shame," the universal South African expression for pity. "Hey, Sue, she must not have a husband."

I could never see what having a husband had to do with one's travel arrangements, but my parents' generation considered a woman incomplete if she did not have a man and children in tow. I was allowed to go to university not because I could study and then have a career, but to find a "professional husband" (preferably a lawyer or a doctor). My father believed if I achieved this, he had done his work as a parent. Single mothers were viewed with pity. Divorce and illegitimacy were considered "*n' skande*," a disgrace, in White communities, especially in Afrikaner circles.

My parents took me once to meet one such "fallen woman," hoping it would extinguish any carnal thoughts in my adolescent mind. Her boyfriend had left her in the lurch when she discovered she was pregnant, so she had to move back home with her judgmental and horrified parents. But instead of finding a sad and contrite object of pity, I met a confident, self-assured young mother with a joyous and flourishing baby. This didn't stop my father tutting about how she had "ruined her life." The whole business, according to my mother, was "a tragedy."

Years later, my status as a divorced, single mother would be met with a mixture of pity and disapproval by my South African family. My father, not known for his tact or sensitivity, informed me that such women were damaged goods and said no man would want me now I had joined the ranks of the divorced and newly single. My determination to remain unattached exasperated him.

Culturally, divorce was considered a sign of failure and something shameful to boot. My mother's brother, a melancholic, alcoholic, seafaring sailor boy, divorced his wife in the 1970s, and throughout my childhood my parents had discussed the subject in hushed and horrified tones with constant speculation as to whose fault it was and who had strayed. I regarded it as sensible that two people who made each other miserable had the sense to go their separate ways. This wisdom eventually served me well, and it was part of the reason I was alone with my children upon my return to South Africa.

The three of us disembarked and attached ourselves to a crowd of fellow travelers. I placed us in the company of other parents bundled together with small children as we made our way through the terminal building. By then, I had British citizenship and the queue moved swiftly through passport control. When I reached the kiosk, I handed over my passport and allowed the children to distract me. The Black clerk looked me up and down, and I watched the spark of recognition light up her eyes as she studied my name and details. She held my glance for a moment and smiled broadly before waving me through, wishing me a happy stay and patting each child on the head as they went past.

But my mood soon fell. If this was supposed to be the new South Africa, it was underwhelming. The "Rainbow Nation" wasn't very colourful. The terminal abounded with White faces, although there may have been a few more Black travelers than I would have expected to see back in the bad old days. I noticed with satisfaction, however, that there were no toilets designated for different racial groups. After all those years, Black and White South Africans could now relieve themselves side by side, in racial harmony.

Prior to departure I had turned down the security detail offered by the London ANC office, or what was left of it, since most exiles had repatriated by then. I thought arriving with a bodyguard would further inflame matters with my family, but this was a decision I began to regret as I entered the arrivals hall.

The Royal Protection Squad could not help me while I was in South Africa. They hadn't been in favour of me going, even though my trip was only for two weeks—a chance for my parents to meet their grandchildren and a chance for me to mend the shattered relationships within my family.

My heart was thumping as we traversed the arrivals hall. Both children were sitting on the luggage trolley with a suitcase in front of them, which would serve both to hide them from the waiting crowd and protect them from bullets aimed from the front. My body protected them from the rear. I knew a sniper could, in theory, take a shot from the upper floor of the hall, where they not only had an excellent angle but also a quick and easy escape route down the stairs at the back of the building. I would have to take my chances.

It may sound like paranoia, but my fears weren't ungrounded. I learned, as I once more surrounded myself with the love and life of Africa—its colour, its rhythm, its vibrancy … purple jacaranda blossoms, wild and sudden thunderstorms, and the sound of crickets in the grass at night—that I was being watched. The white car that was parked outside my parents' house for hours on end was always there, as were its occupants. We politely watched each other from a distance. One evening I felt devilish and raised my hand to the side of my head in a mock salute, and to my amusement the car swiftly did a U-turn and raced off down the road.

They probably wanted me to know I was being watched. Regardless of all the talk about a new South Africa, and the coronation of the ANC government, the nation was awash with vigilantes who possessed an appetite for violence and who had very long memories. But I never said a word. I believed there was little to gain in frightening my children and my elderly parents; our family had suffered enough. I was angry at the imposition, at the arrogance of watching me in broad daylight. I was indignant they had exposed my children to it, but by then any fear had gone.

But first: my father, waiting for me in the arrivals hall.

The feeling in my chest was leaden. A sadness, a grief so heavy I thought it would drag me to my knees in front of the man who had betrayed me in the press, humiliated me, and called me a traitor to my country and my race. The man who would, without hesitation, have joined the Security Police to being me back to Pretoria so I could be arrested, charged, found guilty, and sentenced to years in prison for treason.

This was the man who now cried before me as he looked at the puzzled faces of his grandchildren. The boundless love of my children worked immediately to soften him, but I noticed how he still studiously avoided my eyes. There was no tearful embrace, no welcome home or words of how he loved and missed me. Nothing at all.

My mother and several family members pounced on the trolley and gathered up the children, hitherto only seen in photographs, examining them from every angle, pinching their cheeks (to their annoyance), and ruffling their hair. My family cried and laughed over my children as they embraced. If anyone was watching and hoping for a clear shot, today was not their day. My clucking relatives enveloped me.

My stony-faced father, who had not acknowledged me for five years, stood back from the crowd. He didn't explain his willingness to collaborate with the Security Police and National Intelligence, nor did he apologise for denouncing me in the press. Perhaps he had brought the police with him … perhaps they would swoop in just a few seconds, arrest me in front of my family, and take me away? My children abandoned in a strange country where they didn't speak or understand the language, just as my parents had abandoned me in an Afrikaans nursery with no explanation thirty years before.

I got a hold of myself. That was then. This was now, the new South Africa. Besides, I'd been on the winning side. We'd won the fucking war!

I composed myself and looked my father straight in the eye. But others beat me to it. There in the airport terminal, in full view, my father stared at my children, who were side by side looking up at him. Instead of turning on his heel to go home after seeing what they looked like (which is what he had threatened to do) he stayed transfixed. A small, silver tear crawled down his cheek, and he sniffled.

I swallowed hard and told my children, "Give Grandpa Alvin a hug." Innocently, they obliged, and each child took a hand and walked either side of him as we made for the coffee shop.

Even then I walked alone, a few steps behind them, watching my two children on either side of the tall, greying, muscular man who was my father. Walking ahead of me, on South African soil, were the symbols of my past and my future. I was, as ever, un-belonging—on the outside, looking in. The pain of seeing my betrayer mixed with the joy of coming home as I glimpsed, through tears, the bright blue African sky outside the terminal.

TRUTH, LIES, THREATS, AND RECONCILIATION, 1994-2020

As I GRAPPLED WITH my own reluctance to forgive and reconcile with a parent who had betrayed me, the country was going through the same painful process on a far greater scale. South Africa as a whole was trying, then, to forgive and forget its heinous past and move forward in a new spirit of democracy. As is so often the case, forgiveness didn't come easy. Sometimes the past is just too painful to erase, a lesson I learned as I was going through the process with my own family.

A sincere apology can help one heal, and I never received one. But I overlooked this in the interest of creating strong ties between my parents and my children. While I lost out personally in this process, I did ensure my children had a pleasant and fulfilling relationship with their grandparents. I didn't mind the sacrifice.

All throughout the country, people like me were grappling with the concepts of forgiveness and contrition. The Truth and Reconciliation Commission (TRC), founded in 1995, was a restorative justice body tasked with addressing the pain of apartheid. Its approach was different to that of the punitive justice of the Nuremberg trials held after the Second World War in that the TRC was geared towards dealing with human rights violations after political change.

As a condition of transferring power to a Black majority government, the outgoing regime requested that the commission grant amnesty to those confessing to politically motivated crimes during the apartheid years. They appointed Nobel Peace Prize Laureate Bishop Desmond Tutu head of the commission.

But before reconciliation comes truth. And while the world had always known of the general evil of apartheid, it was only after it ended that the awful specifics were allowed to seep into the public consciousness.

By 1989, around the time I left Namibia, the press had already discovered what was really going on at Vlakplaas. Disclosures in the media added weight to the information I passed on to the Russians and the ANC regarding the death squads that existed to eliminate ANC and SWAPO activists.

Dirk Coetzee, co-founder and first commander of C10—the South African Police counter insurgency unit—was the whistleblower. He told the story behind Vlakplaas, revealing to the world that it was the headquarters of the apartheid state's death squads and much more than just a farm. Coetzee had enough blood on his hands; he was a ruthless killer, and cynics might say his decision to blow the whistle had more to do with the apartheid regime's collapse and his desire to protect himself from the inevitable recriminations, than it did a moral awakening. The bumbling, narcissistic, loud-mouthed idiot that he was, Coetzee spared little detail in describing the gruesome end met by his enemies, including the lawyer and ANC activist Griffiths Mxenge.

Vlakplaas, Coetzee said, employed around fifteen White police officers, several dozen Black police officers, and a number of activists who had been "turned," persuaded to work for the apartheid government. Vlakplaas itself was a squat, ugly, tin-roofed farm west of Pretoria. Over the years, officers based at the unit kidnapped, tortured, and murdered several prominent anti-apartheid and ANC activists. If you couldn't—or wouldn't—be turned, you would be killed. It was here where explosives were used as an execution method, a way of making such a mess no body would ever be identified. Such was the thinking of the kinds of people who called Vlakplaas home.

Coetzee fell out of favour with his superiors after two of his operatives were arrested following a bungled mission. His successor was the dour, dead-eyed Colonel Eugene de Kock, known as "Prime Evil" for his role as interrogator, assassin, and torturer. De Kock was the commanding officer of Vlakplaas from the 1980s to the early 1990s. He had cut his teeth as a security policeman in the eastern Cape before being transferred to pre-independence Namibia, where he played a key role in establishing Koevoet, the ruthless police counter-insurgency group.

There had been several press cuttings and documents relating to Coetzee, de Kock, Vlakplaas, the murder of Mxenge, and the activities of police hit squads hidden in de Bruin's house in Oshakati. At the time I did not appreciate how everything tied together, but now I can see the links between Vlakplaas and Koevoet, not least the de Kock connection. Other similarities included the way they operated with impunity against ANC and SWAPO cadres, sharing a uniform approach to kidnapping, torture, and murder.

In 2015, footage surfaced that showed a man resembling de Kock at Arlanda Airport, not long after Swedish Prime Minister Olof Palme had been shot dead. Palme, who was murdered in 1986, was an outspoken opponent of apartheid and De Kock is on record saying South African forces were involved in his assassination. Others believe Craig Williamson, who was reportedly in Sweden at the time, had something to do with Palme's death. The case has now been closed, and although the police have their suspects, there is insufficient evidence to charge anyone. To my mind, there is a large and unsavoury list of South African assassins who might have been involved.

De Kock was ultimately arrested in 1994 on charges of murder and kidnapping. He testified before the TRC in 1996 and was convicted of 89 charges, including six counts of murder, conspiracy to murder, attempted murder, assault, kidnapping, and fraud. Although he received amnesty for many of his crimes, he was still sentenced to two life terms and 212 years behind bars for crimes against humanity.

De Kock fought tirelessly for parole, his chief argument being that no other member of the apartheid police force was serving a prison sentence. His wife divorced him and moved to Europe with their sons, changing their identities. He was paroled in 2015 and released in 2019 in the interests of nation-building. His whereabouts are currently unknown.

Views of de Kock differ. Some believe he has shown genuine remorse and has cooperated with the authorities. He has helped to recover some of the remains of (some of) his victims. He also met the families of his victims in person and expressed his remorse, asking their forgiveness. In 2012, Marcia Khosa publicly forgave him for killing her mother, the ANC activist Portia Shabangu, and he wrote a much-publicised letter to the family of the lawyer Bheki Mlangeni, whom he had murdered with a letter bomb. Others believed he helped the families only in order to achieve parole, and that he is a master manipulator and a cold psychopath devoid of feeling. This is what I believe.

The embittered De Kock saw himself as a scapegoat and argued that all his orders arrived from "higher up" (that old chestnut) and so he was merely doing what he was told. Whilst I regard de Kock with revulsion and have little time for his anger and self-pity, I believe what he said is correct, that the generals identified who the foot soldiers should go after, and that most of his directions came from his superiors.

De Kock, in his desperation to escape justice, voiced the unease that many of us felt. Press reports had already suggested that President F. W. de Klerk's hands were "soaked in blood," and that he ordered political assassinations and other acts of intimidation during his presidency in the Apartheid era.

The TRC, meanwhile, rumbled on.

Increasing numbers of South Africans criticised the commission for its willingness to grant pardons to those responsible for the most heinous crimes against their fellow citizens. More than an acknowledgement of suffering was called for. The victims and their families deserved more than a sheepish apology or lip service confession from those desperate to save their own skin. They needed justice.

An aim of the commission was to move forward in a spirit of reconciliation in the transition to a new, democratic South Africa. The TRC focused on bearing witness to the past and on the healing that forgiveness can bring, which all sounds very nice on paper but is, in practice, so vague as to be open to abuse and manipulation. The success of the TRC is very difficult to analyse. There is no evidence to prove or disprove that the experience helped South Africans come to terms with the brutality of their past, or that it did indeed motivate them to do so.

The TRC, which was based in Cape Town, commenced hearings in 1996. The aim was to witness, record and, if appropriate, grant amnesty to the perpetrators of crimes that violated human rights. Another intention was to offer reparation and rehabilitation to the victims if they needed it.

Perpetrators of atrocities, meanwhile, could give testimony and ask for amnesty from civil and criminal prosecution. Ordinary South Africans could also express their regret and remorse in a register of reconciliation if they wished.

The commission had the power to grant amnesty to those who fully disclosed the politically motivated crimes they committed, and it heard applications from both sides, from the apartheid state and the ANC. However, amnesty was usually denied if information was withheld, and in these circumstances cases would be forwarded to the criminal or civil courts.

The TRC was a mixed bag. Whilst many agreed it could be helpful to air the injustices of the past, the fact remained there was little that could ever be done to rectify the wrongs of apartheid. In some cases, the TRC served only to open up old wounds.

My frustration with the TRC is that it did not go far enough. Oversimplified and dramatised apologies from generals and politicians with blood on their hands cannot take away the devastating effects of arrest, torture, and murder. Nor can it soothe the physical, emotional, and psychological effect apartheid had on South Africa's people.

For those who fought and died in the liberation struggle, or had loved ones taken from them, a fluffy bit of kiss-and-make-up propaganda is simply not enough. I fear the TRC has created a climate where corruption and wrong-doing are allowed to flourish because people believe they can behave with impunity so long as they confess afterwards. In today's South Africa, there is still a prevailing psychology among the corrupt that they are untouch-able. These people, therefore, believe they are entitled to the excesses of the present because of the privations of the past, an attitude nurtured by the TRC's toothlessness.

I followed the meanderings of the Truth and Reconciliation Commission in exile with a combination of disbelief, anger, and despair that those guilty of crimes against humanity could walk away free. It watered down the horrors of apartheid and forgot those who had suffered and died in a cruel and recent past, the aftershocks of which would rock our battle-scarred country for generations to come.

I think of all those whose blood watered the soil of a free South Africa, and I want to scream when I think of those who killed them, most of whom got away with their crimes. The only consolation is that not everyone was able to evade justice.

In 1997, four former police officers, including Police Colonel Gideon Nieuwoudt, appeared before the TRC and admitted to the killing of Steve Biko twenty years earlier. The commission heard their request but refused to grant political amnesty because the accused did not, or could not, give a motive for Biko's murder.

I wish I could say that South Africa's story had a happy—or even neat—ending. But this is a country of contradictions, and the South Africa of the twenty-first century is languishing still beneath the weight of its past. Old habits die hard, as the saying goes. But how many more people have to die? Racism is still endemic in South African society, and the townships are still brimming with malcontent. There is no overt system of racial division, no "Whites only" signs outside waiting rooms or bus stations, but South Africa is still a country where your race matters far more than it should. Your life will still be easier, safer, and longer if you are born into the White minority. The government is still immoral, as well: it just so happens that the corruption has now spread to the ANC, which has presided over decades of maladministration. It never had to be that way.

Indeed, there was a time, after the release of Mandela and the transition of power, when this new South Africa rode the crest of the wave. It was a time of much backslapping and self congratulation. With the emergence of the TRC, the Rainbow Nation kissed and made up.

The problem with everything that came next, including the fraught reconciliation process, was the lesson it taught South Africans: you could always do your worst and get away with it. It seemed, in this new South Africa, that evil came without consequence, so nobody would ever have to take responsibility for their actions. This perception has since become ingrained in the national psyche. Corruption has turned into a way of life, and once again every man and woman has been left to fend for themselves.

There were times, as a child in that Pretoria garden, when I would bite into a peach and feel the wash of golden fruit juice, its affirming and sweet taste. But there were also times when my expectations would be thwarted, when I would sink my teeth into fruit the texture of cotton, finding only dry and pithy flesh beneath the soft fuzz. If I forced myself to look at the toothmarks I had made, I would often see furrowed holes in the body of the fruit, or—worse—a tiny worm seeking solace beside the pit.

I was horrified to watch as even the ANC, once such a cause for hope and optimism, grew into one of those bad peaches. Worms of corruption were eating their way through the once-golden fruit. The signs had existed many years before, as I found out to my detriment when I was alone and in the field. The origins of "every man for himself" were already there, and if it hadn't been for the Soviets my story would have had a very different outcome.

Today's South Africa has been brutalised by an over-eagerness to forget the painful lessons of the past. It is a natural human impulse to distance ourselves from the things that hurt us the most, but in the case of South Africa it was always necessary to keep the pain close, to ensure we never repeated the awful mistakes we had made. But now myopia, aided and fueled by the Truth and Reconciliation process, has led to corruption and an overwhelming sense of entitlement. The rich have become richer and the poor poorer ... and angrier.

There was a time when the fruit, and the promise it contained, was ripe for picking and sharing amongst all South Africa's people. But the golden sheen turned out to be a trick of the light, an illusion conjured by a hot sun beating forever on a land washed in blood, a beautiful country with a rot at its very core.

THE "PSYCHE OF A SPY"

To betray one must belong,
I never belonged.[1]

> Kim Philby, British intelligence officer turned Soviet spy

AND NEITHER DID I.

In all honesty, it never bothered me. I was so used to being alone and feeling "different" that I became comfortable with it.

I was an only child. Awkward and lacking in social skills, I preferred the company of my radio to the company of other children. The radio was a friend, and an interesting one at that. Its news bulletins carried the promise of exciting places, worlds away from Pretoria and its tired, conservative provincialism.

The brief sense of belonging I had felt when speaking to Ronnie all those years ago in Golders Green had made me feel trapped and claustrophobic. I enjoyed flying solo, and it suited me. In fact, it was the danger of operating on my own that made me feel truly alive. I had to be disciplined, think on my feet all the time. Being an outsider didn't bother me either, and the White South African community was the last place I wanted to fit in. I longed to create something better for my country, to travel, to live abroad, to win the kind of personal freedoms we could only imagine. I longed to push the boundaries.

Espionage writers often suggest that spies feel like outsiders, that they don't belong. This is true, unlike the conventional wisdom that this otherness leads to resentment, anger, and a desire for revenge ... and that these are the factors behind most acts of betrayal. In my case, my otherness was exactly what I needed; it enabled me to maintain self-discipline and focus and to get on with

---

1 Taken from an interview with Australian journalist Murray Styles. Quoted in Johnathan Ancer's book, *Betrayal: The Secret Lives Of Apartheid Spies* (Tafelberg)

the job of betraying those who supported and furthered apartheid. My mistrust of others worked to my advantage.

South Africa in the 1980s was awash with spies and informers. Everyone watched everyone else, and if you suspected someone of being a police spy, they probably were. Several of the crime reporters I sat next to on two national newspapers were on the payroll of the Security Police, and they didn't bother to disguise it because everyone else was as well.

Like rugby and *braais*, spying held South Africa's attention then, and it still does now. Recently, former ANC president Jacob Zuma added to his unpopularity and paranoia by denouncing a number of well-liked and high-ranking ANC cadres as having served as apartheid spies and informers in years gone by. His efforts at shifting the spotlight from himself, and his alleged dubious actions, backfired. His reputation was only tainted further by the torrent of defamation cases that were launched against him.

Yes, a spy lies. Or rather, acts. Spying is a performance art. I lived a legend for several years in South Africa, both before and after my intelligence training. Living it to the letter earned me my ticket to the USSR. It showed discipline, commitment, and focus. The legend must become second nature and must be sustained at all times, but the hyper-vigilance that goes with it is exhausting, and anxiety is never far away.

As with anything else, you have to manage the fear and anxiety. You have to remain composed when remaining composed is the greatest challenge. Swimming in a constant surge of adrenalin sharpens the wits, but such a life is exhausting. Live that way for too long, and it takes a toll on your physical and emotional health. I had to pace myself in social situations, and I needed frequent time-outs to recharge my batteries. I knew tiredness kills in this game … that's when the mistakes happen.

I remained teetotal among my hard-drinking journalist colleagues. Alcohol lowers inhibitions, and I could not take the chance of losing control. For the same reason I tried to have local anaesthetics instead of general, otherwise I would never be certain what had slipped from my drug-loosened lips in the recovery room.

There has been much speculation among espionage writers about what draws spies to the trade. Several have come up with cleverly constructed reasons, like Jonathan Ancer's MICE[2] acronym: Money, Ideology, Coercion, and Ego (or Excitement).

The answer is all of these, and none of these, and something else entirely, far too abstract to define. Dieter Gerhardt, the high-ranking South African naval officer who spied for the Soviets, believed spies had a flaw in their essential character that enabled them to betray others. Personally, as a spy—and in later life a psychotherapist—I believe it takes a type of skewed attachment, or else a lack of attachment entirely to make a successful spy. All other factors are incidental.

Then throw into the mix a passion, an energy, and an ideological set of principles that motivate you to put your life on the line. There is an element of walking on the wild side, living dangerously, which makes you feel alive. In my case, it was also opportunism—taking a chance and flying with it to see where it would lead. To my surprise, one opportunity always led to another, and another after that. And the opportunities I came across were too good to miss, so I put my head down, gritted my teeth and went with it. Spying is about dancing with danger and thriving on it.

All the trappings sound very romantic, dramatic, and exciting, but I believe it is ultimately this flawed attachment that is the key ingredient. With this the act of betrayal is unfettered by guilt, remorse, sorrow, or regret. This trait may indeed give one the sense of not "belonging." As Kim Philby said, "One cannot betray if one does not belong. One cannot belong if one is not attached."

This lack of attachment does not develop because of some deep-seated childhood rejection or trauma, nor is it pathological or evidence of emotional damage. It is merely an inherent trait, something that makes spies different from everyone else—the same way some people are naturally good at painting or arithmetic. Only, in the spy's case, this lack of attachment means you can betray the people you ostensibly care about and walk away without the entanglement of emotion.

I believe spies like Kim Philby, Dieter Gerhardt, and other successful operatives had a skewed attachment or a lack of it towards others. I know I have it to some extent. In my case, this impulse was indulged by distant and chilly parenting, a lack of nurturing and emotion coupled with the pressure of high expectations. It served me well.

---

2 Taken from an interview with Australian journalist Murray Styles. Quoted in Johnathan Ancer's book, *Betrayal: The Secret Lives of Apartheid Spies* (Tafelberg).

Although I am not predisposed to feel attachment towards others, I do at least have a sense of attachment to myself. This isn't something narcissistic, selfish, or self-serving so much as it is an adaptation that has helped me survive. It is a means of self-preservation, and the understanding that I am responsible for myself. For whatever reason, my handler and my organization abandoned me in the field, but I do not blame them for it now. I took responsibility for the choices I made in joining the ANC, and I handled the consequences of that. I owed it to myself to escape and put my life back together.

My attachment flaw enabled the betrayals I committed, but it also served to protect the people I really cared about. I had little time for those supporting apartheid and felt no responsibility towards them. My decision to hide my true self from family and friends was about responsibility, too. I did not want to burden them with the responsibility of knowing, which would also place them in danger. Either way, they would get hurt—and they did.

The backlash, when it came, was bad enough. The Security Police questioned my friends and threatened and intimidated my colleagues. My parents, who were reeling from the negative press coverage, had their modest Pretoria home turned upside down by search parties, who took what they fancied and left them afraid and violated. I felt bad about this, of course. I am not unfeeling. But if that was the price of my small contribution to the end of apartheid, then it was worth paying.

On the other hand, there are spies who exhibit clear and frightening psychopathology, such as apartheid "super-spy" Craig Williamson. We did not have the displeasure of meeting.

Williamson's psychopathy became clear when he spoke of the murder of six-year-old Katryn Schoon. In 1984, Williamson sent a mail bomb to the Schoon household in Angola, intending to kill Jeanette and Marius Schoon, prominent ANC members and anti-apartheid activists. Jeanette and Marius had provoked Williamson's personal ire after they broke his cover to the ANC, allowing the organization to play him without him knowing. Knowledge, as they say, is power, and Williamson was furious and humiliated when it was wielded against him.

Williamson's mail bomb killed the intended targets as well as six-year-old Katryn, who was caught in the blast. The younger Schoon child, Fritz, was three years old when he witnessed the death of his sister and parents. He was found wandering listlessly around the house, confused and severely traumatised. After the bombing he developed epilepsy, from which he suffered for the rest of his life.

For Williamson, the triple murder was something to brag about. To all accounts he remains proud of his achievements and keen to speak of his career. He was one of many monsters let off by the TRC, which granted him amnesty.

As with several of the apartheid spies I have researched, Williamson displays a mixture of psychopathy and narcissism, served with a large dollop of an attention-seeking disorder. A heady and murderous mixture. One wonders if spies are often chosen because of—not in spite of—their mental health issues.

I was never motivated by money, unlike some. The apartheid state paid informers handsomely, which made duplicity attractive. I was never offered anything, and my work for the ANC didn't earn me a cent. My motivation was a desire to build a new South Africa and to take money for a principle that I profoundly valued would have corrupted that principle. I would have felt grubby and greedy if I had ever been remunerated for my undercover work.

Was I better than other female South African spies like Olivia Forsyth and Vanessa Brereton? Well, I chose the winning side, and the more righteous one, but subsequent ANC corruption and misdeeds might leave me wondering about that.

Both Forsyth and Brereton came from backgrounds similar to mine, and we are all of a similar age. We were all active as spies in the 1980s, and to my amusement, we all looked similar. Photographs show serious 1980s-style young women with big hair and a bigger attitude. We were usually glowering at the camera.

I know very little about the real Olivia Forsyth, except that later in her spying career she attempted to become a double agent, and it backfired horribly. She had friends in high places, and it is said her controller was none other than Craig Williamson. Her half brother is, apparently, a certain Heston de Bruin. de Bruin and Williamson were in the Security Police together, and together they infiltrated the student council at Wits in the early seventies. They were rivals professionally, and de Bruin was always resentful of Williamson's charisma and success. It would seem all these characters shared a tangled connection spanning several years.

Forsyth's brief was to infiltrate Rhodes University and spy on the White left, which she did. The information she passed to the police led to arrests, torture, and an arson attack. Other atrocities, as yet unknown, may also have sprung from her betrayal.

Forsyth later claimed to have seen the light, and she tried to defect to the ANC in Zimbabwe. But she was not persuasive enough, and she was reluctant or unable to carry out the tasks she needed to do to prove herself.

The ANC soon ran out of patience with this apartheid spy who claimed to have had a change of heart but had no way to prove it. She was locked up in Quatro, an ANC internment camp in Angola, with other apartheid spies and informers. Ronnie Kasrils intervened, either out of gallantry or because he believed she had seen the light. He moved her to a safe house in Luanda, the Angolan capital, where the ANC kept her. The ANC hoped to exchange her for prisoners on Death Row in Pretoria.

Forsyth escaped (of course) and returned to South Africa where Williamson et al. launched a propaganda extravaganza, hailing her as South Africa's female super spy—the espionage Barbie to Williamson's Ken. Within the ANC, she was thought of as a terrible spy, but back then it was the government that controlled the narrative.

Vanessa Brereton, meanwhile, was a human rights lawyer in the Eastern Cape and a secret member of the ANC. She served as a defender in several high-profile political trials, but unbeknown to her clients she systematically betrayed them to the Bureau of State Security (BOSS). Her betrayal led to wide scale arrests, torture, beatings, and imprisonment.

She left South Africa and settled in the UK before the TRC could begin a chapter of its work examining state intelligence gathering. Reports say she later confessed her true role. Supposedly, she only came to understand the consequences of her betrayals years later, and now she wished to apologise and atone for the suffering she caused. She claimed to have been influenced by her police handler and alleged lover, Karl Edwards. "He made me feel special," was her excuse. Brereton's pact with the Devil may have made her feel all warm and fuzzy inside, but I'm sure those she ruthlessly and cynically betrayed won't feel the love.

Both Forsyth and Brereton are alleged to have had sexual relationships with their handlers. Perhaps this was a modus operandi of the Special Branch when dealing with emotionally fragile but useful young women? I encountered a similar approach from Colonel de Bruin in Oshakati, as he tried to recruit me to the ranks of SWAPOL. I let him play me, and I played him in return. In the end, he had no idea how close he came to having his head blown off with his own revolver on that sweet, jasmine-scented African night.

Forsyth and Brereton found themselves wishing for closure in their later years, and Forsyth went to great lengths to promote her book in South Africa in 2015. I watched her interviews with interest, but something troubled me. It was her lack of passion.

Forsyth's staid demeanor made me think, by contrast, of the gut-wrenching fear, terror, and outrage I had felt as the events of the Soweto Uprising exploded across our TV screen all those years ago. Seeing her made me remember how I had cried in horror as adults with guns killed the nation's schoolchildren, one by one.

Those events lit a flame of passion, a longing for justice that burned within me and sustained me throughout the cold days of my military training. That same flame kept me warm throughout the years of emotional—if not physical—frigidity I experienced while I was in deep cover. In fact, I believe I have never lost that spark. But Olivia Forsyth, whenever I saw her speak, was leaden eyed. There was no spark.

> *It is the world's one crime its babes grow dull,*
> *Not that they starve, but starve so dreamlessly;*
> *Not that they sow, but they seldom reap;*
> *Not that they serve, but have no gods to serve;*
> *Not that they die, but they die like sheep.*
>
> The Leaden-eyed by Vachel Lindsay, 1879-1931

And so I realised what I had: that drive, that spark, that determination. It forged the person I am, and the spy I was. That little, burning, irrepressible, tiny spark is the magic ingredient—the passion that makes a spy.

It is who I am. I am the barefoot, sunburned, blonde child who, years before, reached for a ripening peach in that African garden. In many ways, I never grew up.

In many ways, I never left.

EPILOGUE: ENGLAND, 2021

BETRAYAL IS THE THING WITH LAYERS. Beneath the outer layer is another layer, and beneath that is another. You do not know what each one will bring or what's at the centre. What takes you by surprise is the reaction you have to each one; the discomfort gets worse the deeper you go.

I am the betrayer and the betrayed. All my life, deception was an occupational hazard. Over thirty years ago, I deceived my country and committed high treason, which would have carried a sentence of fifteen to twenty years in prison. I joined the ANC at a time when it was a banned organisation. Not only that, but I was recruited into its explicitly violent military wing, MK, the Spear Of The Nation, and trained in the Soviet Union, the country all South Africans had been raised to hate.

I deceived my family, who did not know what I was doing or what I believed. Hurt as they eventually were by my dishonesty, at the time I spared them the burden of knowing what I did. In doing so, I shielded them from possible intimidation, arrest, interrogation, torture, or worse. Or all of the above. If they knew nothing, they would say nothing. Ignorance kept all of us safe. I had few scruples in betraying those journalists who worked for the Security Police or the National Intelligence Service as informers; those who used intimidation to sway the results of the first free and fair elections in Namibia; or those who informed on activists, interrogated suspects, terrorised local communities, tortured, and murdered. Nor do I regret deceiving a senior officer in SWAPOL. My only regret is that I could not expose more of them.

Yet during the course of my service, I also acquired the bitter taste of betrayal. The betrayal that was the hardest to take was probably my father's.

The Security Police and the National Intelligence Service visited my parents when they discovered my ANC activities. They manipulated my father into joining a proposed team of operatives trying to track me down as I headed towards Botswana. My father agreed to go with them, find me and return me to Pretoria. I would be arrested, and tried for treason. He also gave a series of interviews denouncing me and the ANC in the South African Press. If that's not a betrayal, I don't know what is.

My handler, too, betrayed me. He left me alone in the field with no resources or contacts to fall back on should I need to escape. I had no weapon, no fake documentation, no safe house, nor refuge. There was no route out of South Africa, no funds, and no plane ticket to safety. He ignored my signals, coded messages, and dead letter drops too, despite the increasing urgency. He left me on my own even as the danger escalated and I needed him to make prompt operational decisions.

Ronnie's lack of support was never explained, and neither was I properly debriefed by the organization that recruited me. My theory is the ANC had no clue what to do with an operative who had found her way into the government, interviewed its politicians, and reported on its parliament. At the time my cover was blown, I was about to join State President F. W. de Klerk's press office as a media officer. I was in so deep that even my handler didn't know what to do with me.

I was not the only one denied support. Many ANC veterans living in lonely exile returned to South Africa once Nelson Mandela was released. These exiles, joyful at the prospect of repatriation, faced a rude awakening. They got no help or support from the organization that had been their entire *raison d'être*, and many repatriated ANC supporters died in disillusionment and poverty. Their disappointment was my disappointment. It broke my heart.

I survived only because I made the correct decisions, a consequence of my excellent training in the Soviet Union. When it came to it, it was the Russians who bailed me out, hiding me in their safe house in Gaborone as the South Africans closed their net. It was the Russians who got me on a last-minute flight to the UK, where I claimed political asylum. The Russians debriefed me with sensitivity, and later I conducted a similarly extensive debriefing with representatives of the new Namibian government. The ANC, meanwhile, gave me a notebook and a pen, and told me to "write it all down" as I dealt with flashbacks and PTSD. The heartwarming news was that my old instructors in Moscow sent their best wishes and congratulations for a job well done. After that, I never heard from them again.

The most bitter of all betrayals, however, is the betrayal of South Africa through crime, corruption, vice, and violence. After all my country has endured, these have brought it to its knees once more. Again, my heart breaks.

An optimist might say South Africa is a work in progress. I can relate to that; I am as well.

There is balance within and without. What happens in my life, the changes I face, are akin to the growing, evolving, dynamic developments in the land I come from, the country that made me who I am. After years in exile, I still yearn for the sensual touch of Africa, for its colours and textures, its thunderstorms and dust, the feel of undiluted sun on my bare skin and the smell of the rain as it lashes the dusty ground. I miss the open spaces, the limitless blue sky, the belligerent cries of hadedas and the echo of crickets calling at dusk. I miss the eyes of the night creatures glowing in the *veld* at midnight. I miss the humour, the intricacies, and the innuendos of the Afrikaans language. I long to laugh, as I used to, at the absurdity of it all, the very South African-ness of it.

I feel as though I have "Made in South Africa" stamped on my forehead. I was formed from heat and dust, colour and vibrancy, summer thunderstorms and the blue winter sky. I could not belong anywhere else—not even in the delicate and sorrowful Soviet Union. That longing for the country of my birth is still deep and instinctive.

I wish for peace and progress for all South Africa, but especially for the Black and Coloured population that suffered the most under Apartheid. These are a people with an indomitable spirit. I was always awed by the unbelievable collective dignity South Africa's oppressed majority showed in the face of suffering, and now I am awed further by the courage and determination that has been shown by millions of everyday men and women in the hard work of rebuilding their nation.

Despite my personal setbacks and the horrors of South Africa's past injustices and suffering, there's no reason to stop trying. We may need to find a new way forward, to reevaluate our priorities and principles and take responsibility for the mistakes of our past. Growth can be painful, and it will take time to overcome generations of suffering.

The struggle for a democratic South Africa is not yet over. I have never thought it to be. This process has merely entered another phase, one marked by growing pains and dissatisfaction, self-evaluation and reflection. Our task as South Africans is enormous, a lifetime's work.

We must look forward with renewed hope, always reminding ourselves of the horror of our past and determined never to go back to that. May we never lose sight of the prize. May we proceed with courage and hope. The struggle continues, "a luta continua."[3]

As always, *Amandla Awethu*. "The power is ours."

---

3 A luta continua: the rallying call of the Frelimo movement in Mozambique during the country's war of independence. It is Portuguese for "the struggle continues," and was used by the first president of Frelimo, Eduardo Chivambo Mondlane in the struggle against Portuguese colonial rule in the territory.

POSTSCRIPT

I WAS NEVER TOLD who exactly was behind my training, and I never asked. Information like that was only shared on a "need to know" basis. I didn't.

I do recall my Soviet instructors referring, on occasion, to something they called "the Institute." A Russian researcher specialising in the history of his country's secret service has told me he believes this to be the "Institute of Social Sciences" in north Moscow, an organisation that trained Soviet-friendly students from capitalist countries in the art of revolution.

This name does not hint at the military or operational nature of the training I had. I can only assume that my instruction came under a joint KGB and military operation whose purpose was to train allies of the Soviet Union involved in socialist liberation struggles overseas. My instruction had precious little to do with the study of social sciences, which I suppose was a cover or "legend" surrounding the establishment and concealing its true purpose.

It makes no difference to know who exactly was looking out for me back then. All I know for sure is that I owe my instructors my gratitude for the skills they passed down to me, ensuring my survival in the field.

DRAMATIS PERSONAE

RONNIE KASRILS

Founding member of uMkhonto we Sizwe (MK), the armed wing of the African National Congress (ANC); Chief of Military Intelligence for MK and member of its High Command; Minister of Intelligence Services in post-apartheid South Africa, 2004 to 2008; Member of the National Executive Committee (NEC) of the ANC, 1987 to 2007; Member of the central committee of the South African Communist Party (SACP) from 1986 to 2007; Deputy Minister of Defence, 1994 to 1999; Minister of Water Affairs and Forestry, 1999 to 2004; Sue Dobson's recruiter and handler, 1986 to 1989.

ELEANOR KASRILS

Late wife of Ronnie Kasrils; Met Sue Dobson and assisted her introduction to Ronnie; Met with Sue in London during her exile, before they repatriated her to South Africa and joined Ronnie.

NELSON MANDELA (MADIBA), 1918-2013

South African anti-apartheid activist; Founder member of the ANC; Founder member of MK; Senior member of the SACP; Politician and philanthropist; First President of South Africa, 1994 to 1999.

THABO M'BEKI

Senior member of the ANC; First Deputy President of South Africa, 1994 to 1999; Second President of South Africa, 1999 to 2008.

MIKHAIL SERGEYEVICH GORBACHEV

President of the Soviet Union, 1990 to 1991, making him the eighth and last leader of the Soviet Union; Policies of Glasnost and Perestroika contributed to the lifting of the Iron Curtain and the end of the Cold War.

F. W. DE KLERK

The last president of Apartheid South Africa; Sue Dobson was to be interviewed for the post of media officer in his department before a higher level security clearance revealed her family links to the ANC.

ROELOF FREDERIK "PIK" BOTHA

Foreign Affairs minister in successive apartheid governments; Later cultivated links with the ANC; Interviewed by Sue Dobson for *RSA Policy Review* in 1988/9.

CHRIS HEUNIS

Apartheid minister of Home or Internal Affairs in several apartheid cabinets; Sue Dobson worked for his son, Van Heerden Heunis, on *RSA Policy Review*; Sue Dobson explored his office during an office barbecue at his official residence in Pretoria, 1988.

VAN HEERDEN HEUNIS

Sue Dobson's editor on *RSA Policy Review*; source.

IGOR OLEGOVICH

Sue Dobson's translator and bodyguard; buyer of 'vimmins' ondervear,' 1986 to 1987

VALERY PAVLOVICH

Sue Dobson's intelligence and Military Combat Work instructor.

NINA AND IRINA

The housekeepers of the Gorky Street apartment.

SERGI SERGEIOVICH

Military instructor in engineering, explosives, and weaponry.

(UNCLE) PYTOR

Small arms, pistols, and sniper instructor.

SASHA ALEXANDROVICH

Medical doctor responsible for ANC recruits.

VASILY SERGEIOVICH

Decorated veteran of the Afghan campaigns against the mujahideen; Political instructor and Commissar; Military Combat Work and Politics instructor.

PAVEL ANDREIOVICH

Radio communications and morse code instructor.

HESTON DE BRUIN

Security policeman working for the apartheid regime; security police spy on National Union of South African (NUSAS) Students' Representative Council (SRC) 1973; colleague of Craig Williamson, South African "super spy"; relative of South African spy Olivia Forsyth; Colonel of South West African Police (SWAPOL) in Northern Namibia, in charge of Press Liaison; Introduced Sue Dobson to Koevoet founder "Sterkhans" Dreyer; Source.

LIEUTENANT GENERAL JOHANNES "STERKHANS" DREYER

Founder and leader of Koevoet, a paramilitary force that ruthlessly hunted down SWAPO (South West Africa Peoples' Organisation) insurgents in Northern Namibia.

CRAIG WILLIAMSON

Former South African police Major involved in many assassinations locally and abroad; Involved in kidnappings, burglaries, and "dirty tricks" campaigns for the apartheid regime. Regards himself as a "super spy."

OLIVIA FORSYTH

Former spy for the Apartheid Regime.

VANESSA BRERETON

Former South African human rights lawyer who admitted to being a police spy.

DENIS GOLDBERG

Rivonia Treason Trialist, imprisoned for twenty-two years with other ANC members; released in 1985 and joined his family in London before returning to South Africa in 2002; was a kind and much-loved friend to Sue Dobson during her early years in exile.

ANATOLY ALEXANDROVICH

Representative of the Russian Embassy in Gaborone, who plucked Sue off a Gaborone Street and hid her in the Soviet compound before helping her escape to London.

JOAN AND JEREMY BRICKHILL

Sue's sister- and brother-in-law who were seriously injured in a car bomb blast carried out by South African agents in Harare, Zimbabwe in 1987. When Sue went for the highest level of security clearance for a media officer post in President F. W. de Klerk's office, her connection to the Brickhills was discovered.

JASON AND LINDA BRICKHILL

Joan and Jeremy's children; Sue's nephew and niece.

JANET

Linda and Jason's beloved nanny.

VIKTOR ALEXSEIOVICH

Stand in translator/interpreter when Igor is away.

LUDMILLA

Sue's ward mate at Military Hospital No 1, Moscow; veteran of the Great Patriotic War.

PRESIDENT SAMORA MACHEL

Mozambique's first president after Independence, was known for his Marxist-Leninist leanings. The much-loved president and respected statesman died in an aircraft crash on October 19, 1986, believed to have been orchestrated by South Africa.

ACKNOWLEDGMENTS

I would like to thank and acknowledge those who encouraged and stood by me as I told this story, especially Tom, George, and Guy, who believed in me and helped bring this book to fruition. We encountered some challenges along the way, but truth will prevail, and it has.

I would also like to thank the team at Vine Leaves Press for their encouragement and enthusiasm in bringing this book to fruition. Our collaboration just feels right ... thank you!

I buried my story for many years, believing it was too small and insignificant a drop in the ocean to matter. Through their encouragement and belief in me I realized that every drop matters, and no contribution to something one fervently believes in is too small.

Most of all, I acknowledge those who fought for a new South Africa. It was a privilege to stand with you.

VINE LEAVES PRESS

Enjoyed this book?
Go to *vineleavespress.com* to find more.
Subscribe to our newsletter:

Ingram Content Group UK Ltd.
Milton Keynes UK
UKHW041040160523
421829UK00004B/19